# A PASSION FOR LIVING
## A PATH TO MEANING AND JOY

*Shahan Shammas*

WORTHWHILE PUBLICATIONS
P.O. BOX 8748
LANGLEY PARK, MD 20787

Copyright © 1998 by Shahan Shammas. Printed and bound in the United States of America. All rights reserved. No part of this book may be reproduced or transmitted in any form or by any means, electronic or mechanical, including photocopying, recording, or by an information storage and retrieval system—except by a reviewer who may quote brief passages in a review to be printed in a magazine or newspaper—without permission in writing from the publisher. For information, please contact Worthwhile Publications, P.O.Box 8748, Langley Park, Maryland 20787. First Printing 1998.

Although the author and publisher have made every effort to ensure the accuracy and completeness of information contained in this book, we assume no responsibility for errors, inaccuracies, omissions, or any inconsistency herein. Any slights on people, places, or organizations are unintentional.

ISBN 0-9662028-0-5
LCCN 97-091378

**Attention organizations, spiritual centers, and schools of self-actualization:** Quantity discounts are available on bulk purchase of this book for educational purposes or fund raising. Special books or book excerpts can also be created to fit specific needs. For information, please contact Worthwhile Publications, P. O. Box 8748, Langley Park, Maryland 20787.

Cover illustration: Paul Trattner
Interior design: Agnew's, Inc.
Author photo: Lawrence Johnson
Printed in the United States of America by Thomson-Shore, Inc.

To my wife, Barbara, and my daughters Olivia and Emily

# *Acknowledgments*

I would like to express my gratitude to all those who helped me make this book a reality. I would like to start with Barbara, my wife, for her dedicated support, understanding, and patience, and for her typing, reviewing and editing several versions of this book over many years. Barbara's help and support has been invaluable to me. Next, I would like to thank Joseph Shammas, Steven Pashigian, Gregory and Christine Weber, Gayle and Joseph Dyer, Beverly Levins and Wendy Van Horn for their reviews, comments, and continued support and encouragement. I would like to recognize Amy Pelsinsky for helping with the organization of the book and Joan Van De Moortel, Dale and Sonja Lynn for editing. Their skills helped make this book what it is. I would also like to express my appreciation to my many friends and family members for their patience, understanding and encouragement. A special thanks to several organizations especially the Rosicrucian Order, AMORC for inviting me to speak and conduct workshops and seminars. It was through these efforts that many of the ideas for this book were born and took form. Finally, I want to express my sincere gratitude to Paul Trattner for designing the book cover.

# Contents

**PART ONE**
  **Introduction**    3
  **The Process**    7

**PART TWO**
  **Stage 1**    13
    **Wake Up**
    Opening our eyes • Wakeful living • We do not have to struggle to succeed • We are where we need to be • We have what it takes to achieve • Everyone and everything matters • We are all connected

  **Stage 2**    46
    **Have Something Worthwhile to Live for**
    Having a worthwhile purpose to live for • Defining our purpose • Purpose must be personal • Purpose must be rewarding • Purpose must be motivating • Purpose must be challenging • Purpose must be implemented locally, incrementally, and with global consequences • Purpose must be expandable • Purpose must be a trinity of mission, objectives,

and strategies • Formulating our purpose • My purpose • Embodying our purpose • Write it down • Live it in thought, feeling and action until it becomes your reality • Nurture it • Avoid negative influences

**Stage 3** 80
**Know Yourself**
Knowing ourselves through experience—unusual experiences • Knowing ourselves through experience—common experiences • Knowing ourselves through systems of thought • Knowing ourselves through example • Knowing who we are • We are more than the body • We are in the image of our source • We are creators of value and meaning; transformers of chaos into order • We are seeds in the garden of being—cells in a body • We are in charge of our destiny

**Stage 4** 127
**Decipher the Meaning of Life and Master the Art of Living**
Life and meaning • The blueprint of life and its architect • The cell • Mastering the art of living • Metabolism • Growth • Response to stimulation • Reproduction • Personalizing life • Life as quality • Life as diversity • Life as a journey of self-discovery

**Stage 5** 164
**Understand Why We Age and Die**
Why we age
Improper metabolism, disease, neglect, and abuse • Lack of growth, cancer, or absence of a community sense • Boredom and rigidity •

Withdrawal from engagement and lack of creativity • Indifference, or lack of a positive motive to live • Tyranny of the group, and lack of individuality • Lack of joy in the process of living and the increasing burden of the baggage we carry along
**Why we die**
Birth • Living • Death • A personal experience • Eight reasons we decide to die • I felt tired and needed to rest • It was time to go to bed • I had to get up early the next morning • I did all I could for today—I did not feel like doing anything else • I was bored • It was an accident—I was reading in bed and I just fell asleep • I wanted to sleep and dream • Dissolving the corporation

## Stage 6    239
### Release Your Brakes
Ignorance • Fear • Pain and suffering • Pain and suffering help us wake up • Enable us to let go • Aid our learning and growth • Prepare us for pleasure • Remind us of our ignorance, or "sin" • Polish our character and personality • Link us to humanity

## Stage 7    269
### Take it Easy, Enjoy Yourself, and Do What You Can
Doing what we can • Living like a corporation: clear and focused mission • Action plan • Customer satisfaction • Communication and other skills • Integrity • Empowerment and recognition with a commitment to excellence • Willingness to change

## PART THREE

**A New Beginning:**     299
**Repeat the Seven Step Process—Each Time, Waking Up on a Higher Plane**

Dimensions • The lower dimensions • The first dimension • The second dimension • The third dimension • The higher dimensions • The fourth dimension • The fifth dimension • The sixth dimension • The seventh dimension • Rising to higher dimensions • Acquiring knowledge • Thinking • Adopting an ideal • Practicing detachment • Conscious dreaming • Living the inspired, passionate and creative life • Acts of heroism and noble deeds • Meditation and prayer • Communion • Loving and relating deeply and profoundly

*Part One*

# *Introduction*

When I first heard the story of the Prodigal Son as a child, I was baffled. Why would a son who left his parents' home, squandered his inheritance, and upon his return home, receive royal treatment while the elder son who faithfully remained with his parents, serving and obeying them get the lesser treatment? The elder son complained bitterly to his father about the injustice of it all.

> *"Lo, these many years I have served you, and I never disobeyed your command; yet you never gave me a kid, that I might make merry with my friends. But when this son of yours came, who has devoured your living with harlots, you killed for him the fatted calf!" And he said to him, "Son, you are always with me, and all that is mine is yours. It was fitting to make merry and be glad, for this your brother was dead, and is alive; he was lost, and is found."*
>
> *Luke 15:29–32*

The younger son dared to venture out, make mistakes and through pain and suffering learned the value and meaning of life. He is a far better person because he now appreciates the value of belonging to a family. He knows what it is to be hungry, cold and lonely. He has personally experienced the illusion of chasing worldly pleasures. This son is wiser through his experiences and far more valuable than his elder brother who remained home, safe, secure and protected. While the younger brother learned value by losing what he had, the older brother was surrounded by riches and opportunities he did not take advantage of. All that his father had was his, yet he did not know it, or act accordingly.

The story of the Prodigal Son is the story of life. It is far better to act and experience, to venture forth and err and then ask for forgiveness than to live in constant security, or fear of the unknown. As Alfred Lord Tennyson wrote, "*—it is better to have loved and lost than never to have loved at all.*" It is far better to live and die than to die not having lived at all.

Personal experience is invaluable and there are no substitutes. It is through personal experience that we open our eyes, see and learn. People can describe sights, sounds and sensual experiences to us, but until we touch, smell, taste and experience life ourselves, we do not know. Hence, it is through personal experiences that we should formulate our philosophies of life. We are the ones who must give meaning to our lives and value to our existence through our intentions and actions. Science, art, religion and philosophy are tools we can use to evaluate, understand and explain. But these tools cannot and should never be given the power to strip us of the real value, significance and the validity of our experiences.

My writing, understanding and beliefs are based on my personal experiences, supported by my knowledge of the sciences, religions and philosophies. I do not believe in something because it is written in a certain book, or because it is taught by a system or authority. Through my experiences, I see and know the world from my unique angle as a private, personal and intimate perspective. What I experience, I accept as relatively true until I have a better experience. I keep an open mind about what I have not experienced or do not know much about.

## Introduction

My experiences range from living two years in a monastery on a mountain in Lebanon in the Middle East to serving for three years in the United States Army. I have experienced the challenges of operating my own business and the security of working for the U.S. Federal Government. I have held all sorts of jobs, from medicine to factory work to computers.

I have lived through war and peace and I tell you it is far better to have peace. I have known abject poverty and I have experienced abundance and I tell you I prefer abundance. I was the subject of innumerable abuses and the witness of great acts of love. I have traveled throughout the Middle East, North America and most of Europe. I have known people of diverse religions, philosophies and ethnic origins. From these, I learned the deeper aspects of diversity, cooperation and interdependence.

The first apartment I lived in in Syria did not even have electricity. Now I live in a modern house in the suburbs of Washington, D.C. I did not begin to learn English until I was a teenager. Now I am a Regional Instructor for the worldwide Rosicrucian Order, teaching the creative use of the mind and the development of human potential.

My experiences taught me a lot about life and death, health and sickness, lack and abundance and helped me wake up and live more abundantly with meaning and joy. I intend to share some of these with you so that you too can wake up and experience more of this wonderful and abundant life.

I realize that relying on personal experience alone is not a foolproof method to know reality. No method alone is failsafe. Every system has its shortcomings. Science, religion and philosophy have been evolving and every age thinks that it finally has the correct answers; but, as we progress in our understanding, we realize how limited our past knowledge has been. We only know based on our experiences and the tools we employ. Before the advent of the light microscope, bacteria did not exist for us. Prior to the building of the electron microscope, viruses had no existence. What else lies beyond our reach simply because we have not yet created the appropriate tools to discover them?

We can use our experiences as beacons of light through which we can see and understand. We can supplement our experiences with all that is available to see better, clearer and further. Our experiences are not only what happens to us, but what we make of the events we encounter. Experiences are the food we grow by. With each experience, we learn and see a bit more clearly. We begin to ask wiser questions, act a touch more responsibly and lay another stone in the foundation of our personality. If we continue to build, we will soon find ourselves in a mansion, custom-built by us and for us to live in and experience joy, meaning and contentment.

# *The Process*

*Men are often capable of greater things than they perform. They are sent into the world with bills of credit, and seldom draw to their full extent.*

*Horace Walpole*

To live requires the expenditure of energy. We can get all the energy we need by tapping into our great reservoirs of energy—our passions. Our passions are mighty forces, and like all the forces of nature, must be channeled to avoid being destructive. We can guide our passions by following a path, a process that can help us focus and channel our energies. The path this book proposes is a seven-step unfoldment process. This process, although simple, is not easy to implement. It is, however, most rewarding.

To live fully, joyfully and with meaning, we must wake up to the opportunities life presents us, our unique abilities and the contributions we can make. This awakening will be progressive. It will require courage, patience and persistence. With each stage in our awakening, layers of a "veil" will be lifted from our eyes. We begin to glimpse beyond the illusion, and touch the real and lasting.

Just as the Lord created the world in seven days, we too can achieve the goal of living the abundant, meaningful and joyous life in seven "days." These "days" are stages that we must complete, or steps that we must take to bring about the type of life to which we aspire. Unless we alter the factors that cause our current conditions, our experiences will remain the same. There are no accidents in life. There are only events and responses. We either act or react, assume our responsibilities or make excuses. If we act, we take charge of our affairs, create our future and we live. If we merely react, we allow events to place us on any course, and if we are fortunate, we manage to exist. Ultimately, we have the choice to take what we are given, or to consciously participate in creating and shaping ourselves and our environment.

Life is not a random, haphazard series of happenings. Neither should our lives be. Life is orderly. So should we be. To live full, joyful and meaningful lives, we must act with intent and purpose. We must live like actors and actresses rendering our best. Life is the stage on which we have our earthly experiences. On this stage we can assume any role if we qualify. To qualify, we must develop the required skills, demonstrate our abilities and build relationships. We must prove our qualification through action. If we desire to live a joyful and meaningful life, we must conscientiously plant the correct seeds, in the proper soils and in the appropriate seasons. We must tend to the seedlings until they grow into a magnificent garden that is our individualized form of the Garden of Eden.

We are not privileged to see the ultimate purpose of life. We do not know what lies far ahead. While the farther reaches of life lie dimly, our immediate surroundings are brightly lit. We can take the first step with the advice of Thomas Carlyle: *"Our grand business is not to see what lies dimly at a distance, but to do what lies clearly at hand."* As we dare and proceed, we realize that wherever we go, there is enough light for us to function by. For we are the light through which we see and do. We are our own candle or lantern. Where we are, there also is our light.

Our light is as dim or as bright as we are for our light is a function of our life and we are as alive as we are awake and aware. As we continue to wake up, our light will shine brighter. We will see clearer, contribute more and achieve greater satisfaction. To hasten our awakening, increase our enjoyment of life and live a life of meaning, we can employ a seven-step process:

1. First, we must wake up.
2. Second, we must have something worthwhile to live for.
3. Third, we must know who we are, what we stand for and what makes us unique.
4. Fourth, we must decipher the meaning of life and master the art of living.
5. Fifth, we must understand why we age and ultimately die.
6. Sixth, we must release our brakes so we may glide along the highways and airways of life with the least effort.
7. Seventh, we must take it easy, enjoy ourselves and do what we can.

These seven undertakings—each with its own rewards, challenges and opportunities—will lead us to greener pastures. Life, however, is not a destination, but an ongoing process, a continuing progression to ever-increasing unfoldment. How far we progress along the helix of life is up to us. It is a matter of our awareness, will and actions.

To eliminate the illusion of a final destination, we must add an eighth step to the above seven-step process:

8. Repeat the seven-step process—each time waking up on a higher plane.

*Part Two*

# STAGE 1

## *Wake Up*

*Sleep is the twin of death.*

*Homer*

    *I found myself in a long column of people moving forward. The column was five-people wide and snaked a long way before and after me. I wondered what I was doing in the crowd and where we were going. I could not slow down or get out for the momentum of the crowd. Their forward motion kept me in line and moving. Soon we arrived at an enclosed area with a stairway and began to descend. In front of me, I noticed a lady carrying a baby. Everyone was silent. We continued to descend. In front of us lay a body of water. The people ahead of me continued to descend into the water without any hesitation, or even slowing down to wonder at what they were doing. They descended into the water until they were submerged and out of sight. Everyone followed. I hesitated. I did not want to follow the crowd into the water, but I did not know what else I could do. It appeared almost impossible to turn around and go back. I decided that I should follow, too. I was very concerned as I stepped into the water because I had no idea how long I was going to be under it. I could hold my breath for only a minute or so and I was not a good swimmer. Realizing that no one else was concerned, I decided that my fears were unfounded. If no one* else was worried, why should I be? I took a few deep breaths and went under water. There was no problem at all. I could actually breathe in the water if I remained cool and calm. In fact, everyone adjusted quickly and was doing fine. Everyone, that is, except for the baby. Instead of acting "normal" like the rest of us, it held its breath and refused to breathe in the water. The baby began to cry. The mother was concerned, but did not know what to do. She tried to quiet the baby and encourage it to breathe, but the baby refused to breathe in the water and began to suffocate. I wondered why the mother was not attempting to get the baby out of the water. It was obviously struggling for its life. The baby began to turn blue and its face distorted. A lady nearby saw what was happening to the baby. Her reaction completely took me by surprise. She dashed to the mother, grabbed the baby from her and ran away from everybody else. As she cleared from the crowd, she threw the baby on the floor. When I looked at the baby, I saw that it was dead. I was shocked. "What kind of behavior is this?" I thought to myself, "What is going on here?"

Suddenly, I realized that I was on my own. The crowd had dispersed to chase their own interests. Even though people were everywhere, each was preoccupied with something that caught their attention. Everyone was in his or her own world. I, on the other hand, had only one interest: getting out of the water and breathing air again. I found some stairs and began to climb. I continued to ascend expecting to get out of the water, but there was no outlet anywhere.

I turned and went back to the bottom of the pool where I located the same stairs that had led me into the water. I reasoned that I should be able to use the stairs that got me in to exit. Surprisingly, the higher I climbed, the higher the water rose. Water covered everything, and it seemed that there was no way out of this place.

As I stood way up on the stairway perplexed, puzzled and very annoyed, a lady "official" appeared out of nowhere. She took a key from an invisible wall and inserted it into an equally *invisible lock in the west side of the pool wall. After turning the key, I could see that a "firmament" or a "veil" was covering the water and shielding the air from our view. With a turn of the key, the veil lifted. A man appeared out of nowhere. I sensed that he was ready to leave. He swam up to the surface of the water, lifted his head and began breathing air. He pulled himself out of the water and was gone. Instantly, the veil, the key and the lady disappeared. I was all alone. I went to the wall frantically looking for the lock and the key. I searched for them thoroughly but found nothing. I began to feel distressed. I wanted out of the water. I started to wonder why I came here in the first place. Why did I follow the crowd? How could we all simply follow one another into this place without any knowledge of how to get out of it? What was I to do? I began to scream: "I want out! I want out! I cannot stand it here any longer!* **I want out now** *!" I was getting more and more emotional as the crescendo of my rebellion built up. Just when it seemed there was absolutely nothing I could do, I woke up.*

Why did I have this dream? What is its meaning and significance? Why did I follow the crowd blindly? Why did the people act the way they did? Slowly it dawned on me that this dream represents the world and my life. We live mainly in a dream state. We sleepwalk through life. We follow each other because there is comfort in company. Inertia guides our footsteps. We march to an unknown destination. We are easily influenced by large numbers—"peer-pressure." We feel that if many believe and act in a certain way, there must be truth to their beliefs and acts. We join in since we are *social* creatures. We wear our beliefs like binoculars causing us to have tunnel vision. Some of our beliefs are so strange that if we only stopped to think about them, we would see how little sense they make. Yet we are so accustomed to them that we not only accept them blindly, we also teach them to our children as truth.

We are mostly oblivious to the choices we can exercise to

create our individual destinations. Instead of using time as an ally, we attempt to kill time in the pursuit of trivia. We make excuses for our crazy and senseless acts. We send our children to wars to kill and be killed, calling these acts of bravery and heroism. We force our will on others if we get the chance, yet we would revolt if others attempted to do the same to us. We squander our resources and then complain that we do not have enough. We aimlessly walk about lost and forlorn, yet we wonder why we are not getting where we want to end up. We are creatures of habit and appetite always wanting more, yet we refuse to do what it takes to earn more. We feign happiness and pretend. We live life as a struggle. We age prematurely and die too soon.

Happiness eludes the vast majority of us because we live our lives devoid of meaning. Even though our religions *tell us* that there is value and meaning to our lives, deep down we do not resonate to them. The values we are given are not ours. The meaning assigned to our lives is not of our choosing. We feel helpless in the face of a deity who provides us with free will yet allows us no option to fashion our lives based on *our* will and understanding. How can we be free if the only option we have is to live according to the dictates of religion, or the deity it promulgates? We are threatened with dire consequences if we deviate from *The Ten Commandments*. We will be punished with eternal hell if we sin. How are we not to feel weak, helpless and insignificant in the face of such teachings? We must be careful in what we accept as truth. For we reap in accordance to the seeds we allow in the soil of our minds. If we want different results, we must plant and nurture the appropriate seeds.

What is the value and the meaning of our life? Is our life due to accident and chance as science claims? Or are we God's creation as religion asserts? The answer is both, neither, or either. It all depends on what we accept and believe. Science can only provide theories, hypotheses and postulations—it cannot prove that we are here due to accident or chance. In fact, the more closely we look at all the factors involved, the more we realize that it is almost impossible that we are here by chance. Religion cannot provide any proof either. Evidence is absent from all theological doctrines. Theology is a fiat. We are simply expected to accept the teachings and abide by them.

We rely too much on beliefs. Perhaps this is because our knowledge is limited. Yet if we must believe, let our beliefs be the outgrowth of personal experience and a deep understanding of natural laws. Beliefs based on ignorance are debilitating and act as veils that interfere with clear vision. Unless we remove the veils that block our vision and live with our eyes, minds and hearts open, we will not see clearly and understand. We will remain asleep and lack passion in our lives. We can believe if we need to, but only until we know or can come up with a better belief. If we are sincere and persistent in wanting to know, our experiences will provide us the answers we seek. Even though our experiences are personal and limited, they are our best means to know and wake up. As our experiences and knowledge accumulate, we accrue enough intellectual capital to arrive at answers that resonate deep within us as truth.

Like the baby in my dream, our children are born awake. We soon find ways to discipline them into our ways and lull them to sleep. We sleep and dream feeling good about ourselves for we believe that we are awake and in control. Moving and doing things in our dreams, we reason that we must be awake and that our actions are real and deliberate. Not so. For **while asleep, we can only dream** and **while in the dream world, we cannot be awake. To escape our fate, we must wake up.** In my dream, I could not escape my fate while in the water and asleep. The only escape was to wake up from my sleep. While asleep and dreaming, I could never *know* that I was merely experiencing a dream. It was reality for me. The only way to discern a dream from reality is *after* waking up. If we want to live the abundant life, we must wake up to our abundance. If we want to stop feeling helpless and weak, we must wake up to our strength and power. If we want to feel and know the value of life, we must wake up to our worth and value. Unless we wake up, we will not realize that what we are struggling, fighting and killing for is a mere illusion. In the dream state, we are automatons. There is no thinking, knowing, or causing. Things just happen and we happen to be there. While asleep, we either dream enjoyable dreams or have nightmares. We are so infatuated with our dreams that we "think" our dreams and our understanding of them must be the "truth," the whole "truth" and nothing but the "truth." So, we become "missionaries" forcing our way of dreaming upon everyone who is less fortunate than we. If anyone who is awake tries to tell us that we are merely sleep-acting, we ridicule them. We might even put them to death if they continue to tell us that we can be much more than we are if we wake up. This was the fate of many of our prophets, philosophers and scientists. After killing our true heroes, we excuse ourselves by claiming that they came to die anyway.

One of the "facts" that so many Christians promulgate is the assertion that Christ came to die for our sins. Christ did not come to die. We killed him through our ignorance and sleep-walking. He came to live and show us a life of fullness, meaning and abundance through his example. He stated it clearly in John 10:10 when He said: *"The thief comes only to steal and kill and destroy; I came that they may have life, and have it abundantly."*

If it is true that Christ came so we may have life and have it more abundantly, where is this life? From all indications, very few live it. Is that why Christ came, so only the few may experience abundance? If He came so that we may all have the abundant life, what went wrong? If He came so only those who believed in Him would have the abundant life, that did not happen either. Somehow the abundant life eludes the vast majority of humanity. Why? Is it because

Christ is a level of awareness, a consciousness, that unless we attain it we cannot know abundance? This form of consciousness does not descend on us. We must rise to it by raising our consciousness. Once we do, we will be awake and live a life of meaning, joy and abundance.

We are not on earth as guests invited to a feast. No one owes us anything and we will not be handed the abundant life on a platter. We must create it for ourselves based on what gives us meaning and joy. To live the abundant life, we must take the first step. We must wake up and shake off the dream state. We can choose to wake up willingly, by paying attention to our experiences, environment and circumstances, or be forced awake through pain, suffering and influences beyond our control. We can wake up gradually or relatively quickly. One way or another, we will wake up for that is why we are here. When we do, we will see and know ourselves and others in a new way. We will be transformed to the extent that we have awakened. It is then that we will be able to transmute our sleep-walking into purposeful living and metamorphose our earth into heaven. For when we are transformed, so is everything else.

Waking up begins when we open our eyes and see.

### Opening Our Eyes

Even though we are born with eyes, we are not able to focus and understand right away. We must slowly learn. Even after we grow up and develop our sight, we still only see partially, for our understanding is limited. Seeing is a dual process. We must not only receive the reflected light, but we must interpret it and know its meaning as well. Since neither our eyes nor our understanding is perfect, what we see and how we interpret it is partial and relative to our personal biases, fears, prejudices, culture and environment. Hence, we never see directly and clearly, but through the instrument of the eye and the implement of the mind.

Dr. Deepak Chopra in *Quantum Healing — Exploring the Frontiers of Mind/Body Medicine* mentions experiments performed on kittens. Kittens are born with their eyes shut and their optic nerves undeveloped. The mechanism of sight begins to mature with the use of the eyes. If kittens are blindfolded for the first few days of their lives, they remain blind for life. Psychologists Joseph Hubel and David Weisel placed three batches of newborn kittens in three different boxes. The first was a white box painted with horizontal black stripes; the second was a white box painted with vertical black stripes; the third box was white with no stripes. The kittens were left in these boxes for the first critical few days of their lives. This was enough to condition the kittens for life. The ones that saw only vertical lines for the first few days of their lives, did not see any horizontal lines thereafter and visa versa. The kittens in the white box could not relate to any objects correctly. We, too, see only a few things the first few days of our lives. Are we equally conditioned by, not only what we initially experience, but continue to experience as well?

How do we know if what we see is reality or what we are conditioned to see? Just as we cannot know that we are dreaming until we have woken up, we cannot know that we are seeing partially or because of conditioning until we have begun to see more clearly. Two stories from ancient literature illustrate the process of opening the eyes, knowing and gaining wisdom through experiencing: Adam and Eve from The Bible, and Enkidu and the harlot from *The Epic of Gilgamesh*[1] of ancient Mesopotamia. Let us take a closer look at the story of Adam and Eve (all emphases are mine):

> *The LORD God took the man and put him in the garden of Eden to till it and keep it. And the LORD God commanded* **the man**, *saying, "You may freely eat of every tree of the garden; but of the*

---

1. *The Epic of Gilgamesh*, N. K. Sanders, Penguin Books, 1972.

tree of the knowledge of good and evil you shall not eat, for in the day that you eat of it you shall die." Then the LORD God said, "It is not good that the man should be alone; I will make him a helper fit for him." So out of the ground the LORD God formed every beast of the field and every bird of the air, and brought them to the man to see what he would call them; and whatever the man called every living creature, that was its name. The man gave names to all cattle, and to the birds of the air, and to every beast of the field; but for the man there was not found a helper fit for him. So the LORD God caused a deep sleep to fall upon the man, and while he slept took one of his ribs and closed up its place with flesh; and the rib which the LORD God had taken from the man he made into a woman and brought her to the man. Then the man said, "This at last is bone of my bones and flesh of my flesh; she shall be called Woman, because she was taken out of Man." Therefore a man leaves his father and his mother and cleaves to his wife, and they become one flesh. And the man and his wife were both naked, and were not ashamed.

Now the serpent was more subtle than any other wild creature that the LORD God had made. He said to the woman, "Did God say, 'You shall not eat of any tree of the garden?'" And the woman said to the serpent, "We may eat of the fruit of the trees of the garden; but God said, 'You shall not eat of the fruit of the tree which is in the midst of the garden, neither shall you touch it, lest you die.'" But the serpent said to the woman, "You will not die. For God knows that when you eat of it your eyes will be opened, and you will be like God, knowing good and evil." So when **the woman saw that the tree was good** for food, and that **it was a delight to the eyes,** and that **the tree was to be desired to make one wise, she took of its fruit and ate;** and she also gave some to her husband, and he ate. **Then the eyes of both were opened,** and they **knew** that they were naked; and they sewed fig leaves together and made themselves aprons.

*Genesis 2:15–3:7*

There is a precise sequence to opening the eyes. It begins with temptation. Temptation is primarily an inner prompting that entices and challenges the will. In order to be tempted, we must *see* something that is tempting, alluring, or "a delight to the eyes." Once we are tempted, our minds begin to look for reasons to justify giving in to it. Our minds evaluate and rationalize. Once we clearly envision the outcome of the action and find it desirable, we give in to the temptation and act. The act, in the case of Adam and Eve, was eating the fruit. In Eve's case, the rationalization was that eating the fruit was supposed to make her wise. Once she acted, the results simply followed.

The fact that the fruit was forbidden is not the point of the story. In reality, Eve was never forbidden to eat of the fruit, but it was Adam who was prohibited from tasting it. The relevance of the story is that our eyes will not open until we have an adequate experience. To have an experience, we must find something that is alluring and enticing. We must desire and want. Once we *see and long for* the results, we must *act*.

We see selectively. At times we block out what is clearly "real" and we do not experience it. If we are reading an interesting book or watching a fascinating movie, we do not hear what is going on around us. Other times, we clearly experience something that is not there. If we are anxiously expecting someone, we might hear footsteps that are not there. In the story of Adam and Eve we find the first evidence that we see selectively. For there were two very important trees planted right in the middle of the garden. One was the tree of knowledge, or the *tree of knowing good and evil*, while the other was the tree of eternal life, or the *tree of life*: "And out of the ground the LORD God made to grow every tree that is pleasant to the sight and good for food, the tree of life also in the midst of the garden, and the tree of the knowledge of good and evil" (Genesis 2:9). Anyone who had eyes and could clearly see would have reached for the fruit of the tree of life first and eaten of it. For Adam and Eve were never forbidden to eat of the tree of life that would have given them immortality. The solution to the search for immortality was right before their eyes, yet they did not reach out and eat of its fruit. This tree was equally good to the sight. Yet they chose to eat of the forbidden tree instead. Why?

I believe that Adam and Eve never saw the tree of eternal life, because they did not have eyes that could discern value. It is the mind that sees through the eyes. If the eyes are open, but the mind is not, the mind will not comprehend what the eyes see. Adam and Eve were ignorant of the value of the tree of life. They saw only what they wanted to see based on what *they* considered to be good to the sight, even though all the trees were created equally pleasing to sight. Adam and Eve had a veil, a blind spot, a scotoma that prevented them from seeing the reality of what was before them. It was only after they gained knowledge as a result of eating the fruit of the tree of knowing good and evil that their eyes were opened and they could finally see. That is when they realized their nakedness: *"Then the eyes of both were opened, and they knew that they were naked; and they sewed fig leaves together and made themselves aprons"* (Genesis 3:7). By then, it was too late. The Tree of Life was guarded by an angel and their opportunity to gain immortality lost.

The second story is from *The Epic of Gilgamesh* and is about a man and a woman: Enkidu and the harlot.

> *So the goddess conceived an image in her mind, and it was of the stuff of Anu of the firmament. She dipped her hands in water and pinched off clay, she let it fall in the wilderness, and noble Enkidu was created. There was virtue in him of the god of war, of Ninurta himself. His body was rough, he had long hair like a woman's; it waved like the hair of Nisaba, the goddess of corn. His body was covered with matted hair like Samuqan's, the god of cattle. He was innocent of mankind; he knew nothing of the cultivated land.*

> Enkidu ate grass in the hills with the gazelle and lurked with wild beasts at the water-holes; he had joy of the water with the herds of wild game. . . .

Enkidu lived like the beasts until one day he was tempted by a harlot:

> She was not ashamed to take him, she made herself naked and welcomed his eagerness; as he lay on her murmuring love she taught him the woman's art. For six days and seven nights they lay together, for Enkidu had forgotten his home in the hills; but when he was satisfied he went back to the wild beasts. Then, when the gazelle saw him, they bolted away; when the wild creatures saw him they fled. Enkidu would have followed, but his body was bound as though with a cord, his knees gave way when he started to run; his swiftness was gone. And now the wild creatures had all fled away; Enkidu was grown weak, for wisdom was in him, and the thoughts of a man were in his heart. So he returned and sat down at the woman's feet, and listened intently to what she said. 'You are wise, Enkidu, and now you have become like a god. Why do you want to run wild like the beasts in the hills? Come with me.'

Like Adam and Eve, Enkidu was tempted and gave in to the temptation. He acted and gained the benefits of the experience. As he did, he immediately lost his state of ignorance, or inexperience, and acquired wisdom. Just as in the case of Adam and Eve, Enkidu gained wisdom as a result of experience. He, too, became like a god—*knowing.* In his case, the experience was the sexual act.

Experiencing is the fastest route to maturity. The ancients knew that we must have intimate experiences in order to wake up, open our eyes, see and know. They indicated that these experiences must be encounters as intimate as sex. That is why whenever the ancients spoke of sex, they referred to it as an act of knowing. ". . . *Adam knew his wife, and she conceived and bore Cain.*" When the angel appeared to

Mary with the news that she was going to conceive and bear a child, her response was: "... *How shall this be, seeing that I know not a man?*"

Not only sex, but all experiences can lead to increased awareness. The more personal, intimate and extraordinary our experiences, the fuller the awakening. If a picture is worth a thousand words, an experience is worth ten thousand. Experiences are the windows through which we glimpse reality. The pictures that we see out of these windows are as bright, alive and meaningful as the filters through which they pass to reach our consciousness. These filters are mainly our beliefs and our physical limitations. Even though we might not be able to control our biology, there is a lot we can do about our psychology, the beliefs we form and accept. By adjusting our beliefs, we manage the filters that color our experiences and shape our reality.

To wake up, we must not only see and desire, we must act and cause the results we seek. The more passionately we desire, the more polarized we become and the more rewarding our experiences are. The more clearly we see the end result and the more it appeals to our senses, the easier it will be for us to act. Action is the key that leads to gaining knowledge and wisdom. There is no limit to what we may achieve if we act with knowledge. As long as we continue to desire, experience and learn our eyes will keep on opening. We will grow and mature. With maturity comes wakeful living.

**Wakeful Living**

As we wake up, we realize our nakedness. We see how asleep, ignorant, or "sinful" we had been. We did not see clearly, understand, or know before. We are not what we supposed ourselves to be. Perceiving our "sins", we endeavor to do better. Realizing our ignorance, we pursue knowledge. As we gain more knowledge, we transform a piece of the veil that obscured our vision into a cloth—a "fig-leaf"—with which we cover up our "nakedness," or ignorance.

Full awakening is our aim. Yet, we expect our awakening to be gradual and progressive. Just as the closer we approach the speed of light, the more demanding it becomes to accelerate further, so it is with awakening. The more we wake up, the more demanding we are of ourselves. This is what happened to Saint Paul. The more spiritual he became, the more he realized how "sinful" he was.

> *We know that the law is spiritual; but I am carnal, sold under sin. I do not understand my own actions. For I do not do what I want, but I do the very thing I hate. Now if I do what I do not want, I agree that the law is good. So then it is no longer I that do it, but sin which dwells within me. For I know that nothing good dwells within me, that is, in my flesh. I can will what is right, but I cannot do it. For I do not do the good I want, but the evil I do not want is what I do. Now if I do what I do not want, it is no longer I that do it, but sin which dwells within me. So I find it to be a law that when I want to do right, evil lies close at hand. For I delight in the law of God, in my inmost self, but I see in my members another law at war with the law of my mind and making me captive to the law of sin which dwells in my members. Wretched man that I am! Who will deliver me from this body of death?*
>
> *Romans 7:14–24*

With each awakening, our emotional, mental and psychic organizations change. We become transfigured proportionate to the amount of knowledge and awareness we have gained. Our actions change to reflect our newly gained knowledge. This helps others gain the same knowledge and awareness at an accelerated pace. Through our intentional thoughts, feelings and wakeful behavior, we form an energy field, a "morphic resonance," that covers the globe and makes it easier for others to discover the same knowledge and attain comparable awareness. Simultaneous with our waking up, and to the extent that we become aware, we realize that:

1. we do not have to struggle to succeed,
2. we are where we need to be,
3. we have what it takes to achieve whatever we set our sights on,
4. everyone and everything matters, and
5. we are all connected.

## 1. We Do Not Have to Struggle to Succeed

*It may be that the most interesting American struggle is the struggle to set oneself free from the limits one is born to, and then to learn something of the value of those limits.*

*Greil Marcus*

There are undoubtedly many individuals who live or have lived life fully awake. The Buddha, Socrates, Akhnaton and Jesus the Christ are a few examples. One of the most remarkable demonstrations of Christ's wakefulness is the manner in which He called His disciples to service:

*As he walked by the Sea of Galilee, he saw two brothers, Simon who is called Peter and Andrew his brother, casting a net into the sea; for they were fishermen. And he said to them, "Follow me, and I will make you fishers of men." Immediately they left their nets and followed him. And going on from there he saw two other brothers, James the son of Zebedee and John his brother, in the boat with Zebedee their father, mending their nets, and he called them. Immediately they left the boat and their father, and followed him.*

*Matthew 4:18–22*

> As Jesus passed on from there, he saw a man called Matthew sitting at the tax office; and he said to him, "Follow me." And he rose and followed him.
>
> Matthew 9:9

> The next day Jesus decided to go to Galilee. And he found Philip and said to him, "Follow me."
>
> John 1:43

Jesus simply called His disciples saying: "Follow me." They left everything and followed Him. Even though this appears simple, it is most profound. Jesus must have known what He wanted, who He wanted and what He was doing. He, obviously, called the right people to follow him for they left everything and followed Him. The timing must have been perfect. Jesus must have known exactly what He was looking for. His intentions were crystal clear. When He saw what He wanted, He acted. Life responded. There was no resistance, no struggle, not much effort. Everything flowed as it should, simply, naturally and miraculously. **Lack of struggle is a trademark of the wakeful life.**

Examining my life, I realize that my most important successes came not as a result of struggle, competition, or demand; rather, as a gift from life, flowing to me naturally, simply and wondrously. This is how I was born, left for Lebanon, went to college, came to the United States, joined the Army, found my job and purchased my homes. This is how I found the Rosicrucian Order and met my wife. This is also how we had our children and formed our family. Finding my wife is an experience I will never forget. It is one of those clear instances when I knew that there was more to life than what at first is evident. Instead of struggling and forcing our way, we can make our intentions known, ask for help and when it is granted, accept it graciously.

## Finding Barbara

I had mostly lived a lonely life in Lebanon. Except for the occasional visits with my friends and Aunt Faith, I was mostly alone. I was 24 years old when I entered the United States in 1972 on Valentine's Day. In July of 1972, I joined the U. S. Army for a three-year tour of duty.

Throughout my tour in the Army, I was lonely and in search of a companion and mate. I unsuccessfully struggled through the efforts of dating and even offered to marry a childhood friend in Lebanon. All to no avail.

It was now February 1976, and I was still alone and lonely. Out of desperation, I decided to employ a combination of prayer and meditation to plead my case to the Cosmic Hosts and ask for help. I knew exactly what I wanted—to attract the one most suitable to be my friend and mate. I felt deserving and my intentions were clear. I prepared myself and entered into a meditative state. I was in a highly charged emotional state. I raised my consciousness until I felt I was in the presence of the Cosmic Intelligence. I pleaded my case vividly, intensely and passionately. I asked for help and guidance. I requested a solution to my loneliness. I declared my readiness to meet my mate. I then expressed gratitude and slowly reverted back to my normal state. As soon as I was back, I *knew* beyond any shadow of doubt that I had made contact and that my plea was heard and answered. My request would soon manifest in physical reality.

In April of 1976, the local Rosicrucians held a class in one of the hotels in downtown Washington, DC. I decided to take this class. After walking into the room, I looked around to see who was there. All of a sudden, my heart started to pound loud and fast and a clear voice from deep within thundered forth: "the one you seek is here." Looking at her, our eyes met. I knew she was the one. I walked over and asked if she would have dinner with me that Friday night. She agreed and gave me her address and phone number on a piece of paper.

I had met Barbara earlier, the first time in November of 1975, during the intermission of a Rosicrucian play I was taking part in. I talked with her then, casually. She looked shy and old fashioned, yet bright and friendly. She was wearing a long colorful gown. She asked me many questions about myself. When I met her again, I was surprised that she remembered everything about me, while I could not even remember her name.

I wondered why I felt the way I did when I saw her this time. I decided to accept the feeling and go with it. Meanwhile, Barbara was wondering why she had accepted my invitation so readily and whether or not she should call to cancel. Fortunately, she did not have my phone number.

I picked Barbara up from her apartment in Arlington, Va. and drove her to my apartment in Glen Burnie, Md. where I had prepared stuffed grape leaves for dinner and fresh strawberries for dessert. While driving her back to her apartment later that night, she fell asleep in the car. I stopped the car, got a blanket from the trunk and covered her up. I *knew* Barbara was going to be my wife. It took Barbara a few weeks to even let me hold her hand.

I asked and received a gift. I knocked and a door opened. Yet, at no time was I forced to accept the gift or walk through the door. These were my decisions. Trusting in an intelligence far higher than mine that knows what is best for me, I gratefully accepted the gift. We have been happily married for over twenty years and have two daughters, Olivia and Emily. I have never met anyone whom I would rather have for a wife. Barbara has been perfect for me and, hopefully, I for her.

## 2. We Are Where We Need To Be

*Then he said, "Do not come near; put off your shoes from your feet, for the place on which you are standing is holy ground."*
*Exodus 3:5*

Just as students in a school are in the class they qualify for, we are always where we need to be even if it is not where we want to be; for our current situation is a reflection of who and where we are. The circumstances about us are the necessary environment for our growth and maturation. They shape us, and in return, we incorporate them as aspects of our character and personality. Just as any charged particle cannot occupy space without distorting it, we cannot be in a place without making it a reflection of who we are. We are an integral part of our environment. We can be stuck in it, or we can learn to use where we are as the launching pad for where we want to end up. We can start only from where we already are. This implies accepting our circumstances and ourselves for who, what, and where we are.

Where we are is a school and we are students in the ever spiraling educational system of life. It is we who determine if we will study, learn and graduate. We determine how much time we spend in each class before we move on to the next higher. The passing grade is our level of awareness, understanding and a demonstration of mastery. To gain full mastery, we require several classes, teachers, schools and circumstances. There is only so much we can learn in a class and in any particular school. After a while, we need to take a break and assimilate. When we come back it is either to a new class or to a different school all together.

Where we are is where all of our previous acts have led us and from where all of our future acts will spring. Just as God reminded Moses that where he was standing was holy ground, we must also *see* and *know* that where we are—The Moment—is a holy place, for it is the birthplace of all activities. It is the point where all of our past ends and our entire future begins. If we are not content with where we are, the problem does not lie with the place, or the time; rather, with our awareness, and the use we make of our circumstances. We might complain that we lack time, money, or skills. The problem is not what we lack; rather, what we are doing with what we already have. It is always easy to lay the blame for our shortcomings on others: the government, the system, our jobs, circumstances, or lack of opportunities. The problem does not lie out there. It is right here within us. We should not ask what others are doing to us; rather, we should question what we are doing to ourselves and allowing others to do to us. The answers we seek are right here where we are. We must use our circumstances as the raw material out of which we fashion our future. The future can only be born out of the present.

In Russell Conwell's *Acres Of Diamonds*,[2] a farmer sells his farm, leaves his family behind, and sets out looking for diamonds. Acres of diamonds were eventually found on the same farm that the farmer sold. The moral of the story is that what we seek is often not far away. It might even be in our own backyard where we least expect it. Where we are is also where our opportunities are. To uncover them, we need to dig, not in our backyard, but deep down in our minds. We must start our search for what we desire right where we are. Why go far away if what we seek can be found right where we are? We must build from what is at hand before we ask for what we do not have.

In *The Epic of Gilgamesh*,[3] a king named Gilgamesh sets out to search for knowledge and eternal life—an escape from death which is the lot of common man. Gilgamesh fails. Men have traveled the globe looking for opportunity, wealth and happiness. We all yearn for Shangri-La, Paradise and Heaven, a place where everyone lives happily and abundantly. Is it possible that we are searching in the wrong places? Is it possible that instead of searching for places, we should be looking for states of awareness and being? To find these states, all we have to do is go deep within ourselves or rise high above our circumstances. The road to anywhere starts right where we currently are.

2. *Acres Of Diamonds,* Russell Conwell's Inspiring book About Opportunity. Hallmark Cards Inc., 1968
3. The Epic of Gilgamesh, Penguin Classics, 1972

As soon as we know we are where we need to be, we see that the tree of life and abundance that we seek is already in our midst. We realize that we already have what it takes to succeed. We are engulfed by the circumstances we need to grow. All we need is to trust and act. Where we are is not only where we need to be, but it is the only place we can be. For the place is what it is because of who and what we are. If we change as a result of seeing and knowing, the place and the circumstances will also change. Instead of toiling to be in the right place, we should strive to be in the proper state—seeing who we are, where we are and what is the best we can do in and with our current circumstances.

## 3. We Have What it Takes to Achieve

*The seeds of great discoveries are constantly floating around us, but they only take root in minds well prepared to receive them.*
Joseph Henry

One day I found myself complaining that I was wasting my life. I had to get up early, go to work, engage in seemingly meaningless activities, come home tired, run a few errands, go to bed, sleep, wake up and repeat the same thing all over again. Why can I not have enough time and money to engage in more meaningful activities such as thinking, writing, discovering, learning and teaching? I reasoned that if I only had enough money, I would be free to pursue my passions and excel. This idea of living the life I want impressed itself upon me deeply. It caught my attention. I thought about it constantly over the next few weeks. Finally, I decided to meditate about it to see how I could achieve it.

The answer I received was clear: "unless I become proficient in the use of what I already have, I will not be given more. I must first learn to profitably invest what I have. If I do not know how to manage the few resources I now have, I will not be able to manage the more I am asking for. If I invest my current time gainfully, more will become available to me. The better the use, the greater the returns." Even though the answer was not what I wanted to hear and it surprised me, I accepted it and resolved to comply.

It was then that I remembered the parable of the talents. I realized that I could invest my resources for a 1:1, 1:2, 1:5 or greater returns. It was I who determined the rate of return on my investment. Henceforth, I shifted my focus from asking to receive to knowing how to invest and generate. I wanted to earn and deserve what I was asking for. I began to ask better questions of myself. Instead of asking to have, I began to question what I can give in order to receive. What do I currently have? How can I best invest what I have? With the shift in my consciousness, my focus changed from money and free time to focusing on my skills and abilities. The critical question of the moment became: what is the best use of my time now?

I began having a recurring dream. In this dream, I live in a house. There is nothing outstanding about this house except that somewhere beneath the house, I discover a large hole leading to a passage. I follow the passage. It gets progressively wider as it snakes itself deep underneath the house. Soon I arrive at a wide opening. At this opening I see a beautiful sight—caverns studded with colorful stalagmites and stalactites forming some of the most exquisite figurines and statuettes that I have ever seen. As I walk back up to the house, I see large crowds outside waiting to visit my caverns. However, there is no developed pathway leading to the caverns.

I had to "see" this dream many times before I realized its meaning. I did not need more time or money to attain my heart's desires. I did not have to travel far to arrive at what I sought. I already had what I needed in the form of "rough diamonds." The house in my dream was my mind. If I dug deep inside of it, I would unearth treasures in the form of ideas that could provide me with what I was searching for. I just had to develop these ideas and make them beautiful enough for people to want to "visit" them. Even though what I had to start with was a mere glitter in my eyes, I was sitting on a gold mine. I was the owner of the farm full of diamonds in the rough. With this insight, I saw exactly what I was to do next. I must pave a way for people to visit my caverns. I need to transform the ordinary stones I had into precious stones. Clear insight propelled me into action. I began to think and write. The idea of this book was born.

We have what it takes. Even though most of what we have is not fully developed, we can develop whatever we have. Everything we need to succeed is within us, or surrounding us. The more our eyes open, the more we realize that we are surrounded by what we need. We must start from where we are, evaluate what resources we already have and then we must *engage* ourselves. We must act, experience, learn and continue to improve. If we want more out of life, we must do more ourselves. We *can* do more, but we must start with what we already have and where we are. We have each other and mother earth. We have our skills, abilities and relationships. We have this very moment with its challenges and opportunities.

Even though everything appears ordinary around us, there is nothing "common and ordinary" in life. EVERYTHING IS A MIRACLE. We get used to things and become accustomed to their wonder and then we take them for granted. Living becomes a habit and a routine and our senses of curiosity, wonder and amazement get dull. We should not look at things as they are. Rather, as they can be if we transform them through our creativity. Words, stones, wood and people can be transformed into prose and poetry, cathedrals and family. We are gods in the making. The more we create extraordinary from the ordinary and uncommon from the common, the more of our true nature we reflect.

We live in the world, but the world lives within our

minds. Our minds are like gardens. Each garden—mind—has many plants growing in it. Many people allow weeds to grow in their gardens. If these weeds take over, they will hide and suffocate the good plants, the ones that bear abundant fruit. We all have some weeds in our gardens hiding between the good plants. Weeds grow naturally. It takes effort, care and dedication to have a healthy, productive garden. We must learn how to be effective gardeners by weeding the undesirables and feeding the favored. We must become cultivators of our minds.

There are four rivers flowing in the midst of the garden of our mind: habits, attitudes, expectations and beliefs. These four rivers water our minds. Rays of sunshine and bursts of creativity invigorate the life of our garden. We must spray our garden with the water of our passions and add fertilizers in the form of hopes, dreams and aspirations. We can employ visualization on a regular basis to kindle our desires. We must keep on weeding, feeding and pruning our gardens for we are as alive, healthy and vibrant as the gardens of our minds.

There are also two main trees in the midst of the garden of our mind. One of these trees is The Tree of Knowledge, the other is The Tree of Life. These two trees are central to our being. They are the two pillars that hold our temple, the body, together. These two trees are intertwined. For as long as we live, we should want to know and for as long as we crave knowing, we will live. If we nurture our minds, we will grow the crops we want: joy, laughter and love; peace, health and contentment; abundance, value and meaning.

We are familiar with Aladdin and his magical lamp. You rub the lamp and a genie appears to do your bidding. We carry such a lamp within us. It is our mind. Yet this lamp is mostly hidden with its light dimmed, saved for special occasions, usually under duress. We seldom use our minds creatively to solve problems, challenge ourselves and live the life we want. We must always keep in mind that the genie always fits the lamp. If the lamp is tiny, the light (the genie) will be dim. We will not have enough light to work with and we will become content with mediocrity. If, however, we fully realize that it is *we* who determine the size of the lamp in which we place our genie, we can expand the light of our lamp by acquiring more knowledge, sharpening our skills and mushrooming our abilities. There is no limit to how much we can expand our light. We set our own limits. We are a universe unto ourselves, contracting or expanding based on our involvement and effort.

We are told that we use about ten percent of our minds. Perhaps it would be more accurate to say that we use our minds to no more than ten percent capacity. We use all of our minds, but at minimum capacity. Our minds are like automobiles that can take us places, except that our minds are capable of moving us not only at the maximum speed of a regular automobile, but at the speed of light. Unfortunately, we drive our minds at no more than 55 to 65 miles per hour due to some artificial laws we impose on ourselves and accept as cosmic law. We have more neural networks in our brains than there are stars in the galaxies. If these worked together, harmoniously and cooperatively with a single purpose in mind, we could perform wonders and demonstrate miracles, not occasionally, but at will and regularly.

The state of the world at large is a reflection of the condition of our minds. The colonial mentality rules. Divide and conquer! Our minds are divided against themselves. The world is divided against itself. This division is mostly out of ignorance and some of it is out of malice. Either somebody keeps our houses divided in order to rule over us, or we do it to ourselves out of fear, ignorance and insecurity. As long as people and nations remain divided, very little can be accomplished.

> *"If a kingdom is divided against itself, that kingdom cannot stand. And if a house is divided against itself, that house will not be able to stand."*
>
> Mark 3:24–25

We have choices in life. We can choose to function at high or low levels. We usually sabotage ourselves, compete with others, fight for survival and waste our natural and acquired resources on trivia that appears very real and important at the time. We lose track of the fact that we have made these what they are and we have given them the values that they assume.

To have time for great works of art, breakthroughs in science and medicine and the accomplishment of lofty deeds, we must rise above the level of satisfying our primary needs. Why is it that our needs for food, shelter, medicine and comfort have not been met after all these years of existing as a civilized society? Are we incapable of eliminating hunger, disease and wars? Are we incapable of living the noble life instead of the savage life? We will not be "civilized" until we begin to "drive at higher speeds," remove the artificial barriers and obstacles from our paths and use our skills, abilities and relationships to create for the benefit of humanity at large.

We can never get to Heaven until every individual values himself or herself enough to pursue their passions. Heaven is a measure for how far we can stretch ourselves and how high we can reach. Heaven is being the most we can be, doing the best we can do and creating miracles in our lives and in the lives we touch. We cannot do our best unless it incorporates our passions, aptitudes and ideals. By seeking to fulfill our passions, we develop our potential and contribute our best to society, the country and humanity.

We have what it takes to achieve. Having it is not enough. We must proficiently use what we now have and from it fashion what we aspire to attain.

## 4. Everyone and Everything Matters

*Every action of our lives touches on some chord that will vibrate in eternity.*

*Edwin Hubbel Chapin*

Everything and everyone in our lives *does* matter. Every act is important. Every thought counts. Every feeling has an impact. Every individual has a place. Every event can be utilized for some good. What we do with ourselves matters. It matters whether we are thankful or resentful, appreciative or complaining, loving or hateful. It matters whether we drink water or alcohol day after day. It matters whether we nourish and nurture ourselves and each other, or deprive and abuse ourselves and each other day after day. It matters whether we gossip, connive and quarrel or we think profound thoughts, give thanks and praise others day after day. It makes a difference what we do with our time and abilities and whom we associate with day after day. It all adds up and makes a difference even if it takes a long time for the results to become evident.

It is easy to see the impact of an act on our lives when that act leads to an obvious result such as when you buy a lottery ticket and win. I know a young lady who accepted a ride from a teenage neighbor and ended up in the hospital with a severe concussion. Obviously, not all decisions lead to such dramatic results—at least not immediately. But the repetition, over a long period of time, of the smallest of our acts, thoughts and feelings can lead to dramatic consequences. Dripping water may not have a significant impact, but continued over eons, it will leave its mark on the hardest of terrain. Our results are determined by the choices we make day after day.

In ancient Egypt, it was believed that after death the soul of the departed was weighed against Truth, or *maat*, represented by a feather. The soul was placed on one of the scales and a feather on the other. The deceased was rewarded or punished based on the result of the weighing. This Judgment Hall, which according to the ancient Egyptians we will face at the end of our physical life, is merely a process for tallying the results of the many small judgment halls we face while alive on Earth. Each day and every moment we encounter decisions as to how to invest our resources of time, abilities and relationships. If we make a wise choice, we add to our "good" scale. If we make an unwise decision, then we add to our "bad" scale. We progress if the "good" scale outweighs the "bad" scale. However, if we learn from all that we engage in and experience, what would have been added to our "bad" scale is added to our "good" scale instead. Since we can learn from all of our experiences, everything in our lives *does* matter. Let us be aware of what we think, feel and do. We must watch out for the habits that we form.

We are, at any given moment, faced with the choice of what to do with ourselves and our lives. We hold the keys to our success or failure. Based on the decisions we make and the actions we take, we create abundance or scarcity, meaning or meaninglessness, Hell or Heaven for ourselves and others. We decide if someone is important or unimportant, view an activity as tedious or exciting. By controlling the level of our knowledge, awareness and understanding, we decide the level at which we function. We are the result of all the decisions we have made thus far. If we want to change our status in life, we must expand our usefulness and do what it takes to qualify for and deserve whatever we crave. By taking simple steps in the right direction, beginning right now and repeating them daily, we move toward our desired destination.

## 5. We Are All Connected

*The universe is one of God's thoughts.*
*Friedrich Von Schiller*

We are all connected; to each other, to nature and to God. We are all children of the one life. Our mother is earth and our father is the sun. Just as all water creatures are connected through the medium of the water and all air creatures are connected through the medium of the air, all humans are connected through our humanity and all life forms are connected through the life that courses through their being. We share the same elements of earth as nourishment. We build our bodies by consuming other life forms. We evolve by experiencing each other. We rise from the same source and to that same source we return.

We are all engaged in transforming the simple into the more complex, the inefficient into the more efficient and the chaotic into the orderly. Not only is no man an island unto himself, no thought, feeling, or act is limited to itself. Everything is both a wave and a particle (wavicle) in nature. As a particle, it is local. As a wave, it is global. Through the media, a story in one country is known everywhere else. Through commerce; books, music and products from one country are distributed to all other countries. Acts of generosity, philanthropy, crime and barbarism in one country impact the consciousness of everyone else.

If our connections are not apparent to us, it is because we only see what our level of awareness enables us to see. Just because we have seen, touched, smelled, tasted and studied an item does not mean that we *know* that item and realize our unity with it. Perhaps what we need to go through to see fully is the type of experience that Saul went through to transform him into Paul: *"And immediately something like scales fell from his eyes and he regained his sight. Then he rose and was baptized" (Acts 9:18).* Our scales must come off, not only from our eyes, but from our hearts and minds as well. Once these are opened, all the secrets of the universe will lay naked before us. We will see that what we once considered common is anything but common and what we viewed as separate and apart is in fact intimately connected to us and we to it. Not too long ago I saw and for a fleeting moment comprehended, the deeper reality of a not so ordinary garden tomato.

### The TOMATO

I picked a tomato from my garden and looked at it. I did not look at it casually, but with a deep desire to really *know what is this thing we call a tomato?!*

I remember planting the seed. Then, after an ambiguous period of not knowing what was taking place in the soil, I saw a tiny seedling break the surface of the soil. It was as if it was declaring silently but resolutely *"I am here and I am alive!"* The plant grew in width and height until it became fully mature. It acquired many stems, branches and leaves and even though I could not see the roots, I knew they were there. Then many tiny yellow flowers formed beside the leaves on the stems.

After a few days, I saw tiny bulbous structures at the base of the flowers. At first small, hard and green, they grew to become large, soft and red.

I now hold one of them in my hand and look at it attentively, curiously and lovingly. What are you?

Red, soft and round.

The colors green and red displayed by you are not inherent in you. Color is due to light, absorption, refraction and the structures of my eyes and brain. At night, your color is not there, for it never was in you even when I saw it there. What I see as color is what you do not absorb when the rays of light reach you. You reflect the color I see. What you reject, I consider an essential aspect of you. What I see tells me as much about me as it does about you.

I cannot know how hard or soft you are until I touch you. By touching you, my own structure, my nervous system and how it functions, are revealed to me. I interpret my own sensations, thoughts and ideas as qualities of yours.

Looking at you when you were round, but small and green, I could not understand how you would be able to slowly transform yourself into a much larger round structure with a different color—red. I could see you getting larger on a daily basis. Even though, logically, I understand how you do that, I still do not fully realize the magic unfolding before my eyes.

I am told that you are a bunch of cells grouped together in a specific way. But these cells are not the same cells that formed you a while ago. When you were a tiny bulbous structure you had very few cells compared to now. How did you know how to create all these extra cells and add them to yourself? I am told that you are constantly changing and that you have been adding to yourself from the soil, the air and the sun. If life progresses only from life, how could the soil, the water, the air and the sun add to your body and life? How can you take inert elements and give life to them? Or, are all these elements and the sunshine alive as well?

Your journey from a tiny, green, knot-like structure until you became the red, soft and large tomato I now hold and observe, lasted about four weeks. During this journey, you constantly changed your features while extending in the three dimensions of space. During this time, you were also extending in the fourth dimension of time. Your journey appears to have started from when you were tiny, green and knot-like, but for your journey to begin the plant had to be first. For the plant to be, the soil, seed, water and sunshine had to be first. Where is the real beginning?! All beginnings and endings are mere apparent starts and ends. Since you are always in a state of change, your journey is ongoing. Your beginning with me was the seed I planted. That seed had to come from somewhere. It had its own journey. Your seeds and cells will have their own journeys as well. In a way, you had no true beginning and are not going to have an ultimate end. The cells that formed you were part of some other structures. Now they are going to be part of another. Before I picked you up, you were part of the plant. To remind me of your previous connection, you carry a "scar" the same way that I carry a belly button to remind me and others of my previous connection. The same way that I came from my mother, you came from your mother—the plant. The plant is connected to the soil just as you were connected to the plant. The soil, in turn, is connected to earth. Earth is connected to the solar system. The solar system is connected to the galaxies and the universe.

Where does it all end or start? Your atoms and cells, just like mine, are always combining, breaking down and recombining. Since nothing can be created nor destroyed, all that now is, has always been, only in different combinations, assuming different forms and existing in diverse spaces and times.

I look at you again. What makes you now must have been a part of everything else, one time or another; from the beginning, now and forever.

Behold, when I look at you, I see eternity.

Slowly I lift the tomato up and bring it closer to me. Now it is seen as separate and apart, as a tomato. I open my mouth and reverently consume the tomato. It is now part of me. The eternity that was the tomato is now part of the eternity that is me. The journey continues. What constituted the tomato is now breaking down. The particles of the tomato will recombine and reappear in a different form. They will no more be known as a tomato, or seen apart by themselves. Henceforth, the particles will be called by a new name. They will take on my identity and the journey will go on until I, too, am dissolved, absorbed and recombined into other forms. Then, I too will appear in a different garment and be known by a new name.

I take a long and deep breath.

What is true of the tomato is equally true of the air I just breathed in and the sun whose rays are shining upon me.

Soil, air and sunshine forming the tomato; tomato, air and sunshine forming me.

I am always becoming with everything else. Is air part of me? Is water or food part of me? They are not until I take them in and then they are.

How can I be so dependent on these elements and yet proclaim a separate existence? This is the paradox of the ages. I am, yet without all else, I cannot be.

Can I have a body without what I consume? Can I have emotions without others to interact with and an environment to respond to? How can I depend so much on others to stimulate and cause my emotions and yet think that I have a separate existence of my own? Is not my intelligence activated and developed as a response to my environment? Did not my senses form as a result of being in this world, immersed in earthly experiences?

I am in the image of my environment and my environment is in my image. Environment and I, like chicken and egg, have always existed and coexist. We both assume various garbs, colors, shapes and form numerous associations. We take on unique identities for a while and then exchange them for new ones. As we exchange, we change, wake up and grow.

# STAGE 2

# Have Something Worthwhile to Live for

*This is the true joy in life, the being used for a purpose recognized by yourself as a mighty one; the being thoroughly worn out before you are thrown on the scrap heap; the being a force of nature instead of a feverish selfish little clod of ailments and grievances complaining that the world will not devote itself to making you happy. I am of the opinion that my life belongs to the whole community and as long as I live it is my privilege, my privilege to do for it whatever I can. I want to be thoroughly used up when I die for the harder I work the more I live. I rejoice in life for its own sake. Life is no brief candle for me. It is a sort of splendid torch which I've got ahold of for the moment and I want to make it burn as brightly as possible before handing it on to further generations.*

George Bernard Shaw

We are reminded that the vast majority of people "live a life of quiet desperation." We hear about violence, drugs, promiscuity and crime permeating society. We are inundated with conflicts, diseases and despair. Meaninglessness abounds. Even though we are advancing technologically and living longer, we are not becoming any happier. Life has become too demanding and complicated. As the pace of change accelerates and we are faced with many options, we lose sight of what is essential. We waste precious time wading through the many trivial choices we face which, because of their large number, assume prominence. We find ourselves living for the distractions instead of the vital. Yet, inwardly, we know that there must be more to our lives. Not knowing what to do, we get discouraged. Struggle becomes a normal way of life. We lose hope and give up our dreams. With the lack of something meaningful to live for, we despair and die having never really lived.

We are not victims of our circumstances. We can be victimized if we allow ourselves, or we can wake up and live the life we choose. For life to have meaning and a lasting significance for us we must live purposeful lives. We assign a purpose to our lives through our intentions, knowledge and actions. Without purpose, our lives will lack meaning. Without meaning, we cannot be motivated. Without motivation, we lack the will to fully live. We sleep-walk through life.

Even though we are powerful, we mostly live a powerless life. On rare occasions, usually under extreme circumstances while performing altruistic acts, we exhibit extraordinary powers. People walk for distances, scale high mountains, swim for hours, withstand extremes of temperature, walk on fire and endure days of hunger and thirst for the sake of a loved one, or to accomplish a passionate mission. We need to learn to tap into and use, at will, the tremendous powers buried within us. I believe the key for tapping into our source of great power is to live a life of purpose in service to others. This is how Christ lived and used his powers—to serve the needs of others. Jesus never performed miracles to flaunt his powers, impress others, or exalt himself. It seems natural to call on these hidden forces when we are attempting to serve others while living our purpose.

Ralph Waldo Emerson stated that, *"Nothing great was ever achieved without enthusiasm."* There is no enthusiasm without passion, for the two are one and the same. Doing what we passionately love and loving whatever we do allows our energy to flow freely—this flowing energy of love can be tapped to achieve whatever we seek. Once we have love, the most powerful of emotions, we can use it to heal, build and perform miracles. When we do, we live the miraculous life.

To live for something worthwhile beyond our limited self, we must strongly believe in it. It must either spring from our core passions, or we must learn to love it and make it our core passion. While we have a vast selection of things to live for, we should strongly consider an ideal. Each religion, science and philosophy, has its own set of ideals to promulgate. To decide which ones are for us, we must examine our purpose for living, then use that purpose as the measuring stick to evaluate the various ideals. We select the one most in harmony with our nature, aptitude and circumstances. Once we decide on an ideal, it becomes easy to evaluate systems of thought we encounter against the ideal we established for ourselves. The ones in harmony we encourage, while those in discord we leave alone to wither and die on their own.

**Having a Worthwhile Purpose to Live for**

For several years now, I have been trying to grow a fig tree in my back yard so I can enjoy some fresh figs. The first winter I tried to protect the small shoot by covering it with leaves in a plastic bag. The leaves rotted and with them the shoot. The next spring, the plant started growing once more from the ground up. It grew about three feet but produced no fruit. That winter, I wrapped foam insulation around the shoots. The plant survived the winter and in the spring grew to over eight feet but still bore no figs. While fertilizing my small garden in my back yard, I decided to use the same fertilizer on the fig tree. That was a big mistake. The beautiful leaves of the fig tree started to wither and die. Within a few days almost all the leaves were lost. No figs this year either.

The next winter was much colder than usual. It killed the fig tree. Fortunately, the roots remained alive and in the spring the tree came to life again. Even though the tree grew, it produced no figs. One more season of disappointment.

The tree is a good ornament, but that is not why I planted it. Unless the tree produces figs, there is no justification for me to keep it. The tree must produce to serve the purpose for which it was planted and is taken care of.

*And he told this parable: "A man had a fig tree planted in his vineyard; and he came seeking fruit on it and found none. And he said to the vinedresser, 'Lo, these three years I have come seeking fruit on this fig tree, and I find none. Cut it down; why should it use up the ground?' And he answered him, 'Let it alone, sir, this year also, till I dig about it and put on manure. And if it bears fruit next year, well and good; but if not, you can cut it down.'"*

*Luke 13:6–9*

We are not unlike the fig tree. We cannot just *be*. If we want to stay alive and not be "cut down," we must *be* for one or several reasons. We must produce fruit. We must contribute. If we want to remain alive for a long time, we must bear fruit for all the time we are alive. The easiest and best fruit we can produce are the ones in accordance with our nature.

Just like fruit trees, we are known by the fruit we produce. Unlike the fig tree, however, we bear different fruit at different times and we decide what the fruit will be. We can produce fruit two ways: haphazardly based on circumstance, or intentionally based on awareness. The fruits we produce are our contributions to the society in which we live. We always contribute even while "asleep." However, not all of our contributions are of equal value. While "asleep" in consciousness, we mostly contribute anger, hate, malice, violence and destruction. We are on an ego trip. We view ourselves as the center of the universe. We demand the best from everyone, yet we are not required to give much in return. While "asleep", we are selfish. We cause and contribute to negativity. As we wake up, we shift the focus from self to others. We realize that there is no getting without first giving. We become convinced that service is the greatest source of joy and contributor to meaning in our lives.

Life *is* a stage. On this stage all of us play, with some winning and others losing, some leading and others following. There are two ways to play. We can choose a role and a life style we want for ourselves and live accordingly. Or we can live haphazardly, tossed around by various stimuli, whims and wishes, if we choose to do nothing and allow events to determine our roles and fate. We can live the life we choose if we decide on a worthwhile purpose to live for that is exciting enough to keep us inwardly motivated. This will be our reason for waking up every morning and with a passion for living. If we do not create our own reasons for getting up each morning, we will soon run out of external stimuli to keep us going. When we do, we age quickly, wither and die.

Living is not a simulation or a rehearsal. Each act is a one time deal. Therefore, we must live with awareness. We have free will to the extent that we exercise it and choose. We can choose to pretend that we are not important and that our contributions do not make a difference. This, however, does not change reality where everything is interconnected and matters.

In the movie "Defending Your Life," actor Albert Brooks and actress Meryl Streep find themselves defending their acts while alive on earth to a judge and jury in heaven. They have to prove that they lived without fear and took advantage of every opportunity to live their lives as well as possible. If they are judged to have learned their lessons, they will be allowed to move on to another plane of existence. Otherwise, they have to return to earth to live again and again until they learn from their experiences and take full advantage of their opportunities. Living a purposeful life is the best way to take full advantage of our opportunities. For we not only look for opportunities, but we create them as well, often out of obstacles. Unless we learn to take full advantage of our opportunities, we, too, might have to return to earth, again and again, until we wake up and recognize that to live a life of purpose is the only worthwhile way to live. It is then that we realize our "obstacles" for what they are—opportunities to exercise our ideal and express our purpose.

To succeed in life, we require energy, a plan, tools, resources, will, action and persistence. Mere success, however, does not lead to happiness. We could succeed doing the wrong things. We can set goals and reach them only to discover that our ladder of success is leaning against the wrong wall. Choosing a worthwhile purpose to live for, is to create and occupy our niche in life. It is to recognize the unique challenges that have been placed in our path. As we live a life of purpose we find meaning in everything we undertake. We cease searching for the ultimate meaning and purpose for life. We conclude that love and joy are good enough reasons in and of themselves. Once we have joy and love in our hearts and understanding in our minds nothing external can babel or confuse us. We work together and build ourselves a true and lasting City of Peace—a new Jerusalem. This city will have a new Tower of Babel at its center. We build this "Gateway to God" gradually employing people with different "tongues," talents, customs, nationalities, creeds, races, beliefs and abilities. As we work together with joy and love we bond together. We form a new body and become a new individual. We achieve our ultimate goal—returning home and regaining Paradise Lost. Once home, we will be robed, jeweled and the fatted calf will be served as the celebrations begin.

## Defining Our Purpose

Life without purpose is unbearable once we wake up. Yet, having a purpose is not as difficult as it might seem. We are slowly led to our purposes through our circumstances. Each experience, each ability and each desire is like a piece of a puzzle. Once most of the pieces are in their places, a picture begins to emerge and our purpose in life begins to unfold. As this purpose unfolds, it becomes self evident. It points to where we can make a difference.

Any purpose we accept for our lives must incorporate the following features:

### 1. Purpose must be personal

Our purpose must be our own, based on our needs, understanding, values, commitments, likes, and loves. It must be an unfoldment of our inner nature like the unfoldment of a seed in the process of maturation. Our purpose should be like our clothes, home, or job. It must reflect our personality.

We should not live our entire lives for the sake of others, based on their needs, wants and expectations of us. We should neither live to prove ourselves, nor to gain the approval of others. Only humans seem to live to prove themselves to each other. Plants and animals live simply as an expression of their being. Living to prove ourselves is labor intensive, stressful and can never be carried out fully and to the satisfaction of all. We should rather live to express our individuality. In order to live our lives, we must live according to our individual choices doing what we value most.

It is not easy to live a life of purpose unless that purpose is personal and we are passionate about it. Personal, however, does not mean just one purpose for our entire life. One primary purpose is not of greater value than many secondary purposes. Additionally, we can change our purpose as our understanding and circumstances change. It is the nature of life to go through stages. As infants and children, our purpose is mostly to receive and survive. As we grow up, we begin to focus on giving and living.

People with well defined personal purposes live powerful lives. They see no obstacles in their way, only opportunities. They seem impervious to what cannot be done. They are always ready, determined and committed to do whatever they really want. These people are results-oriented. Their entire being is integrated and harmoniously cooperating to allow them the best chance to succeed. Their intent is so clear that either people move out of their way or join in and lend them a helping hand. These people possess the complete faith that whatever they seek to do is as good as done.

## 2. Purpose must be rewarding

Living a purposeful life is not the easiest way to live. It is, however, the most rewarding. These rewards are: abundant energy, health and vitality, gratification and peace of mind. Since every purposeful act is a stone we lay in building the cathedral of our lives and the realization of our dreams, every act and experience becomes rewarding in itself. We do not have to wait for a final reward upon completion. This changes our lives from living for delayed gratification to one in which we derive instant fulfillment from any act we undertake that is aligned with our purpose.

## 3. Purpose must be motivating

To the degree that we decide on something worthwhile to live for, to that degree we are motivated. It is easier to be motivated when we mentally see, hear, touch, smell and taste the life we want to experience. The degree of our motivation and the amount of energy we have for an activity is directly proportional to the value of that activity. We assign the highest values to our core passions. If our core passions are the same as our purpose, then the anticipated fulfilling of our purpose breaks down all barriers to inactivity. We act because we are pursuing our deepest passions, the pillars of our purpose. Our purpose, when based on our core passions, is powerful enough to provide us with all the motivation we need to carry out any task. If we anchor our purpose to a personal ideal in addition to our passions, then that purpose becomes our wellspring and the source of our power.

Like a rechargeable battery, we require frequent recharging. If we do not learn how to keep our batteries charged, we run down, tire and stop. As we exert, we use up energy. As we enjoy the fruits of our labor, we recharge our batteries and are ready for more action. We are told that the human brain is a goal-seeking organ. Unless we are motivated to carry out an activity, we do not. We are naturally motivated when we do what we value.

Until we know value, everything is worthless. Once we know value, everything becomes valuable. The more we do what we enjoy and learn to love what we must do, the more energy we will have. It has been said there are no dull activities, just dull people. We must add value and find meaning in whatever we do. The more excited we are about the activities we engage in, the higher the rate of our vibration and the more energy we have. We get tired and feel depleted out of boredom, fear and worry. We get energized doing what we enjoy and find meaningful.

Years ago I used to believe that I could only work for a number of hours before I got tired. I also believed that unless I slept a certain number of hours every night I would feel tired and sleepy the next day. For several weeks, while working at Walter Reed Army Medical Center in Washington, D.C. I had been working longer and sleeping fewer hours than I believed I needed. I felt more and more tired. One Friday morning, totally exhausted, I decided that at the end of that day, I would go home, unhook the phones, lock the doors, get in bed and sleep until I naturally woke up.

After work that day, as I got ready for bed, the phone rang just before I could turn it off. I was tempted not to answer, but I did. It was my sister-in-law. Sounding very concerned, she told me that my brother was in critical condition with Legionnaire's disease at the navy hospital in Charleston, South Carolina. My brother was on duty as a navy medic and while answering an emergency call, attempted mouth to mouth resuscitation on a dead woman. Unbeknownst to my brother, the woman had Legionnaire's disease. A few minutes later, I was in my car.

The eleven-hour drive seemed like four. My mind was racing and I completely forgot about my fatigue. All of a sudden I had all the energy in the world. All I could think about was my brother.

When I saw my sister-in-law, she informed me that my brother was in isolation and that I would not be allowed to visit. I insisted on going to the hospital. I saw my brother in the isolation room hooked up to different gadgetry and in deep sleep. I went into the room and sat there until my brother opened his eyes and saw me.

I spent the rest of that day with my sister-in-law helping with the children. That evening I drove back. When I got back, it was Sunday evening. I was still full of energy and my mind was highly animated. I felt no fatigue.

From this and other experiences I learned a few valuable lessons:

- **The importance of value in providing motivation and energy.** I came to realize clearly that emotion is but energy in motion. If I considered an act valuable, I was

enthusiastic and had the energy I needed. Even though it is easier to be enthusiastic about activities I value, I realized that I could also feign enthusiasm. I could fool my mind into generating all the energy I needed if I acted enthusiastically and with conviction that an activity was valuable.
- **The detrimental effects of certain limiting beliefs.** I used to believe that I required a certain number of hours of sleep to remain energetic. I do, but not as much as I thought I needed. I have managed quite well on very few hours of sleep for several days. At times, two hours was all I needed. At other times, I required six. I no longer place conditions on my body. I allow my body to determine what it needs and when it needs it.
- **I often confused boredom with lack of energy.** If we find an activity to be boring, or has no value for us, we lose interest and with it our energy.

## 4. Purpose must be challenging

The purposes we select for our lives should not be easily attainable. They should be difficult enough to be challenging yet remain within reach. They should require our total commitment, involvement and skill. They should cause us to stretch, grow and mature. If we remain challenged, our minds have something to focus on. With our minds occupied with worthwhile challenges we have no time for trivia or boredom.

You and I are too valuable to waste our lives. We need challenges to stay alert and to achieve what we want and are capable of. There is a difference between simply existing—doing what it takes to earn a living to pay for necessities—and passionately pursuing what we crave and love.

If we are in the image of our creator, we must create. What we create must challenge us and bring out the best of what we have and are. Our creations are in the image of what we dwell upon. If we focus on the base and the ugly, then that is what we create. If, on the other hand, we focus on a worthwhile ideal, then what we create is challenging and worthwhile.

## 5. Purpose must be implemented locally, incrementally and with global consequences

Our happiness is a measure of our *progressive* realization of our purpose. The best way to implement a purpose is to introduce incremental changes that lead to the desired end. After several frustrated attempts and over four billion dollars in spending, the agency I work for concluded that a massive change in its direction was not desirable and perhaps impossible to implement. What is true of an agency is also true of an individual. We must position ourselves to realize our purpose one act at a time. Small acts tallied together add up to the realization of our purpose and the expression of our ideal. We should enjoy every incremental step and celebrate every minor achievement. They all add up and contribute to our overall unfoldment, growth and maturation. Instead of waiting for a grand implementation, we must fulfill our purpose as our abilities permit. One act committed at the right time, in the right place and with the proper attitude can have a tremendous impact on the lives of many.

We know of many great thinkers such as Socrates, Akhnaton, Jesus, Mohammed, Buddha and Jefferson who affected not only their immediate environments but the future as well. We must be aware that our thoughts and actions even though they are local, can have global consequences, now and throughout time. At a minimum, we influence our family, friends and those we come in contact with. Through them we influence all whom they come in contact with, thus indirectly influencing the larger community.

### 6. Purpose must be expandable

Our purpose must reflect our infinitely expanding universe. If our universe is limitless and we are part of this universe, then we are limitless as well and so must our purpose be. We are the limits of our achievements. Regardless of the degree of success we attain, there must always be room for growth. We should never be able to fully realize our purpose.

The best way to have a purpose that is infinitely expandable, is to align it with an ideal. Ideals are absolutes. Like the speed of light, absolutes can be approximated, but never fully attained. While it is easy to begin living a life of purpose, as we proceed it becomes progressively more demanding.

### 7. Purpose must be a trinity of mission, objectives and strategies

Purpose, like knowledge, is powerless unless it is expressed and lived. We must, not only know what our purpose is, but how we intend to implement it as well. Hence, our purpose must be a trinity of mission, objectives and strategies.

The *mission* is the *why* of our purpose. Why do we have a purpose? Why are we selecting this particular purpose?
The *objectives* are the *what* of our purpose. What activities will we pursue to accomplish our stated mission? In what specific avenues will our efforts flow?
Our *strategies* are the *how* of our purpose. How will we achieve our stated purpose? How will we execute our plans to attain our goals?

## Formulating Our Purpose

*He who has a why to live can bear mostly any how.*
                                               Nietzsche

    Since we are alive, we must decide what we want to live for. We can choose to drift, or we can select something worthwhile to live for. Some live for money, power and prestige. Others live for fortune, fame and recognition. For most, their reason for living is not well examined. They live haphazardly, changing their reasons for living from one circumstance to the next, or adopting reasons that are not congruent with their natures and deep-rooted desires. If we are going to live, we might as well live the life we choose and enjoy it. To enjoy something, it must be what we really want. What good would it do us, what a wasteful life it would be, if we select a purpose for ourselves and after great effort and struggle attain it, only to find that it was not what we really wanted after all?

    Our life could be an example of greatness, or of mediocrity and insignificance. The role we choose to play in our society and the world is critically important. If we pick the appropriate purpose to live for and an ideal to live by, we can make a difference not only in our life and the life of our community, but in the entire world as well. For we are in the world, of the world and are intimately connected to the world.

    Many turn to books to find their purpose in life. We need to turn to the book of life instead. This book is within and without us. It's language is clear even though it is symbolic. If we open our eyes and see and if we open our minds and comprehend, we will realize that we are here for a reason. We are an integral part and parcel of the body that is humanity. We are part of life, a unique and magnificent expression of the creativity of God.

    Our purpose in life is not to satisfy the whims of others. It is not something that is predetermined either. We formulate our purpose as we live. We can use our circumstances to determine our purpose, or we can accept what others tell us. Many use the Bible to find their purpose in life. These people mistakenly are guided to believe that their purpose is to save their souls from eternal damnation. Our souls do not need saving. They are part and parcel of God. What needs saving is our minds from ignorance. Even if we use the Bible to find our purpose in life, we can still find a purpose that is uplifting. In Genesis, the purpose for which God created human beings is clearly stated:

> *Then God said, "Let us make man in our image, after our likeness; and let them have dominion over the fish of the sea, and over the birds of the air, and over the cattle, and over all the earth, and over every creeping thing that creeps upon the earth. . . ."*
>
> Genesis 1:26

It is our destiny to wake up and be in charge of our lives—how we live and what we live for. We can choose to accept our destiny or ignore it. We have a choice. We do not have to settle for the crumbs when we have invitations to the feast. We can even choose to give the feast ourselves if it is part of our plan for our lives.

The world is full of the accounts of individuals who made a difference. These individuals had a mission for their lives with objectives and strategies. Jesus the Christ is an example of one such individual who made a tremendous difference.

Jesus had one *mission:* love. Through love, show humanity the way to life and abundance.

He had one *objective:* live love and demonstrate it through words, action and example.

He had one *strategy:* service. Give love freely and generously, expecting nothing in return.

Christ's life had an impact because He lived a life of purpose. How about you and me? How do we know what to live for? To formulate our purpose, we need to:

a. identify what it is that we love to do, clarify our values and prioritize them according to their relative importance to us;
b. recognize our innate abilities, talents and aptitudes, then analyze our past high achievements and determine the skills we used;
c. determine what is important for us and note our special challenges and opportunities;
d. discover what we are good at and what makes us happy;
e. listen to what others say about us and find out what activities we enjoy and have enjoyed as children; and finally
f. recall the events that moved and touched us in the past.

To these we add the answers to what we would do if money was not an object and we had a short time to live? What would we be if we could relive our lives and the right opportunities had presented themselves? If a genie could grant us one, two, or three wishes, what would we ask for?

We can blend these together to come up with a purpose for our life that embodies our uniqueness. To associate this purpose with an ideal, we must clarify our philosophy of life by answering the following questions:

**Why were we born?**

Was it an accident of nature that molded us and pushed us onto the stage of life to struggle, compete and survive only if we are deemed fit? Or, are we born to assume certain challenges, settle upon a purpose, for which we can live and from which we can derive pleasure, meaning and value? Why do we wake up every morning, day after day? Is it to kill time, or to build a life? Knowing that we might not wake up the next time we fall asleep, what would we do that we feel is vital?

**What is the best way for us to live?**

What can we do with our time, abilities, energy, talents and relationships? What is the best investment we can make with these? How can we best use our challenges and opportunities?

**What legacy do we want to leave behind?**

How do we want to be remembered? What contributions are we willing to make for living and receiving benefits? What rent or mortgage are we willing to pay for using earth as our home base?

**My Purpose**

I was in Beirut, Lebanon at the American University during the summer of 1969, when I decided on my first worthwhile reason for living that was more than mere day-to-day survival. Since I had little money and could not find a job, I had rented a room in one of the poorest areas of Beirut—one room, with an inner doorway that led to a bathroom. I could not even afford electricity. One Saturday, I invited my sister and my two youngest brothers who were in orphanages to spend the weekend with me. When it got too dark inside, we went to the roof of the apartment and sat under the moon to talk while eating grapes and bread for dinner.

I encouraged my brothers and my sister to not despair, even though things looked bleak. I told them that one day we would all live better lives in better places. When they asked me where we might possibly live, I said, "We are all going to go to the United States and start a new life. I do not know when or how, but it will happen. These hardships we are going through now will only be memories we will look back on."

I was in a different state while I was talking. Somehow I knew that it would come to pass. This new vision became our shared dream. We had something to look forward to, something to hang on to, and a worthwhile reason to live for.

It did not matter that we were born in Syria and that there was no way Syria would ever grant us passports to immigrate to the United States unless we served in its military first. It did not matter that we were in Lebanon temporarily, only as long as we were students. It did not matter that we had no contact with my father in Syria and that I was the only adult in my family in Lebanon and without my father's permission my brothers and sister would not be able to leave the country legally. I did not let the fact that my father would never permit his children to leave him and go far off get in the way of my having a new reason to live. I did not let the fact that I could hardly pay the meager rent for this shabby place stop me. Nor did I allow the fact that we needed passports, visas, plane tickets, a place to stay and money to cover expenses get in the way of our decision. The four of us bought into our dream and were hopeful. Somehow, we were going to the United States.

This vision of a new country and a new life became our incentive to endure, hope, persist and wake up every morning to face our challenges. Our consciousness was transformed. Nothing mattered as much as our shared dream. All that remained was for this dream to become a reality, for the vision to take form and dwell among us as a physical actuality.

We are in the United States now and that purpose is realized. Now that we are less concerned with survival, we can devote ourselves to more altruistic purposes. We can graduate from fulfilling needs to expressing wants. Having received, it is now time to give. Having grown and our fundamental needs taken care of, we are ready to devote ourselves to living our passions and expressing our ideals.

On July 9, 1994, I woke up, in the middle of the night, with a purpose for my life so well defined and impassioning that

I got up right away and wrote it down in detail. This purpose encapsulates all the elements for a successful personal purpose. It is highly *personal, rewarding* to implement and *motivating to* live by. It is *challenging* and it *can be implemented locally, incrementally* and with *global* **consequences**. It is *expandable* and it is a trinity of *mission, objectives* and *strategies*.

## Mission

From an early age I yearned to learn, understand and know. I often wondered about the nature of things, underlying causes and the deeper nature of reality and existence. Like the constitution of a country that rarely changes, my mission basically remained the same. I want to know and understand. I want to discover and learn. I love to share and teach. Thus, my mission is to discover, learn and teach. These constitute the *why* of my life—the stated, specific reasons for my being.

To discover, I think and contemplate, read, write and meditate. I set time aside, at least once every week, for study. I experiment and observe myself and others carefully. To learn, I practice what I discover and seek to incorporate it into my behavior and everyday life. I practice what I learn by being a living example. To teach, I participate in meaningful discussions, hold classes, engage in public speaking and conduct workshops and seminars.

## Objectives

I will write, be a public speaker, produce books, videos and cassettes. I will conduct workshops, seminars and training sessions. These are *what* I do—the specific avenues along which my efforts will flow. I do these to serve my purpose which is aligned with three ideals: Peace, Love and Harmony.

**Peace**

I want to live in a peaceful world, my world and the world at large. I understand that peace starts with me—I must be peaceful myself before I can expect peace anywhere else. In fact, I know that if I am not peaceful, there cannot be peace elsewhere. I *will* live a peaceful life and I *will* express this peace wherever I am. The peace I want is absolute. I realize it is impossible to achieve this. I will still attempt to approximate it as much as I possibly can and I want to surprise myself as to how close I can get.

I will not cause acts of war, nor act in ways that destroy peace. I will live the peaceful life, for that is the best way to live, for me and everyone else. Once we live the peaceful life, we can use our resources for enlightenment, creativity and improving our lives, instead of wasting them on violence, war and destruction.

I would rather live in peace than feel powerful, superior and important. It is far better for me to give and share for peace than waste valuable resources in defending what I think I own. I will support acts of peace wherever and whenever I encounter them. I will not subscribe to systems of violence and aggression regardless of their source, even if that source is believed to be a god.

**Love**

I am love and I will always demonstrate this love. I will love myself and everyone else, for love keeps me young, motivated, energetic and on course toward my ultimate unfoldment. I will love, for love is energy and through it I can create, transform and heal. I will love, for love is experiencing my essence and sharing it with the essence of others. I will love for that is my true and deeper nature. I will love, for love is life and life is love. I will love, for love is my god and I am an aspect of that god. I will love diversity, for god manifests as variety. I will love the young and the old, the white and the black, the healthy and the sick, the tall and the short, the pretty and the ugly, for all are stages that I have gone through or will go through at some point along my evolution and unfoldment. I will love the plants, the animals and mother earth.

Everyone needs not only nutrition, rest, cleanliness and activity, but also touch, affection, appreciation and above all, love. Therefore, I will love and I will allow myself to be loved.

**Harmony**

Harmony is beautiful music. It is balance, style, culture and multiplicity functioning as unity. Harmony is a reflection of the deeper aspects of life. Harmony is individuality thriving in an environment of collectivity and the group benefiting from the contributions of individuals. Harmony is the condition that fosters creativity, respect, appreciation, music, joy and love.

I will live a harmonious life, for that is the healthy and creative life. I will encourage and uphold the spirit of harmony, for that is the music of life and being. I will foster harmony, for it eliminates discord and chaos while it instills order and accord.

These three ideals constitute my objectives. They encapsulate my values that support my mission and drive my strategies.

**Strategies**

My strategy is to publish several books beginning with this one and to conduct at a minimum two workshops a year. I will proceed incrementally. I will expand my seminars and workshops by increasing the numbers and the geographic areas I cover. I will volunteer my services for as long as I am employed. Once I retire from my current job, I will pursue my purpose full-time and with unrestricted passion. I realize that in order to teach, I must continue to learn myself. My education should never stop. I also know that the best way to teach is to be a living example. Therefore, education and example are the two critical factors for me to successfully achieve my purpose. These are my strategies, the specific avenues of *how* I will achieve my stated purpose.

**Education**

Since life is helical, ever spiraling toward more awareness, harmony and effectiveness, I will also live a life spiraling ever upward. Through education I participate in knowledge transmittal. I learn from those who discovered before me. Likewise, I must contribute to the education of others. I must educate myself before I can educate anyone else. Education is a deep understanding and an inner appreciation for reality as it is and as it can be. It is the ability to think clearly and see with as little veil clouding our vision as possible. Education is an ever-increasing degree of freedom gained from knowledge. Education is refinement, culture, lasting power, character and personality.

Everything we touch, think about and do becomes a permanent part of ourselves and life. It gets "written" in our consciousness and the collective consciousness from which anyone and everyone can draw. Education is the staple of life. Without this staple, we will starve, wither and die. Education is the true food not only for the individual mind, but for the human species as a whole.

I am a student and a teacher, a reader and a writer. I read to learn and write to teach. I write on the consciousness of everyone I touch throughout my life. The first place I write on is my own consciousness.

**Example**

I will live my life as an example of the peaceful life. I will live my life as an example of the loving life. I will live my life as an example of the harmonious life. Even though

I will be far from perfect, I will not despair or get discouraged. From my shortcomings, I will learn how to improve, what to avoid and compassion for those who have also failed. Through my attempts and struggles, I will grow stronger and become wiser, making it easier for me to succeed in subsequent attempts. Unless I attempt and fail, I will not succeed. I will not only be an example of success, but someone who has also failed and learned from mistakes.

I will not live for a religion, a science, or a philosophy. I will live for my ideals. I will live for quality of life and abundance. I will not live to defend a system nor will I live to establish a new one either. Whatever gets in the way of living and expressing my ideals, I will leave alone and will not empower. Any system, science, religion, or philosophy that espouses Peace, Love and Harmony I will support, for they are aligned with the nature of my being. Peace, Love and Harmony will be my beacons and guiding light. Through these I will measure my progress and find meaning and value for my life.

I will learn from those I can use as an example and I will teach by living an exemplary life myself. If I fall short, I will attempt to do better and share what I have learned with my fellow citizens of the world. I will journey through life expressing and establishing Peace, Love and Harmony in my life and everyone that I touch.

What I accept or reject will only be based on content, not source. Indeed, many destructive systems of thought come from so-called unquestionable sources purporting they are the word of God. I will persist and I will insist on living my ideals. There can be no exceptions.

## Embodying Our Purpose

Unless our purpose gets incorporated into our consciousness as part of our belief system, it has little power to propel us into action. We must embody our purpose and express it in our daily living if we want to live a purposeful life. Just having a purpose is not enough. It must become *The Arc of the Covenant* that we follow. To embody our purpose, we must:

1. *write it down;*
2. *live it in thought, feeling and action until it becomes our reality;*
3. nurture it and
4. *avoid negative influences.*

## 1. Write it Down

> When schemes are laid in advance, it is surprising how often the circumstances fit in with them.
>
> Sir William Osler

Our consciousness is like a library. Our beliefs are the books in this library, written into our consciousness, spelling our identity. They color who we are and how we function. We write indelibly when we think, feel and act passionately, with awareness and intent. Actions repeated turn into habits, attitudes, expectations and beliefs. As we write, we create the software that directs our activities.

We should never allow others and circumstances to program our minds for us. Humans are easy to indoctrinate. Why allow others to indoctrinate us when we can do it to ourselves and live the life we choose? Unless we act in our own interest, we will be slaves to other people's interests. Why not take control of our software by writing down what *we* want? Once we do, our inner self will take over to help us get what *we* want out of life.

We must carefully choose and prepare the proper background for writing into our consciousness. Dr. Georgio Lazanov of Bulgaria[1] has shown that words integrate better in the mind if they are carried out as suggestions with the

---

1. See *Superlearning* by Ostrander and Schroeder Delta, 1979

proper background music. Slow, rhythmic music, and a relaxed state, enhance our ability to soak up the messages spoken. Music quiets the left hemisphere of the brain, allowing the right hemisphere to transform the body through images, music and words. Ritual plays a major role in preparing the mind to accept the words recited. We experience the effects of ritual during such ceremonies as weddings, funerals, mass, baptisms and graduations. It is also extremely valuable to look at ourselves in a mirror while writing into our consciousness.

How much we write at one time is up to us. We can choose to write the entire message all at once or, we can choose to record one aspect of our message at a time, repeating it until it is mastered, before going on to the next. Benjamin Franklin is well known for tackling one item at a time. He had thirteen virtues he wanted to master: Industry, Frugality, Temperance, Silence, Order, Resolution, Sincerity, Justice, Moderation, Cleanliness, Tranquillity, Chastity and Honesty. He spent a week on each virtue in a cyclical fashion. Slowly and surely, he progressed toward his ideal character and personality.

## 2. Live it in Thought, Feeling and Action Until It Becomes Our Reality

*Every human mind is a great slumbering power until awakened by a keen desire and by definite resolution to do.*
Edgar F. Roberts

Just having a purpose and writing it down does not bring it to life. We must daily express our purpose by the way we live. The ideas behind the words we write must be lived, expressed repeatedly with feeling and we must act in response to the impulses they generate. We must do this until the ideals become second nature.

The best way to write into our consciousness is to first write our purpose down on paper and then regularly read it to ourselves, intentionally and with feeling. Since what we think, feel, and act becomes our beliefs and these are automatically written in our consciousness, we must believe in what we are saying to ourselves. If we believe in our purpose, then our bodies act accordingly. Napoleon Hill in his famous book, *Think and Grow Rich,* states that what the mind can conceive can be achieved and what the mind dwells upon the body acts upon.

What we achieve in life is directly related to what we believe is within our power to attain. We received many of our beliefs from our parents while we were young and impressionable. This is how we inherited our religious beliefs. Now that we are grown, we must examine our beliefs carefully weeding out those that debilitate us while nurturing the ones that empower us. Even though we can believe in whatever we want, it is best to formulate our beliefs based on knowledge, experience and utility. If we have several belief systems that we can choose from, we should adopt the ones that best serve our purpose and ideals.

What we believe in are the "facts" we create for ourselves. If we can believe in Samson and the power that was in his hair, we can believe in the power underneath our hair. If we can believe in Noah's ark and that two of every creature fit in that ark, we can believe in the ark that is our mind. If we put correct thoughts, feelings and beliefs in the ark that is our mind, we attain lasting security, prevail against any storm and glide toward the achievement of our purpose—living a life of meaning and abundance and making a worthwhile contribution. Our mind, unlike Noah's ark, cannot hold tigers and lambs together. All of our "creatures" must fit together harmoniously and coexist. No contradictions are allowed in the ark of our mind. Additionally, our ark is not limited in size, shape, or functionality.

## 3. Nurturing Our Purpose

Seeds dropped in the soil of the mind, if nurtured, grow and produce fruit after their kind. Deciding on a purpose and writing it down is merely planting the seeds. There is a time lapse between planting the seeds and harvesting the crops. We must care for and nurture the seeds through their feeble stages until they grow into strong plants and bear fruit. We nurture our seeds (purpose/ideal) when we:

### a. Maintain positive expectations

We must always *expect* to realize our purpose. The expectations we have for ourselves set our mental framework. We must expect to succeed in order to succeed. We must know that the life we want to live is in fact at hand. It is not a far away state. It's beginning is where we are now. We cannot see its full implementation because it is currently at the seed stage.

Expectations are light versions of beliefs. We can enhance our positive expectations through visualization, self-talk and prayer—repeated with feelings. As we expect, believe and know that it is within our reach to live the life we want, we do. By planting the right seeds, we reap the appropriate harvest.

Since the assumptions we make about ourselves influence our expectations, we must question our assumptions regularly and make sure that they are not counterproductive. We cannot assume that it is impossible to achieve our purpose just because what we seek is difficult or has not been done before. Obviously, there are limits to what we can achieve, but no one knows what these limits are. That something has not been done before is no proof that it cannot be done. We did not know we could fly until we tried it and after many failures we succeeded. We did not know we could fly faster than sound; yet we broke the sound barrier. We did not know we could go to the moon and now that we have, we know we can go anywhere we choose. Living the life we want is obstructed by comparatively minor barriers. We can break these as well.

## b. Intensely visualize the life we want

High achievers routinely use visualization, coupled with self-talk, to enhance their performance. They first intensely visualize what they want to achieve and then they repeat the messages they want their subconscious to accept. Their bodies then attempt to actualize the visualization. The *sequence of achievement* is visualization with self-talk, (mental simulation) followed by actual enactment. The performance is often reflective of the clarity and intensity of the mental images. Realization will follow visualization unless sabotaged with self-doubt, fear and worry.

The brain cannot distinguish between a vividly imagined experience and a real one. We know this to be true because we react to dreams, phobias and mental suggestions. If we allow our imagination to run unchecked, we can even be overtaken by paranoia. The brain reacts to pictures based on their emotional content. Thus, if we vividly imagine ourselves living the life we want, our mind will direct us to act accordingly. Once we act, results will follow and our visions become our reality.

Visualization is an art and a science. It is the art of painting pictures on the screen of the mind that we want the mind to act on and, in time, actualize. Since visualization employs the senses, the more we understand and fully utilize them, the better results we can achieve. Each sense is composed of sensory components which in turn are made up of a very large number of sensory bits of data. **Sight** has two basic sensory components: *hue* which relates to color and *saturation* which measures intensity. **Hearing** also has two main components: *pitch* which relates to frequency and *volume* which measures loudness. **Touch** has three basic components: *temperature* which relates to how hot or cold something is, *pressure* which gages how light or heavy something is and *liquidity* which senses how wet or dry something is. **Taste and**

**smell** are related and have four sensory components: *salty, sour, sweet and bitter.* If we become adept at manipulating the "dials" that control these sensory components and paint our pictures vividly and with an abundance of emotions, we help shape our reality and manifest our destiny.

**c. Act confidently**

Our behavior is guided by the concepts we accept as true. If we are confident and believe that we can attain our objectives, then we will. If, on the other hand, we believe that we are incapable of attaining our goals, then we will not attain them whether or not we are in fact capable of attaining them. Acting boldly, we take advantage of what life brings our way. Acting confidently, we increase our chances of success. To boost our confidence, we can engage in self-talk on an on-going basis.

**d. Set goals**

Since we are goal-oriented beings, by setting goals, we give our mind something to aim for. Hence, it is important to know what the intermediate steps are for achieving what we want out of life. Our goals should focus on what we want to achieve and when. The method of achievement could vary and should not be part of our goals. It is far more important to know what we want than how we are to achieve it. Let the end result, not the means of achievement, be our goal.

**e. Keep at it until it becomes reality**

We must persist until we succeed. Persistence requires fortitude and the right habits. Habits form as a result of repetition. Thus, repeating the right acts, thoughts and the messages we compose for ourselves will form the habits we want. Most habits require a twenty-one day repetition cycle before they are established.

We are creatures of habits. In his book, *The Greatest Salesman in the World,* Og Mandino states that the difference between those who succeed and those who fail is the difference in their habits. If we want to succeed in living a meaningful and joyous life, we must form the appropriate habits. Once we form the habits we want, we get rid of the ones we do not want; for the desirable habits will replace the undesirable ones. Once we form a habit, we give it control over our life.

> *Sow an act and we reap a habit.*
> *Sow a habit and we reap a character.*
> *Sow a character and we reap a destiny.*
>
> Charles Reade

### f. Employ self-talk on an on-going basis

Self-talk, along with visualization, is the process of writing new programs in the mind. Experts tell us that we talk to ourselves several hundred words per second. We talk to ourselves while "awake" and while "asleep" through our dreams.

What we say to ourselves is very important. The books we read, our prayers, and even the songs we listen to have an impact on our lives. Unfortunately, most of us talk and write into our consciousness while we are half asleep. We are seldom aware of what we are telling ourselves or the effects these scribblings are having on our experiences and rewards in life.

Self-talk is a commercial that we play automatically, naturally and repeatedly to ourselves. Self-talk works because commercials work. Businesses pay handsome fees for good commercials because they know that commercials are effective, especially if repeated at opportune times and associated with someone or something familiar to the audience. We get much better results if we script and edit the language we use for our self-talk. By carefully selecting what we feed the mind, we can influence our habits, attitudes, expectations and beliefs. The more feeling and value we package our statements with, the deeper these statements sink into the recesses of our minds and the more we repeat them, the more effective they become.

The following is a sample self-talk to use. Write your own words for your personal message. Should your needs change in the future, you can change the message to match your new needs.

*I live a purposeful life.*
*I live a meaningful life.*
*I live a joyful life.*
*I live an abundant life.*

*I have a wonderful mind.*
*I have a miraculous mind.*
*I take good care of my mind by keeping myself challenged.*
*I discover, learn and teach.*

*I have a wonderful body.*
*I have a miraculous body.*
*I take good care of my body by keeping it fit and flexible.*
*Through my body I experience, commune and share myself.*

*I appreciate my body, mind and emotions.*
*I enjoy the challenges of my environment.*
*Through my body, mind and emotions I relate to my environment and achieve my purpose.*

*I live the meaningful life by living for my purpose and ideal.*
*I live the joyful life by thinking and feeling exquisite thoughts and emotions.*
*I live the effortless life by developing excellent habits.*
*I live the miraculous life by forming superb attitudes.*
*I live the content life by regulating my expectations.*
*I live the healthy and wealthy life by cultivating empowering beliefs.*
*My life is my own.*

*I am in charge of my life.
It is I who decides how well, meaningfully and abundantly I live.
This is my life and I live it as I see fit.
My life is my own and the ones I choose to share it with.
I will live as well as I want.
I will live as long as I want.
I determine the quality of my life.
I decide the duration of my life.
My life is my own private journey.*

*I live a purposeful life.
I live a meaningful life.
I live a joyful life.
I live the abundant life.
And I do it with vigor, joy and creativity.
All the while, I am living my chosen purpose and expressing my ideals.*

## 4. Avoid Negative Influences

*A greater sculptor than a Rodin or a Michelangelo is Thought. What a man thinks in his heart he advertises with his face.*
Thomas Dreier

Negative thoughts are like weed seeds that get thrown on our path. If these seeds find fertile soil in our hearts and minds, they sprout quickly, grow and can take over our garden. Some become trees bearing undesirable fruit of self-doubt, worry, tension, stress, fatigue, phobia and disease. Negative thoughts abound. We hear them everywhere. Those who are either failures or are afraid try to scatter negative thoughts to ensure that others meet the same fate. If they cannot succeed, no one else deserves to, either. Misery loves company.

Most of us grow up with negative influences. As children, the word we hear most often is: *don't*. Thus, we grow up unsure of ourselves. Safety and security are encouraged at the expense of all opportunities for taking risks. We are discouraged from loving ourselves. In fact, many of us grow up ashamed of our bodies, believing them to be evil and bad. Thus, we seldom look at ourselves with appreciation and love.

Ignorance is the root cause of many negative thoughts and feelings. Even though there are several systems that engage in negativity, some of the best I encountered were religious. I have had so many people try to convince me how sinful I am. One morning as I was heading up from the metro station in Rosslyn, Va., on my way to work, a man was standing outside the metro station passing out leaflets. I took one and later read the leaflet, entitled "WE ARE ONE HEART BEAT . . . FROM HEAVEN OR HELL." The subject of the leaflet was that we are all sinners and unless we call upon the name of the lord, we shall not be saved. The first four verses, all from Romans, read:

> . . . *as it is written: "None is righteous, no, not one . . ."*
> *Romans 3:10*

> . . . *since all have sinned and fall short of the glory of God . . .*
> *Romans 3:23*

> *Therefore as sin came into the world through one man and death through sin, and so death spread to all men because all men sinned . . .*
> *Romans 5:12*

> *For the wages of sin is death, but the free gift of God is eternal life in Christ Jesus our Lord.*
> *Romans 6:23*

The leaflet's message is clear: *we are all sinners. There is not a single person who is righteous. On our own, we are hopeless. We all deserve to die and will die because of our sins.* Even if individu-

*ally we have not sinned, we still are guilty by the mere fact that the ones we came from (Adam and Eve) were sinners. The only way we can be saved is to do what we are told.* Many oblige because of ignorance coupled with low self-esteem. Instead of using our God-given abilities to think, reason, live and experience, we submit and follow. We allow others to interpret the word of God for us. We forget that we are the *work* of God and whenever the word of God and the work of God meet, the work of God takes precedence for it is direct, requiring no translation.

It is sad indeed that many people believe in the above quotes. These people cannot live lives of meaning and purpose. In fact, they are mostly dead. For to be alive is to touch life and be touched by it intimately and profoundly, without fear or guilt, but with joy. For what is the value of our lives if we are engulfed by fears and demeaning beliefs? What meaning can our lives have if we cannot think? What purpose can our lives serve if we are controlled by debilitating low self-esteem? We must first shake off these states and wake up to the deeper reality of who and what we are. Once we do, we save ourselves from ourselves and begin to live, perhaps for the first time.

# STAGE 3

# *Know Yourself*

> *Nay, be a Columbus to whole new continents and worlds within you, opening new channels, not of trade, but of thought. Every man is the lord of a realm beside which the earthly empire of the Czar is but a petty state, a hummock left by the ice.*
>
> Henry David Thoreau

On the portal of the Oracle of Apollo at Delphi, Greece the Seven Wise Men have engraved the injunction: "Know Thyself." Knowing self is *the cardinal knowledge*. As we know ourselves, to that extent we can know all else. Examining the world in which we find ourselves, we see a kaleidoscope of human beings with a tremendously diverse level of awareness and self-knowledge. Some think, will and use tools to construct; others think, will and use tools to destroy. Some believe that we are creatures even above the angels; others declare that people are merely dust in the wind. Some hold that we are powerful, the product of love and intimacy; others believe that people are hopelessly weak, conceived and born in sin. Some believe that we are the directors of the elements, rulers of the planet, shapers of our destiny; others believe that we are naught but creatures of habit, appetite, environment and circumstance.

Which are we? What describes us best? We are all, at

different times and during different circumstances. We are never the same, one finished product. We are always becoming. We have the capacity to make ourselves into whatever we choose within the limitations we find ourselves in and these limitations are only real due to our limited knowledge. We have it within us to take a catastrophe and challenge ourselves to derive the most good out of it. At the same time, we can take the best opportunities for creativity, joy and self-fulfillment and turn them into a disaster. Ultimately, we are not what others think us to be. Rather, we are who we *know* ourselves to be. Our true power is not only in knowing what we currently are but in knowing what we can be and doing what it takes to achieve it.

To know our deeper reality is not easy for we are not born into this world with instructions as to who we are and what we can become. We are given a name and we grow up thinking that is who we are. We see our bodies and we believe that we are them. We experience emotions and thoughts and we tend to identify with them. As we grow up, we observe the adults around us. We imitate and acquire their concepts and, more or less, become just like them.

The world is a marketplace and time is our commodity. We can use our time to chase trivia, or we can invest this precious resource to discover our world and learn about ourselves. The more time we spend experiencing, learning and growing, the higher the return on our investment. The only lasting gains we can make are the knowledge and skills we can incorporate into our character and personality. It is far more important to focus on what we are becoming than what we are acquiring in worldly goods. If we have the right knowledge—knowing ourselves and the circumstances in which we exist—we can acquire whatever goods we want. To paraphrase Christ: *of what value is it to acquire all the goods when we do not know what we already have in ourselves? It is of little merit to know everything else when we do not know our own true self.*

Knowing ourselves involves understanding everything about ourselves. We must know if we have a soul, why were we born, if we lived before, and whether we will live again. We should know why we are the way we are, have the preferences that we do, and love or hate the people that we do. We need to understand why we are in our current situation, what is going on with our lives, why do we act the way we do, and what do our dreams mean. Since we know ourselves and others through our experiences and these are limited, we do not know as much as we think we do. Out of the entire spectrum of vibrations available, we only perceive what our senses have evolved to perceive. This is a minute segment of reality. Additionally, much of what we know, we learned as children. If we observe how children learn, we realize that the vast majority of what they learn is through mimicry of adults and the particular culture in which they find themselves. We are still children when it comes to knowing. We mostly copy, adapt and use what we observe others are doing. We seldom think and experience the AHA of discovering. This is why there is so much belief and tradition in the world instead of knowledge, intelligence and wisdom.

To know ourselves, we must question, observe and listen until we are guided to the answers we seek. If we want to know, we will know. If we persist in asking, we will receive an answer. If we do not prematurely give up knocking, the doors will be opened for us. We must want to know ourselves and persist until we undergo an experience or arrive at an answer. We must beware not to prejudge the answers we receive or bias them by deciding what they should be. We can start learning about ourselves by examining all that is available for us beginning with our experiences. Experience *is* the best teacher and unfortunately, it cannot be granted; it must be lived to be obtained. For example, now that I am a parent, I can clearly understand what my parents must have gone through. I often try to explain my role as a parent to my children. Even though they say they understand what I mean, I know there is no way they can relate to what I really mean until they become parents themselves.

In addition to our own experiences, we can use the accumulated knowledge of our species to learn about ourselves. We can learn through what others have already discovered. Finally, we can use the examples of enlightened ones who knew who they were to find out who we are. Hence, there are three main avenues for knowing our self: **experiences, systems of thought** and **examples**.

## 1. Knowing Ourselves Through Experience

*We should be careful to get out of an experience only the wisdom that is in it — and stop there; lest we be like the cat that sits down on a hot stove-lid. She will never sit down on a hot stove-lid again — and that is well; but also she will never sit down on a cold one anymore.*

*Mark Twain*

Living is creating memories through experiencing. It is like writing a book. This book, however, is not a finished product. It is a living book in the process of being written. Experiences are what gets written in this book. Therefore, our experiences are our true and lasting assets. Each experience is a letter, a word, a sentence, or a paragraph that adds to the overall meaning of the book that is our lives.

Since what we are today is because of all the experiences we have had so far, it follows that whatever experiences we live through are used to build our character and personality. This includes those experiences we perceive as "good" and those we describe as "bad." We need to train ourselves to see the true significance of our experiences. While life molds us with its circumstances, we create ourselves through what we make of our experiences.

Each experience is a trinity of three elements: the event,

the consequences and the knowledge gained. These three are the trinity that Hegel spoke of as thesis, antithesis and synthesis. The event is the thesis, the consequences are the antithesis, while the knowledge gained is the synthesis. In the case of Enkidu and the harlot for example, the event was the act of sex, the consequence was the loss of his state of innocence, while the knowledge gained was the opening of his eyes and becoming like god knowing good and evil.

Thesis and antithesis, or event and consequence are of complimentary polarities. If one is the male aspect, then the other is the female aspect. Synthesis (learning) will not result, or a child will not be born until the two aspects interact and a threshold is reached (pregnancy). This threshold can be reached through one seminal experience or might require several encounters which is often the case. That is why we do not learn the valuable lessons of life from one experience. Once the threshold is reached, change takes place. We wake up and are transformed. This synthesis (knowledge) contains elements of both event and consequence the same way that a child contains elements from both parents. The child (synthesis) grows more polarized and soon becomes a thesis of its own, attracting an antithesis, interacting with it and giving rise to a new synthesis. This helical process of experiencing and learning continues ad infinitum. With each ascent on the rung of the helix, we wake up into a higher state of being and functioning. We move from ignorance to knowledge, from darkness to light, and from "sin" to "holiness." The helical nature of life is clearly demonstrated in the structure of the DNA, the basis of our genes.

Most of our experiences simply happen to us. Few of us intentionally create the experiences we need to sculpt our lives. Additionally, we create the value of an experience by the use we make of it and this value changes over time. Hence, the value of an experience is relative. Einstein's theory of relativity applies not only to physics, but to all aspects of life. Experiences may start as painful, puzzling and disappointing, but over time, these values change. What was once painful is no longer painful. What was once puzzling is now clear. What was once disappointing is now seen as a blessing. Unless we learn how to evaluate our experiences in terms of our entire lives, we will not be able to discern the triviality of some events or see the deeper meaning of others.

Our experiences are of two types: unusual and common. Even though not many of our experiences are unusual, the insights we gain through them are invaluable. Our ordinary experiences are innumerable and what we learn from them depends on the effort we put into learning from them. We can learn a lot or hardly anything.

## Unusual Experiences

*I have but one lamp by which my feet are guided; and that is the lamp of experience. I know of no way of judging the future but by the past.*

*Patrick Henry*

I am fortunate that I had some interesting experiences early in my life prior to being indoctrinated into a system of thought. My parents were too busy trying to survive to concern themselves with educating me, so that when I had my first few unusual experiences, I was pristine. Thus, I can live my life based on philosophies developed as a result of my personal experiences.

I grew up in a Christian sector of Aleppo (Halab), the second-largest city in Syria, approximately 70 miles east of the Mediterranean Sea. It has a population of about one million, most of whom are Moslem Arabs, with a few scattered pockets of other ethnic and religious groups such as Armenians, Assyrians, Arameans, Kurds, Druze and others. I am half Armenian and half Aramean.

We had no cars, so I did lots of walking, and none of the

modern appliances we are so used to in the Western world: telephones, refrigerators, ovens, showers, washers, dryers, televisions. The first rental unit that I remember we lived in near the edge of Hay El Syrian, the small Christian community, did not even have electricity. We used kerosene for light, cooking and heating water for a bath in a corner of the kitchen.

At the age of four, I went to school. The children in my school were mostly like myself. Their families could hardly afford the tuition, and the only thing on everybody's mind was satisfying the immediate necessities of food, clothing and shelter. Few had the time or the inclination to discuss matters of the mind or the soul. I, too, lived mostly in a state of oblivion. Yet, whenever I had the opportunity, I would allow my mind to roam and imagine a life vastly different.

We lived in a rental house with two other families. Each family had their own bedroom, but shared the same kitchen and bathroom. One family was an Armenian couple with grown children who lived elsewhere. The other family was that of Simon, the caretaker of our church, his wife and son.

My first opportunity to question the nature of my being came when I was nine years old with a visit from my Uncle Jacob. He handed me the Bible he was carrying and asked me to read a passage to him. He pretended to be testing my ability to read, but he made sure that everyone heard the passage that I read. To this day I am not certain if he wanted me to read that passage for himself, to bring it to my attention, or simply to make everyone else aware of it:

> *I said in my heart with regard to the sons of men that God is testing them to show them that they are but beasts. For the fate of the sons of men and the fate of beasts is the same; as one dies, so dies the other. They all have the same breath, and man has no advantage over the beasts; for all is vanity. All go to one place; all are from the dust, and all turn to dust again. Who knows whether the spirit of man goes upward and the spirit of the beast*

*goes down to the earth? So I saw that there is nothing better than that a man should enjoy his work, for that is his lot; who can bring him to see what will be after him?*

Ecclesiastes 3:18–22

How did my uncle find this passage, anyway? No one in my family, or anyone else I knew for that matter, read the Bible. We merely went to church and heard the Bible read to us. This incident triggered my desire to know and understand myself. My reading of the passage did not seem to affect anyone other than myself. My young mind could not accept that I was just as the beasts are and that I had no advantage over them. Could the beasts think, talk, read and write? I reasoned that since I was endowed with all these extra abilities, it was not all for naught. I *must* be more and different. But why was I so different and what did it mean?

My first experience about the nature of my being took place when I was in second or third grade. I came back from school one day and my mother was not home. I looked for my mother in the court yard but could not find her. I was hungry. I waited and looked for her for what seemed like a long time. I was getting very frustrated and much hungrier. My mother was nowhere in sight.

I saw that the kitchen door had the big, iron key in it. I was too short to reach the key and turn it to unlock the door. Struggling to get a foothold on the ledge under the door, I finally managed to turn the key and open the door. Looking for something to eat, I saw a large box of detergent sitting on the counter. Stepping on a pot, I got hold of the box.

I shook the box to find out what was in it, wondering if the white granular stuff was edible. I deliberated for a while, then poured some out and started to eat it. I did not eat much because it did not taste good. I knew right away I had done something I should not have. Wanting to wash the taste away, I reached for some water and drank it. Foam began to come out of my mouth and nose. I panicked because I could not breathe. I ran out of the kitchen to the yard, and passed out.

The neighbor (the church caretaker's wife), seeing me lying motionless on the ground, started to scream: "The boy is dead! The boy is dead! Where is his mother?" I could not speak or move any part of my body. I knew that I was not dead, but there was no way I could convey that message. That was when I noticed that I was not in my body. I was about eight feet above, looking at my small body lying there motionless on the ground. I was aware of what was happening yet I could not communicate. I was confused and did not know what to do. *I see my body and the lady, yet here I am up here. What is going on?* The lady quickly fetched a bucket of water and poured it on me. I do not remember exactly what happened next, or how much time this whole incident took. Somehow I got back in my body and could move my limbs again. Perhaps the foam had settled by then and the shock of the water being dumped on me caused me to breathe.

I never forgot this experience for it left an indelible mark on my consciousness. The two most lasting memories are those of bi-location and my inability to move my body. When I experienced myself outside of my body, I could not move my body. Now I look at myself and wonder at how easily and effortlessly I move about. How do I move about? My body seems to have a life of its own. I cannot order it around and have it simply obey. I cannot demand that any body part move or behave in any way I choose. I cannot, for instance, tell my feet to jump and how high, and have them obey. When I am ready and want to jump, I simply jump, seemingly without giving any command. I always marvel at people. It is a profound source of pleasure and joy to watch how they move about, talk, laugh, sit, get up, sleep and wake up. It all happens so effortlessly, perhaps as a result of extreme habit.

I now know that I and my body can be separated and are not one and the same thing. *I am the mover of the body. I am what gives the body its life.* It is I who is aware through the body. The body on its own is an organized system that will eventually return to its original form. Even though I do not know what caused me to be in the body in the first place, or why I leave it, I do know that there are two aspects of me: the seen and the unseen. While I cannot form a philosophy of life from merely one experience, I, and others close to me, had several similar experiences over the years that shed more light on the nature of our being. Two examples illustrate:

> My first experience with someone I knew who died was that of my great uncle. My parents explained to me that he went on a journey never to return, and I simply accepted their explanation. I was about five years old. However, when my mother died, it was a different story. I was thirteen years old. My mother had six children: five boys and one girl. I was the second oldest. My older brother was fifteen, while my sister was about two-and-a-half years old.
> 
> When I came home from school there were many people in our room. I was very shy and did not know what to do. I knew that something was wrong but did not know what. I went to my Aunt's house nearby. I kept wondering what was happening inside our one room. Why were so many people crammed inside it? And why were so many of our neighbors waiting outside looking sad with tears in their eyes?
> 
> I came back from my Aunt's house a couple of hours later to even more people there. Some of them told me that my mother had been asking to see me and that I should go right in. I was too shy to step in with so many people there. Besides, I was on the verge of crying, and I knew that if I went in, I would. I felt that, being a "big boy," I should not cry in public. So I stayed outside and out of the way. My mother lay on the floor, on a mattress,

with covers all over her except for her head. Relatives and neighbors were continuously coming to see her before she died. Somehow they all knew she had a few hours to live. They were all in tears and some were singing very sad songs about how her children needed her and would not be able to manage without her. Soon she passed away. She was thirty-seven years old.

I learned later that while I was at my Aunt's house, my mother asked to see her children for the last time. She saw everyone except me, kissed them all, and said her good-byes.

I never knew what exactly happened to my mother. Somehow she got sick and within a few days passed away. No diagnosis of her illness was made because we did not take her to see a doctor. None of us ever saw a doctor, for we could not afford one. When we got sick, we allowed nature to take its course. Even when my mother had her children, the only one to assist was the local midwife whose only knowledge was hands-on experience.

The next two days I stayed at my Aunt's house. I kept on going to school. The funeral was on the third day. I went to school on that day, too. However, I was called home to attend my mother's funeral. In those days I always went to school, unless my father specifically told me not to. Since I had not seen my father, I had no instructions as to what to do. My father had always been a strict disciplinarian. We were routinely beaten for much less serious offenses than skipping school.

When I came home early, my mother was already in a casket. I later learned that one of my uncles paid for the casket because my father was too poor to afford it. There was a large crowd inside and outside the house. I had no idea what to do or where to be, so I did what I could to get out of the way.

As the procession started to the local church, about a mile from where we lived, I followed from a distance until they were inside the church. When I hesitantly walked inside the church, a relative saw me and took me in to join the group of mourners near the front of the church.

In the succeeding weeks and months, the enormity of the loss of my mother finally began to settle in. My entire life changed. My father seldom had time to care for us, concern himself with what we did or what happened to us. Occasionally, and mostly in the first few weeks, my Aunt came over, gave us a bath and cooked for us. As time went on, we were more and more on our own. We were alone, filthy, hungry and forlorn.

A couple of months after my mother's death, I realized that unless I did something for myself and the rest of the family, no one else was going to. As soon as school was out for the summer, I took a job at my uncle's bakery (my mother's brother). I earned enough money to care for myself and do what I could for my brothers and sister.

My mother's family blamed her death on my father. He was brutally abusive and they believed that her death was due to years of physical abuse from my father. The two sides of the family seldom talked to each other. So I had to keep my job a secret from my father.

My uncle's bakery was famous for its pita bread. We delivered bread to many restaurants and institutions all over Aleppo. My uncle's wife and my grandmother also worked at the bakery.

One day I was asked if I would go with Jack, a young man who worked for my uncle, to deliver bread to a restaurant. This was to be my first delivery. Jack stacked the bread on a flat board and placed the board in front of him on the handlebars of a motorcycle. I sat on the back seat holding onto him. That was the last time I went with Jack or anyone else to deliver bread.

One minute I was riding the motorcycle holding onto Jack, the next minute I was back at my uncle's bakery. When I regained consciousness, I found myself soaking wet lying on the flour sacks in the back room. This back room was used to store the flour sacks, knead the dough, allow it to rise, cut the dough into small round pieces and let them sit until it was time to flatten them into the round pita dough.

I tried to sit up but could not move. I was in excruciating pain. I did not know who I was—I could not remember anything, including my name.

There was a young man and an older man cutting the dough. I asked one of them what time it was. He told me the time. I asked him again what time it was. Again he told me the time. I asked him once more what time it was. He looked at me carefully, and told me the time once more. But it was all useless. My brain could not hold onto the information.

I started to cry. Soon my grandmother came in, surprised to see me awake, perhaps even alive. She started to talk to me. I understood her as she talked, but instantly I forgot all that I heard. The old lady looked very familiar, but I had no idea who she was. I realized I should know her from somewhere. She left, but she kept coming back once in a while to check on me.

I lay on the flour sacks for what seemed like a couple of hours. Eventually, and with much difficulty, I managed to sit up, slide down and slowly walk out. I noticed that one of the long boards on which pieces of the round dough were placed was sticking out of the stack. I tried to push it back into position, but could not. I had no strength.

My uncle started to talk to me, asking me about the accident and what exactly took place. He, too, looked familiar, but I did not know who he was or what he was talking about. Somehow, I knew I should try to go home, but I had no idea where home was. I could not even ask for help. I did not know who I was, what my name was, or where I lived.

I sat in front of the bakery on a stone, leaned against the

wall and started to cry once more. What was I to do? After my grandmother finished her work, she came over and asked me if she could take me home. I was glad for her help. Slowly, we walked. I let her lead. When I got home it was early evening, and my father was busy doing something. I sneaked in, went to bed and slept until the next morning.

Slowly, over the next few days, I began to remember who I was, where I lived and what I did for a job. I still had no idea what had happened.

Shortly thereafter, sporadic fragments of pictures began flashing through my mind. Gradually, the flashes increased in duration and intensity. Initially, all I could see were random pictures of me riding on the bike holding onto Jack. Slowly, I saw more details connecting the pictures together. Jack was driving carelessly. He kept looking back and talking to me. I was scared. He was assuring me that everything was O.K. The last time he did that, he was in the wrong lane. There was a car coming towards us. I saw the car and tried to warn him. Jack turned and saw the car. He pulled on the brakes as hard as he could, but it was too late. The motorcycle skidded, got hit and was thrown against a parked car.

Later, through the years, I pieced together more details. Several eye witnesses told me what they saw. The motorcycle was destroyed. Jack was injured, but not badly. When people found me, I was pinned under the motorcycle by the parked car. I appeared to be dead. My head was dangling down. They could not keep it upright on my shoulders. The people thought that my neck was broken. I was taken to my uncle's bakery and water was poured on me. Not responding, I was laid on the flour sacks in the back room of the bakery.

I do not know why I was not taken to a hospital. Probably because, as with my mother, no one could afford it.

Each flash of memory was like a piece of a puzzle. A

clear picture did not emerge until I had enough pieces, and after I placed them in their proper order and sequence. So it is with life and its flashes we call experiences. Until we have enough of them and place them in the proper order, a clear and meaningful picture does not emerge.

A couple of years after my mother's death, my father re-married. He already had six children, and we were in the way. Slowly, he got rid of all but one. He placed the two youngest boys, Joe and Toros, in an orphanage in Aleppo; he assigned his four-year-old daughter, Jeanette, to the care of Faith Winger, the Presbyterian missionary who was her godmother. Continuing his purge, my father banished his oldest son, Serge, from the house, and sent me, then 15 years old, to a monastery in Zahle, Lebanon. He kept my younger brother John at home with him. He either did not know where to place John, or kept him perhaps as a reminder that he once had a family.

I began studying to be a Christian monk at the monastery of the Syrian Orthodox Church of Antioch in Zahle. Life was unlike anything I had known. It was quiet, simple and secure. The monastery itself was away from the city, on top of a mountain. Winters were cold and summers breezy. Everything we did was related to prayer and study.

We got up at 6:00 a.m. every morning and we prayed until 6:30 a.m. At 7:00, we had breakfast. From 8:00 to 11:30, classes in the Bible, theology, literature, Aramaic, Arabic, Church history and some sciences. Lunch at noon. Afternoon classes from 1:00 to 4:30. Dinner at 5:30. From 6:30 until 7:00, evening prayers. From 7:30 until 9:30, individual studies. Around 10:00, we went to bed. On weekends, if we had some free time, sometimes we were given permission to go for walks in the mountains of Lebanon. Regardless of what day it was, we never missed the scheduled prayer and evening study periods.

## Know Yourself

One evening while sitting in the study hall with my book open in front of me, I realized that I could not study. I tried to force myself, but could not. I was very restless and wanted to lie down. I asked if I could be excused and go to bed. Normally, no exceptions were granted from prayer or study unless one was sick, and I was not. To my surprise, I was granted permission to leave.

I slept in a large room with eight beds in it, arranged in two rows facing north and south. My bed was the third in the first row. I was the only person in the room. It was dark and very quiet, unusually still. All of a sudden I sensed that my mother was in the room. I perceived a movement; like from a heavy, dense, swishing wind. I *knew,* beyond any doubt, that my mother had come to visit me.

As far as I can remember, I had not been thinking of her or missing her. I lay very still in my bed. Even though I could not see anything or anyone, I could keenly sense her presence. Feeling to me like dense wind, she came closer to my bed. Soon she was completely covering me. I could feel the pressure on me, and the sense of her presence was overwhelming. I knew from deep within that she came to visit, comfort and reassure me. Finally, with her visit in the monastery, my mother got her chance to say good-bye to me. Through this experience, I became aware of someone who had departed their body while previously, I had become aware of myself outside of my body.

Do we then have an existence independent of our bodies? What is our relationship to the body? Slowly I began to glimpse answers. It soon became clear to me that what appears evident is merely what is at the surface. Life is like a gigantic iceberg; the portion we see is the part above the surface. Just like the iceberg, life has depth. No one knows how deep life is. We are only aware of a certain portion of it and even of that portion, our knowledge is very limited. In my next experience I saw, with my inner eyes, the actual link that connects the two "bodies."

It was a hot, sultry Friday night. Tossing and turning in bed, I finally fell asleep. I was in deep sleep when my alarm went off. I could not believe it. Why would the alarm go off on a Saturday morning? I thought that I must have forgotten to turn it off when I went to bed the night before. The alarm was very loud. When I tried to reach over and shut the buzzer off, I could not. I was tangled up in the white sheet covering me. The alarm was very annoying. I became frantic. I *had* to turn it off. I struggled to free myself from the white sheet. Finally, I reached the clock. I extended my right index finger and tried to push the alarm button off. To my utter amazement, my finger went through the clock.

*What is happening?* I tried again, and again my finger simply went through the clock and the alarm would not shut off. I was fully aware of what was transpiring. I could vividly sense my emotions as my finger went through the clock. I cannot be in a dream state, I thought, this is too real. I was totally engrossed, when all of a sudden I realized that I was not in my bed. I was *over* my bed. I looked down and there lay my body in bed still wrapped in the white sheet. I was astonished. Soon the realization that I had experienced this kind of thing before caused me to relax and be aware of my circumstances. There I was, floating over my bed, in the middle of my efficiency in Glen Burnie, Maryland.

I realized that this was my chance to study myself and conduct some experiments. I wondered if I could go anywhere I chose. I thought I should try. Suddenly, I found myself in a store full of electronic gadgets. The room was a storage place for old equipment that needed repair. I hovered over the pieces studying them. I soon realized that there was a "cord" coming out of the back of my head. This cord extended all the way back to my body in my bedroom in Glen Burnie. I focused on the cord. I wanted to know what it was. I saw that it connected the forehead of my body in bed to the back of my head in this state and at this store.

After a while, I thought to visit my next door neighbors and impress upon them my visit while still out of my body. They were a young couple that I knew only superficially. I felt some doubt whether I really should visit them, what to do or say. I hesitated, not knowing what else I could do or try out. That is when I snapped back into my body and the experience was over.

I now KNOW that I live in my body. The body is my abode while I am the house-keeper. My true nature is "essence," "spirit," "awareness," "consciousness," "soul," or whatever else we want to call it. I know that my body without me is lifeless. It is organized matter that remains organized for as long as I animate it. Once I leave it, it will break down and revert to its natural state: disorganization and a lower state of functioning. My body is dust and when I leave it, it will go back to dust. Dust to dust. I, however, am not dust. I am what gathers the dust together into a suitable abode through which I experience, learn and unfold.

## Common Experiences

*Our lives teach us who we are.*
                                    *Salman Rushdie*

Our potential is vast. To actualize this potential, we require a variety of experiences. This is why, in each life time, we have different experiences under a variety of circumstances. We assume various roles and participate in a kaleidoscope of activities—whether a child or parent, an employee or employer, a teacher or student, an athlete, a musician, a public speaker, an administrator and a host of other positions and occupations. Each position we occupy provides us a window through which we can peek at ourselves. Each window presents us with a different vista and allows us to see and experience a "mini" self within the one overall self.

Each experience is a window of opportunity to find out more about ourselves. To see through these windows into ourselves, we must look beyond the window into the vista. Unless the windows are clear, we cannot see beyond them. If we are more interested in our ego than the experience itself and the lessons it may impart, we will be looking at the window itself rather than the view it provides. If we tend to defend ourselves and assert our will rather than go through the experience, we will not learn. To get the most out of an experience, we should remain detached, observe and be honest. An example to illustrate:

> I abhor a "mess." I took it for granted that my neatness was simply part of my character. This went on for a long time and would not have led me to know more about myself had it not been for my family. I can tolerate only so much mess and for only so long before I reach the limits of my tolerance and find myself in a state of rage.
>
> Once, after a spell of rage, I stopped and thought about my action. It did not make much sense. While I was enraged I acted as if I were possessed—not myself, unable to control my actions readily, yelling and demanding neatness. How did neatness assume such a prominence in my life, I asked myself? Is neatness more important to me than the quality of my relationship with my family? Why do I get enraged when I see a "mess?"
>
> I finally had a revelation as to the origin of my action, or more appropriately, reaction. When I was a young boy my mother often sent me to our neighbors' homes to clean up

their mess for which I was paid a paltry amount. I resented having to clean up after other people. Why can't people clean their own mess? The only reason I cleaned their mess is that I was poor. I resented that I had to work from such an early age while none of my other friends did. Additionally, the other boys and girls whose homes I cleaned did not do anything to deserve the better life. They were simply born into richer families. They could mess all they wanted and all they had to do was pay someone else a few nickels and dimes and have their mess cleaned. I considered it demeaning to be the one to clean their mess.

These thoughts and feelings were etched into my consciousness from childhood. Though the markings were evident, their causes were soon forgotten. After a while, I did not know why being neat was so important. It simply was. Not only was I very neat, but I resented anyone else who was not. Not knowing the real cause of my obsession with neatness, I simply reacted to mess violently once my tolerance was exceeded.

To learn from our experiences, we must care enough to take the time to ask the right questions, ponder and not dismiss the experience until we understand the real causes behind our actions. The more we want to know ourselves, the more our experiences reveal to us. Experiences seem to come at critical junctions when we most need to know ourselves. Sometimes it is hard to know whether we are experiencing so we learn, or whether we are simply ready to learn and our experiences act as a trigger. Either way, when we are ready to learn, our eyes open and we see our experiences for what they are.

Recently I was invited by the local Parent-Teacher Association (PTA) to speak on *Raising Emotionally Healthy Children*. Two days prior to the presentation, I overheard my wife and younger daughter arguing:

Wife: Why don't you pick a dress for Easter and put it aside? We will be going to Michigan in a few days and you will need a nice dress for church.
Daughter: I do not have any dresses I want to wear for church on Easter.
Wife: What do you mean you do not have any dresses? Your closet is full of nice dresses. Here, let us pick one together.
Daughter: I do not like any of them.
Wife: What is wrong with this dress? It is new and you have never worn it. Why don't you wear this one for Easter?
Daughter: I don't like it.
Wife: What don't you like about it? I bought it for you. I spend time and money to buy you nice clothes and all I get from you is complaints.

The argument continued for a few more minutes. When my wife left my daughter's room in tears, I was enraged. I dashed to my daughter's room and yelled: "What is going on here? Why is your mother crying and why are you complaining so much?"

When my daughter attempted to explain that she did not like the dress, I demanded to know what exactly she did not like. When she answered that she did not like the buttons, I was furious. I grabbed the dress and looked at the buttons.

Me: They look fine to me. In fact they look lovely.
Daughter: But I don't like them. I want to take the dress, cut the top off and wear it as a skirt. That way I don't have to see the buttons.
Me: Why would you take a beautiful dress that is perfectly fine just the way it is, cut it up, simply because you formed an opinion in your head that you do not like the buttons?

I was taken over by my rage, yelling louder and then I slapped my daughter. As I hit her, an eerie sensation came over me. I was not in control of myself. Someone or something else was.

I felt terrible. I began to apologize. It was useless. The damage had been done. My daughter's feelings were hurt and she refused to forgive me.

I spent the next few hours wondering what caused me to over-react. Why did I behave the way I did? Why didn't I reason with my daughter? I felt especially bad at the thought that in just two days I was going to give a talk to parents about raising emotionally healthy children. I toyed with the idea of canceling the presentation. What a terrible example I am on the subject. I felt like a hypocrite emotionally damaging my daughter and then pretending to be an expert on the subject. Perhaps my talk should emphasize what not to do.

Several attempts to make up with my daughter failed. That night I could not sleep. I felt guilty. I still could not believe my response. What caused me to over react and lose control?

Suddenly, the eerie feeling returned. I heard my mother's voice in my head. She was crying and pleading with my father to stop hitting her. I was standing there feeling helpless. I wanted to do something to stop him from hurting her, but I was too young to face my father and I was terrified of him.

The voices in my head changed. I was now hearing the cries of my wife. This time, I am grown up and I am not helpless. I react. No, I over-react. Unfortunately, the recipient of my fury is not my father; rather, my daughter.

The voices in my head changed again. I was reliving my childhood experiences. I remembered how my father would lock me in a room and keep on hitting me, kicking me with his boots, striking me with his wide leather belt, and other times using a whip. He would keep on hitting while my mother and brothers stood outside looking from the window. My mother would plead with my father to stop. He would ignore her and threaten her with punishment. The memories of many abuses against me and my mother rushed into my consciousness. I saw how brutal and savage my father had been and how helpless and worthless I felt.

The scene changed. I am now hitting my daughter, but it is not really me hitting my daughter. Rather, it was my father doing it through me. I hear myself yelling at my daughter, but it is the voice of my father yelling through me. My father is not dead. He lives through me. The sins he committed are visited upon me and my children.

When the scenes ended, I felt relief and was at peace. I could finally fall asleep.

The next morning, choked with emotions and amid tears, I told my wife and two daughters my story, shared with them the abuses I experienced as a child, explained why I lost control the day before, talked about my father, my mother, and other painful incidents that I recalled. Finally, I made a solemn promise that what happened the day before would never happen again. Once more I asked my daughter's forgiveness. We hugged, kissed and cried. I was free at last.

Understanding myself and the forces that at times attempt to rule my life, I am better prepared to deal with them. I will attempt to eradicate their effects from my life. I will not allow the chain of horror to continue. This line of evil ends with me.

Our habits, attitudes, beliefs and actions affect not only the here and the now, but the future as well. We reach into eternity through those we influence. The examples we set for our children will carry forward into future generations. Let us beware of what we do and say, how we act and react.

The imprints we leave behind are not on sand. They are in the minds and hearts of all whom we encounter. We will never know the full impact of all that we do or choose not to do.

## 2. Knowing Ourselves Through Systems of Thought

*It is said that desire for knowledge lost us the Eden of the past; but whether that is true or not, it will certainly give us the Eden of the future.*

*Robert G. Ingersoll*

We can learn a lot about ourselves by studying biology, chemistry, physics, psychology, sociology, computer sciences, engineering, history, literature, religion, philosophy and a host of other arts and sciences. Through these systems of thought we mostly learn about the facts, the *what* of self. We go to school to learn about ourselves and our environment. What we learn are generalities. Individually, on the other hand, we are not generalities. We are specific instances. Even though it is easy to study and predict group behavior, it is impossible to exactly predict the behavior of individuals. This is true of electrons, atoms and people. We are similar to everyone else in most ways, but the conglomerate that we are, is unique. We are unique because our bodies, thoughts, emotions, attitudes, expectations, beliefs, knowledge, needs, wants, hopes, dreams and aspirations are unique. We are unique to the extent we highlight our individuality.

We are a world unto ourselves. To know our world, we must study ourselves and use every available system of thought as a tool. Each system makes a unique contribution to elucidating our nature and reality. It is obvious that the more intimately we know the arts and the sciences the better we can understand ourselves. What is not as obvious is that we can learn about ourselves from almost any system. We can know ourselves better by immersing ourselves in life, by observing others, how we react to situations, what we like, dislike, the people we associate with, the organizations we join or do not join, the countries we like, the foods we prefer, and the pets we keep. The way we relate to people, countries, songs, and foods tells us a lot about our selves. If we **study** our surroundings and *observe* the environment that we create for ourselves, we get to *know* a lot about us. In fact, any occasion can serve us to learn more about ourselves if we are aware, observe and experiment. Here is an example of how I used a simple luncheon to learn more about myself:

In a Chinatown restaurant in Washington, DC, I noticed that the place-mat was imprinted with the Chinese Zodiac. It was headlined:

> Charming, Witty, Gallant, Wise - Recognize Yourself?
> Stingy, Selfish, Cunning (must be someone else!)

The Chinese Zodiac is based on a twelve-year cycle, each year represented by an animal featuring certain qualities. People generally determine their sign by their birth-year and read the qualities associated with that sign. I was ready to do the same, when an inner prompting urged me to use the animals that generate strong feelings within me instead. I quickly identified three.

> The Buffalo is by far my favorite animal. The sight of a buffalo has stirred deep emotions within me since my first glimpse of one in a movie as a child.

> The Rabbit is my favorite pet. For several years now we have kept one. I often hold him when I am relaxing, watching television, or just walking around in our back yard. Tender and loving feelings stir within me when I see a wild bunny as well.

The Snake is the only animal I am uncomfortable with and toward which I harbor subconscious fear.

The qualities under the signs associated with these three animals are:

**Buffalo**   A born leader, you inspire confidence from all around you. You are conservative, methodical and good with your hands. Guard against being chauvinistic and always determining your own way. The Buffalo would be successful as a skilled surgeon, general, or hairdresser.

**Rabbit**   You are the kind of person people like to be around—affectionate, obliging, always pleasant. You have a tendency, though, to get too sentimental and seem superficial. Being cautious and conservative, you are successful in business but would also make a good lawyer, diplomat, or actor.

**Snake**   Rich in wisdom and charm, you are romantic and deep thinking and your intuition guides you strongly. Avoid procrastination and your stingy attitude towards money. Keep your sense of humor about life. The snake would be most content as a teacher, philosopher, writer, psychiatrist and fortune teller.

Even though one sign can never fully describe a person at all times, in my current stage of life, the qualities of the above three animals describe many of my natural proclivities. The descriptions associated with each animal are general and can apply to many people. Never-the-less, we can learn a lot about ourselves by studying our favorite animals and their traits. It is interesting how our two daughters are so similar and yet so unlike. This is clear from the pets they keep and the animals they prefer. Olivia loves horses, dogs, birds and bunnies. Emily loves turtles, pigs and frogs. Is it a mere coincidence that we have the feelings that we do toward certain animals? Or, is it because we see a reflection of ourselves in their eyes and an echo of our souls in theirs?

## 3. Knowing Ourselves Through Example

*Example is a bright looking-glass, universal and for all shapes to look into.*

Michel de Montaigne

One of the easiest ways we can learn who we are is to study someone else who knew who he or she was. Instead of learning through trial and error, we can shorten the process by following the example of someone who has already gone through their own trials and tribulations and learned. Just as if we want to be successful, it is easiest to emulate those who are successful, if we want to know ourselves, it is best to imitate those who do. It is even better if we can have them as mentors. If we do not have a living example, perhaps we can study the biography, or autobiography of someone who knew themselves much better than we do, and from their examples, get to know ourselves better.

There are several individuals who, through experiences that elevated their consciousness, had glimpses of their true nature. These include: Akhnaton, Socrates, the Buddha, Christ, Muhammad, some Sufis and mystics. Since most people are familiar with Christ, I will use Him as an example of someone who knew His deeper self and inner reality.

Christ believed Himself to be the Son of God. This was His reality and guiding light. It is of little consequence whether or not Christ was truly the Son of God. Since the mind cannot distinguish between a real and a vividly imagined event, and since Jesus **believed, knew** and ***acted as if He was the Son of God,*** then for all practical purposes, He was who He said He was as far as He was concerned.

Christ knew that His essence was love. He dedicated His life to reflect His essence and be an *example* of love. He identified with love so much that He personified it. His life was a reflection of love—the ideal He lived for. So, He loved Himself and everyone else completely and unconditionally. He loved the poor and the rich, the sick and the healthy, the

Gentile and the Jew. He loved the tax collector, the prostitute, those who accused Him and those who served and loved Him. He even loved His enemies. By living love, this ideal became an integral part of His character and personality. After a while, no one, not even Jesus, could tell the two apart. He embodied love so deeply that He became one with love. Since God was Love and He was Love, He and God became one and the same.

*I and the Father are one.*
*John 10:30*

*He who does not love does not know God; for God is love.*
*1 John 4:8*

*Philip said to him, "Lord, show us the Father, and we shall be satisfied." Jesus said to him, "Have I been with you so long, and yet you do not know me, Philip? He who has seen me has seen the Father; how can you say, 'Show us the Father?' Do you not believe that I am in the Father and the Father in me? The words that I say to you I do not speak on my own authority; but the Father who dwells in me does his works. Believe me that I am in the Father and the Father in me; or else believe me for the sake of the works themselves. Truly, truly, I say to you, he who believes in me will also do the works that I do; and greater works than these will he do, because I go to the Father."*
*John 14:8–12*

*Jesus said to him, "I am the way, and the truth, and the life; no one comes to the Father, but by me."*
*John 14:6*

Can you imagine the effect of such a *self-image* and *self-esteem*? I and the Father are one! No one goes to the Father except through me! I am the way, the truth and the life! What a consciousness, what a mind, what a belief and what an environment he surrounded Himself in! The seeds He dropped in His own mind were Truth for Him. He saw Himself as the Son of God, the product and personification of love. What He knew and believed to be true, His mind accepted and acted upon. If we believed as profoundly that we, too, are the Child of the Almighty, we would live the miraculous life as well. While we are not the Christ, we are in a position to do even as much as Christ did, as He Himself stated:

> *Truly, truly, I say to you, he who believes in me will also do the works that I do; and greater works than these will he do, because I go to the Father.*
> 
> John 14:12

> *And Jesus said to him, "If you can! All things are possible to him who believes."*
> 
> Mark 9:23

Christ is the example of what we can be. He is the potential of humanity. When Christ used the words: "I am . . ." He was representing us. He was speaking for us. Obviously, Christ was not referring to His body when He said: *I am the way, and the truth, and the life.* He was referring to His essence, His inner reality; **who** He is and not **what** He is. We, too, can be as He was if we know, believe and act with confidence.

Belief is a mental conviction based on an acceptance of a truth without proof. Belief without knowledge can be dangerous. It can lead to fanaticism and destruction. Knowledge is also a mental conviction. This conviction is based on insight and understanding acquired through experience. Obviously, not all beliefs are equally potent. Beliefs based on superstition and hearsay are not in the same category as beliefs based on knowledge and as a result of personal experience. While beliefs based on knowledge are empowering, beliefs without knowledge are empty. So is knowledge without action. It is powerless. It is useless to know and not act accordingly.

Christ lived the miraculous life because He knew who He was, believed in Himself, and He understood the laws of nature. He had confidence in Himself and in what He could do based on what He knew. We are different from Christ in what we know, believe about ourselves and the level of our confidence. Fortunately, we can do something about these. We can get to know ourselves, strengthen our faith and we can act with confidence.

**Knowing Who We Are**

*He knows the universe and does not know himself.*
*Jean de La Fontaine*

Using experience, available systems of thought and the examples of enlightened ones, I am led to the following conclusion about the nature of our being:

1. we are more than the body,
2. we are in the image of our source,
3. we are creators of value and meaning; transformers of chaos into order,
4. we are seeds in the garden of being—cells in a body, and
5. we are in charge of our destiny.

**1. We Are More Than the Body**

*Your body is the church where Nature asks to be reverenced.*
*Marquis de Sade*

We are more than our bodies. That is why we do not live just to eat, drink and be merry. We yearn for meaning, value and belonging. We are as much social beings as we are individuals. We do not seek to only serve ourselves, but our species as well. As we interface with others and the environment, we have the power to influence them, and through them, shape and mold ourselves.

There is a difference between knowing who we are and what we are and between knowing ourselves and knowing about ourselves. *What* we are is visible—the body with its emotions, mind and circumstances. *Who* we are is invisible—living essence, core and the *breath of God* within us. We are much more than our bodies. We are a living self with a unique identity and individuality. Our *self* is ensconced in its source which is SELF—The Cosmic Intelligence, or God. We can never see or know our self face to face and directly. We cannot point a finger at self and say "this is self." Self is not a thing. It is not matter bound by space and time. Self is the *still small voice* and the I AM—timeless, boundless and causative. Self cannot be experienced directly for self is the one who experiences. It cannot be observed directly, for self is the one who observes. Self cannot be known directly for self is the one who knows. We can know self indirectly through its expressions which act as a mirror reflecting back to itself the nature of its creativity.

*What* we are is of earth, while *who* we are is of heaven. We are a visible, tangible, material body and an invisible, intangible animating factor. This is evident if we compare a living being to a corpse. The corpse does not have life. We are alive. We are sensitive, aware and can function. We live for as long as we are both, the life principle and the material through which this life principle expresses itself. Hence, we are changeless core and changing periphery. Individually, we are a breath exhaled as an emanation from our source. Yet, we remain anchored in our source as we extend out and undergo experiences as a unique individuality. At the source, we are the one who experiences. Away from the source, we are the experiences and the potential for more experiences. As we extend away from the source through our experiences of the world, we establish our individuality and identity. We become a unique soul personality.

Who and what we are, are two aspects of the same reality. Like matter and energy, they are interchangeable. What we are is of a lower rate of vibration than who we are just as matter is of a lower vibratory rate than energy. Our core (*who* we are) vibrates at such a high rate that for all practical purposes, it stands still. What we are vibrates at varying rates. Our physical body vibrates at the lowest rate followed by our emotional, mental and finally the spiritual "body." Just as matter is constantly changing and assuming various forms and shapes so it is with what we are. It is constantly changing. Just as energy is the source from which matter forms and to which it returns, so it is with our body. It arises out of SELF, experiences, grows until it eventually becomes the SELF, thus returning to it.

Just as there is a lot we can know *about* God, there is a lot we can know about self through its manifestations. Our knowledge of God is a reflection of our knowledge of our core—the self. Since this knowledge is constantly evolving with the evolution of our consciousness, our knowledge of self is also evolving. Since we are constantly becoming, so is our knowledge of ourselves, our source and God. Like God the Father, who cannot be seen or known except through the Son, the expressed, our essence can only be known through its manifestations—the body with its mind, emotions and circumstances.

To know ourselves, we must know *who* and *what* we are. We know what we are if we scrutinize our bodies; our cells, tissues, organs, systems and our environment. By studying our actions, reactions, passions, relationships, needs, wants, dreams and aspirations we can have a good understanding of what we are. We know what we are through our senses. These senses function between specific ranges. Reality is very confined for us because of the limitations of our physical senses. Fortunately, we can develop and use our psychic senses. By delving deeply into *what* we are, we soon arrive at an understanding of *who* we are. In all cases, it is our experiences that lead us to know ourselves. Our experiences are pointers to what we are and what we are becoming.

## 2. We Are in the Image of Our Source

*If God has created us in His image, we have more than returned the compliment.*

*Voltaire*

We are in the image of our source. Since we are body and core, our body is in the image of its source, nature, while our core is in the image of its source, God. The atom is the basic building block of nature and all material expressions. The atom is a trinity of three stable particles: electrons, protons and neutrons. Trinity pervades nature. Matter is solid, liquid and gas. Water, the most abundant substance on earth is ice, liquid and vapor. Since materially we are of nature, we too are a trinity of "solid" body, "liquid" emotions and "vaporous" mind.

Our essence, self, is a trinity as well. We are a trinity of actual, potential and a state that separates the two. What separates the actual from the potential is the changes that we must go through in order to grow up, mature and actualize our potential. As more of our potential becomes actual, we display a greater resemblance to our source.

Our potential self is infinite just as God the Father is. Our actual and manifest self is finite just as God the Son is. The changes that we must go through to transform our potential into actual binds our two aspects together just as the Holy Spirit binds the Son to the Father. We are in a constant state of change because we, as self, are on our way to becoming SELF, our possible and *ideal self*. What we now are is a reflection, a ***changing image***, of what we can be. This is our *self-image*—the present snapshot of SELF. Change is what we must go through to have the experiences we need to transform our current reality, our *self-image*, into our possible self, *ideal self*. The gulf that we must traverse to bridge the divide between our actual and potential selves is not in space and time; rather, in awareness, abilities and mastery. What must change is our knowledge of self—the way we see, feel and know our self. As we know self and reflect more of its capabilities, the value and meaning we assign to self and our circumstances will change. The more we know our self, the higher our *self-esteem*. If we liken our *ideal self* to God the Father, and our *self-image*, the manifest and changing self, to God the Son, then the relationship between Father and Son, or *ideal self* and *self-image* is the Holy Spirit, or Love. This love arises out of *self-knowledge* and is *self-love*. Hence, who we are expresses itself as a trinity of *ideal self*, *self-image* and *self-love* or *self-esteem* in the image of God, our source, who is a trinity of Father (potential), Son (actual) and Holy Spirit (Love).

**Ideal Self**

We are not only our past and present, but the future as well. Our future state is the potential to become more than we currently are. It is to actualize ourselves. Self-actualization is based on what we have to work with and what we decide to attain. What we have to work with changes as we gain knowledge and awareness. Equally, what we desire to attain is ever unfolding. For as we attain one goal, we realize that we are hungry for another. Hence, we never fully actualize ourselves. For the more we know ourselves, the more we realize how much more there is to know and do. Knowing ourselves is an eternally spiraling process. Like space, time and the universe, it is ever expanding.

Our ideal self is the God aspect we house within, the higher dimension into which we are constantly extending. As we extend, we change and become. We get an inkling of what we can be by being aware of what we have become since infancy. As babies, we were helpless and capable of very little. As adults, we can think, use tools, compose, relate and create. This is only the beginning. For we achieve to the extent that we use our minds, act and gain mastery of our circumstances. Our mind is an aspect of the overall mind in nature. It is a reflection and an image of the *mind of God*. This mind is mostly dormant and asleep within us like the intelligence that is asleep in a seed waiting to be planted to begin the journey of unfoldment. If there is no limit to our universe, there is no limit to our mind, and there is no limit to our potential. Therefore, we must strive to convert more of our potential into actual by extending ourselves, taking calculated risks, and by expanding our skills, abilities and relationships. As the level of our awareness increases, so does our knowledge of self. The more we know our self, the higher the level of our awareness and with it, the more mastery we express and the better we reflect our source.

Our ideal self is like a seed buried deep within us. It is up to us to nurture this seed to grow, unfold and mature. Our unfoldment involves two stages: an unconscious phase where nature is at the helm and a conscious deliberate phase where we are in charge. The second phase happens only if we wake up and take control of our lives. By constantly nurturing our bodies, emotions and minds and by selecting and shaping our environment, we create the conditions for our ideal self to express itself. The more transparent we become by purifying ourselves, the better we will hear the *still small voice* within us and the more of our *ideal self* we will reflect. Furthermore, as we are guided by our ideals and practice meditation and prayer, we open up the avenues of communication between our ideal self and the actualized self. The more we attempt to commune with our inner self, the more the ideal self expresses itself through us. We can draw upon our ideal self for power, guidance and inspiration.

## Self-Image

We are a *self*. This *self* is an *image* of **SELF (God)**. For an image to be a true reflection of its source, it must maintain contact with its source. If something comes between the image and its source, the image ceases to reflect the source. Instead, it reflects and is an image of what came between, the impostor. If we allow selfishness, greed, jealousy, dominion over others and avarice for worldly possessions to become the source we reflect, then instead of living a life of purpose, meaning and joy we merely survive through struggle and competition. We lose our feeling of connection to our true source. We become the prodigal child, lost and orphaned.

Our self-image is how we see ourselves, where we are and the circumstances we find ourselves in. Our self-image is always changing based on the decisions we make and the actions we take. We polish our self-image as we expose our lives to the bristles of experience. It matters greatly how we see ourselves. If all we see is limitations, pain and struggle, that is what we reflect back onto others and nature. If, on the other hand, we see ourselves as noble, loved and limitless, then that is what we reflect as well. We must see and know ourselves, not as a freak accident of nature, rather, as the miracles that we truly are.

We act based on how we see and understand ourselves. Just as we are a reflection of our source **SELF**, our current status in life is a reflection of our *self*. To reflect more, we must see ourselves as more and act based on this new vision. We must learn to see ourselves not as we are, but as we ***want to be.*** By acting and living the way we aspire to be, we will surely attract or create the circumstances that will give us the opportunity to form our desired reality. By continuously keeping our sight on where we want to go, and by moving in that direction, we gradually get there.

Even though we are an image of our source—God, what

we reflect is not God. We are a gross and an imperfect mirror. Instead of reflecting love, often we reflect our own impurities—greed, hate and dominion. This is why we worship the gods that we do. These gods are a reflection of ourselves. They are our creations instead of us being the reflection and creation of God. Hence, it behooves us to carefully examine our views of God. Is God the ideal that we wish for all and ourselves? Do we then go about living life translating that ideal into daily action? Or is God a tyrant who, through anger and jealousy destroys and punishes and therefore we do the same?

What we accept, believe and reflect makes all the difference in the quality of life for ourselves and others. Within us is the spark of divinity. The manner in which we reflect this spark is our self-image—how we view ourselves, others and God. Let no one, especially not us, deny us the right and privilege to live life reflecting the best we are capable of. As we reflect more of our true source—love, we become children of this source and live with confidence and with joy. Let this be the self-image we see and, through living, reflect.

**Self-Esteem**

A gap will always exist between our current self—*self-image*, and our possible self—*ideal self*. The way we *feel* about this gap is a measure of how satisfied or dissatisfied we are with our self. How much we *love, appreciate and value* what we are even though we are not yet what we can be, is a measure of our *self-esteem*. Our *self-esteem* is a function of our awareness and acceptance.

This gap between what we are and what we can be is the force behind our evolution. It manifests as an inner urge to stretch and unfold like a seedling in the process of becoming the plant it can be. This potential difference between what we are and can be acts as a force that ever spurs us to experience, unfold and become what we are capable of becoming. We continue to change until our *self-esteem becomes self-knowing* and *self-love*.

Accepting or rejecting ourselves with all of our achievements and shortcomings is an indication of our self-esteem and psychological maturity. If we have high self-esteem, we totally and unconditionally accept ourselves and others physically, emotionally, mentally and spiritually. Accepting others means allowing them to be what they choose for themselves. We treat them with respect and dignity. By accepting ourselves, we treat ourselves gently and with affection. We harbor no hate, resentment, jealousy, shame, or fear.

The degree of our self-esteem determines how happy and content we are and the value we assign to our lives. It determines the way we relate to others and to change. Our self-esteem is more like a barometer than a stable indicator. This indicator rises and falls based on the way we feel about ourselves and the way we relate to our environment. Our self-esteem manifests as **emotions** which bathe the body and color the mind. We display a kaleidoscope of emotions the quality of which varies based on circumstance and the manner in which we respond to our thoughts and events. Our emotions are the source of our energy and are the link between ourselves and our environment. Since emotions are a reflection of self-esteem, the way we feel often controls the way we think and act.

Low self-esteem is the root cause of many of society's ills. It leads to failure, abusive behavior, hate and crime. Individuals with low self-esteem are easily controlled and manipulated by their own emotions and by external factors. Individuals with high self-esteem, on the other hand, are confident, happy and loving. The highest form of self-esteem is self-love. We can enhance our self-esteem by:

a. being true to ourselves, acting accordingly and enjoying our activities; doing only what we want to do and doing it as best as we can;

b. making only commitments we want to keep;
c. eating the food we want to eat, wearing the clothes we want to wear, and working at a job of our choosing;
d. never going against our inner feelings;
e. being genuine, honest and truthful;
f. treating ourselves lovingly;
g. getting involved, playing, laughing and having fun;
h. living lightly—consciously and within our means.

## 3. We Are Creators of Value and Meaning; Transformers of Chaos into Order

*In all chaos there is a cosmos, in all disorder a secret order.*
*Carl Jung*

Our environment is vibratory energy which we perceive as sensory impressions (texture, color, sound, . . .). Many of us know that secondary qualities such as aroma, taste, color and sound do not exist as we know them. These are received as vibrations which the mind interprets into sensory impressions we can relate to and understand. We perceive each other, ourselves and the world as solid objects. In reality, all that exists is energy. However, what we perceive is not energy. We are aware of people, animals, plants, rock, sand, water and fire. Energy is data. Like data, energy is a meaningless form of vibration. For data to become information, and for energy to become people, animals, plants, rock, sand, water and fire, a translation must take place. Meaning must be added to data to transform it into information. Like a television or computer screen that receives energy vibrations and translates these into sounds and pictures before we can see and understand them, we translate the energy vibrations we receive from the environment before we can understand them. What we *receive* through our sense organs is data—vibratory energy. What we *perceive* is information—sound, sight, touch, taste and smell. Somehow we translate the data we receive into information. Thus, we create value and meaning.

As we live, we incorporate into ourselves matter, energy, time, habits, attitudes, expectations, beliefs, knowledge, abilities, skills, relationships and memories. We transform impressions into memories; food, water and air into cells and tissue; energy, space and time into material realities. We translate energy into matter, data into information, chaos into order and meaninglessness into meaning. We are the molders and shapers of our perceptions.

We do not exist in, for, and by ourselves. We are social beings. We are intimately connected to our environment and to each other. What we do to ourselves affects others. What we do to others is a reflection of ourselves. All of our actions have impacts. They create or destroy. One way or another we transform all that we touch. As we interact with others and our environment, we transform parts of them into ourselves. In turn, we impart portion of ourselves to them. Progressively, we are all becoming reflections of each other.

As we build our society, we transform rock, wood and metal into buildings, simple elements into complex compounds, raw material into cars, computers and rockets. All life forms are engaged in the same activity: transforming the inorganic into the organic, the less organized into higher forms of organization, and the "chaotic" into the orderly. As we touch and shape events and things, we leave our unique imprint on them. The imprints we leave behind are not made up of letters and hieroglyphics, but of our intentions. As we pass through the world, we form a trail. This trail is that of the values we created and the transformations we brought about.

## 4. We Are Seeds in the Garden of Being—Cells in a Body

*The kiss of the sun for pardon,*
*The song of the birds for mirth,*
*One is nearer God's Heart in a garden*
*Than anywhere else on earth.*

Dorothy Frances Gurney

Life is a garden, and we are gardeners. What we put in as seeds, we reap as products and services. The results we are experiencing today are the seeds we planted yesterday. What type of thoughts, feelings and acts are we sowing today? If we want something specific tomorrow, we must plant the correct seeds today. Plant garbage, receive garbage—or, garbage in, garbage out: GIGO. Plant value, receive value—or, value in, value out: VIVO. VIVO is life, GIGO is useless garbage.

We are immersed as seeds in the soil of our environment. We are in the process of becoming a plant with flowers and fruit. The flowers and the fruit are potential in the seed, yet cannot be born until certain experiences are had and a particular stage is reached. Unlike a seed that must assume the shape dictated by its genes, what we are becoming is only one possibility from a sea of possibilities. We have a say in what we become based on what we think, feel and do. To actualize our potential and produce the best "flowers and fruit" we must experience until we mature.

Maturity is not a matter of age alone. It's ingredients are experience, awareness, knowledge and eyes that see value. Even though I have lived over half a century, in many respects, I am still a baby. Obviously, I am much more mature now than during my early years in the United States. I had a much narrower view then as evidenced by my search for an adequate job and career. The only opportunities I looked for were in the biological sciences. After all, my college degree was in biology and I considered myself a biologist. Even though it was difficult finding a job in my chosen field, I refused to look elsewhere. There were many opportunities to find other jobs, but I did not even investigate. When my brother offered me a job with Digital Equipment Corporation, I would not even consider it. "Computers?" I told him, "You must be kidding, I am a biologist."

After joining the Army, working for seven years in a medical laboratory and after several eye-opening experiences, I gradually woke up to the realization that the only reason I considered myself a biologist was because of my training, education and on-the-job experiences. Nothing else distinguished me from someone in a different career. Since these traits are acquired, I can be anything I decide on being. As soon as I realized this, my views broadened. My vision began to change from a "tunnel" to a "funnel". I stopped calling myself a biologist. Henceforth, I declared that I was whatever I chose to be. All I had to do was get a new education, acquire training and develop new skills. This realization allowed me to change careers, get the training I needed and start a new profession in computers.

Just as a plant needs the sun to grow, we require experiences to mature. Hence, we are not here to prove ourselves to others, but to experience and unfold more of our innate potential. We are on a journey, but not to a destination, rather to a state of maturity as expressed in our mastery of ourselves and circumstances. As we progress to maturity, it appears that we are being reminded of truths that we had forgotten. Plato taught that we have the answers within us. We simply cannot access them for we do not remember, or know how to retrieve them. That is why he often acted as a midwife when he taught. He helped people remember, or give birth to, what was already within them. Experiences help us remember who we are.

We are a seedling immersed in the soil of our environment. Being a seedling, we contain within us the same intelligence that is in our parents, the source from where we sprang. Unlike a seedling, however, we have free will and this intelligence can only guide us to the extent we allow it. Without the conscious awareness of this intelligence and its guidance, we follow the path of least resistance. We live subject to the weather with all of its inclement conditions. As we wake up, we begin to allow the intelligence within to guide us. We live not only as a seedling immersed in its environment, but as a conscious living being who is able to shape its environment and circumstances.

This intelligence within is our Self nurturing and guiding our self. Our Self is aware of the bigger picture. It knows our purpose in being here on earth. Therefore, it weaves the events surrounding us to give us the best opportunity to learn and demonstrate mastery or to fail and have an opportunity to prepare and get ready for the next event. The more in tune we are with this intelligence, the more in harmony we are with the intelligence of life.

My life is replete with examples of the handiwork of this intelligence. During my darkest hours, this intelligence whispered to me as a *still small voice* and guided me through my trials and tribulations. It was this intelligence that created the circumstances for me to go to the monastery, leave it later and go to high school. While in high school, it urged me to take the college entrance exam and apply for admittance, even though I had no realistic chance of ever going to college due to my lack of finance. It was this same intelligence that arranged my meeting with Jean Holladay (Grosback) and all the circumstances that made it possible for me to go to college.

It was My Self—the intelligence—that spurred me to emigrate to the United States, and as a *still small voice* impelled me to join the U.S. Army, take the foreign language test, apply for the science and technology program, and later get my first significant job in the U.S.A.

It was this same voice that thundered within me to join the Rosicrucian Order, meet my wife and form my family.

After we were married, both my wife and I wanted to have four children. But it was this intelligence that revealed to us that we only needed two. This intelligence and voice has been fundamental to my life. Its influence on my thinking, teaching and writing this book is undeniable.

This intelligence is always within us. It is like a comet circling our day-sky. To see its brilliance, we must dim the other lights, the "lights" of fear, doubt, confusion and haste. Once we dim these lights, we see this intelligence waiting to guide our steps and illumine our way. It is expecting us to ask so it may guide us. It is anticipating our questions so it may answer. Ask and it shall be given. Knock and it shall be opened. Dare and take the first step and all the gates will be opened, one at a time and as we are ready and willing to go through them.

We are not only what we appear to be. We are not just a seedling. We are all of our connections as well especially to our source. We are more than a plant. We are a tree in a forest, a cell in a larger body. We are connected. We are cared for. We are important; for without the cells, there is no body. Being a cell in the body, we have access to the intelligence, protection and guidance of the entire body. This is the secret of our higher reality and source of our true, amazing and immense power.

## 5. We are in charge of our destiny

*Destiny. A tyrant's authority for crime and a fool's excuse for failure.*

*Ambrose Bierce*

The power of choice is the greatest power we have. How we choose to feel, think and act determines what we become. Unless we exercise our will and choose, our decisions will be made for us. Unless we mold ourselves, circumstances will. We are in charge of our destiny to the extent that we will and act. Yet, too often instead of taking charge of our lives, we blame many of our shortcomings to environment or heredity. We fail to see that our shortcomings are our opportunities to take charge and shape our destiny.

Environment and heredity play major roles in our lives, but the extent of these roles is usually overrated. No one has tested the limits of how much we can influence our genes based on the environment we can manipulate. Our genes are very adaptable especially at the early stages of our development. Our chromosomes contain a tremendous number of genes, the vast majority of which never get expressed. Our environment plays a decisive role in *which* genes are expressed, and how our brains develop.

It is true that genes determine our features, but what we do with these features is often far more important than the features we possess. Even though our genes enable us to talk, see, hear, touch and think, it is up to us to choose what to say, what to look at, what to listen to, what thoughts to entertain, what feelings to express and what acts to carry out. Even though our genes allow us to laugh and cry, encourage and discourage, sympathize with another or gossip, they do not decide which to do, when, how and why. Knowing what to do with what we have, is as important as what we inherit. Our genes and environment provide us the raw materials with which to work. These are like air, wood, stone and soil. What we do with these is up to us. We can transform the air into living tissue, the wood into homes, the stones into cathedrals and the soil into magnificent gardens, or we can pollute the air, use the wood to crucify our opponents, hurl the stones at others and poison the soil. What we choose to do makes a difference.

In the April 20, 1992, issue of the *Washington Post*, there was an article in the Science section entitled: *"Choosing the Right Mutation? Tests Suggest Cells React to Environment by Altering Genetic Code. OMNI* magazine reported on the same subject in an article by Pamela Weintraub: *Natural Direction, Extraordinary new findings suggest that life forms may literally direct their own evolution.* In these articles, bacteria and yeast determine what mutations to make based on the environment in which they find themselves. *"It is generally accepted in biology that if a phenomenon happens in microbial cells, it also happens in the cells of 'higher' organisms."* These articles suggest that it is possible for higher organisms like us to direct their evolution, determine how to change, and in fact be the directing agent of their own unfolding drama. Obviously, not everyone in the scientific community concurs with these dramatic conclusions.

If the bacteria can direct their evolution, why can't we? If the lilies of the field can adorn themselves with so much beauty, so can we, especially inner beauty. If the birds can overcome the pull of gravity and fly high, we can conquer the pull of our lower nature and soar.

Use it, or lose it is a truism we can apply to direct the course of our evolution. If, for example, we emphasize care and compassion, love and cooperation, industry and frugality and use these qualities repeatedly until they gradually get incorporated into our character and personality, we change our state of being. Since our characters and personalities are shaped by our thoughts, feelings and acts and these we can control, we can play a critical role in the process of Natural Selection through the choices we make.

We differ from all other life forms by our higher degree of self-awareness. If we intentionally become more aware of our choices and select behaviors that we want to foster, we take part in directing the course of our evolution, shaping society and ultimately the world. We can do wonders if we exercise our choices properly. We must habitually focus, not only on what we are, but what we *can* be; not only on what we have, but what we *are becoming* as well. As we take the helm and direct the course of our affairs, we live the life we choose.

It is not an accident of nature that we are each a unique living being, as individual as our fingerprints and as distinct as our genetic code. Our uniqueness is an indication that we are uniquely qualified for at least one activity that we can excel at. We must find out what this is and do it. Our experiences prepare us to carry out this unique activity. We must not shy away from difficulties. By tackling these, we gain strength. Let us not be fooled by our current circumstances, either. One stage of our lives cannot define us adequately. We are not powerless just because once we were children. We are not weak just because sometimes we feel weak. We are not confined and restricted just because physically we are. Emotionally, mentally and spiritually we are as free as we want to be. For through thoughts, dreams and visualizations we can project our consciousness through space and time. We can float in the air, jump over trees, go forward or backward in time. We can see ourselves as noble, powerful, mature, or any other way we choose. Once we accept responsibility for our lives, we take charge of our destiny.

## STAGE 4

# Decipher the Meaning of Life and Master the Art of Living

*Life is the art of drawing without an eraser.*

*John Christian*

One of the main traits that sets us apart from machines is that we are social beings. We belong to a community, a family of kin. We yearn to love and be loved, to serve and be served, to give and to receive. We have an innate sense to commune and belong. This sense is as strong as our sense to seek food and shelter, find a mate, procreate and care for our young. Unlike machines, we cannot just stay busy. We must find meaning in what we do. We cannot just exist, we must find value and joy in our lives. We must know that our contributions make a difference.

To find meaning in our lives, we must know and accept our lives as valuable. We must have satisfactory answers to the questions of why we live, why we die, and whether or not we matter. We must learn to deal with the fact of our mortality. We must decide how to best use our limited amount of time adequately. We must be clear about who we are going to spend our time with and for what causes. We must also settle on what legacy we intend to leave behind.

To find personally meaningful answers to the difficult questions of life is not easy, but it can and must be done. For without a solid philosophy and a commitment to do that which we find meaningful, we will drift, struggle, and die prematurely having hardly lived. To live meaningful lives, the meaning of our lives must be clear to us.

## Life and Meaning

> *Life is filigree work. . . . What is written clearly is not worth much, it's the transparency that counts.*
> Louis-Ferdinand Céline

As I leave home everyday, I pass by an odd-shaped lot that has been ignored for several years. One morning I noticed heavy equipment on that vacant lot. Day after day, I noticed ongoing activity. Soon the ground was dug up. I had no idea what was transpiring. I asked my wife, but she did not know either. I followed the progress of the activities with interest. I wanted to know what was taking place. As time went on, I realized that something was being constructed there. Initially, I thought the lot to be too small and awkwardly shaped for a house. After a while, I thought anything was possible. Soon the construction began to take shape. I still did not know what it was going to be. A few months later, a beautiful house stood there with a fully fenced yard and new grass growing in the lawn.

If we had the luxury of observing life from beginning to end, we might know what is being constructed through our living as well. We do not see our lives in their entirety. Each life is but one step in the unfolding drama of being. To see the meaning of our lives, we must be able to see the complete picture—the entire structure after it is completed. The reason we can tell that a house is being built before the construction is completed is that we have seen houses before and can figure out what is being built by merely observing what is unfolding. We cannot do the same with our lives. We have never seen the complete edifice of a concluded life. We have nothing to go by. If we have never seen a butterfly, we can never know what a cocoon will transform into. It is easy to deduce and infer if we know the end result. It is extremely difficult, if not impossible, to do the same having never seen the final product.

Our lives are like lines in a gigantic painting that is being drawn. We can only see through the opening that our level of awareness provides. We only see where we place our awareness and that is only a minute segment of what can be realized. It is as if we are faced with a painting that is completely covered by an opaque cloth with only a few tiny holes. Even if we move the cloth around and the holes reveal other aspects of the painting, it is still very difficult to know the nature of the covered work of art. Even if we spend our entire lives analyzing the tiny isolated fragments of the gigantic picture, we will not arrive at a complete understanding of the value and meaning of that painting.

We are in the dark about the meaning of our lives because we stand in the world shining a tiny light—our awareness—at our surroundings expecting to see and understand all. Instead, all we glimpse is a limited view. If we stand in a dark room and shine a feeble light at only a few isolated spots, regardless of how well we study those spots, we will not arrive at a complete understanding of what is in that room. We look at life with eyes covered with "scales." These scales are the result of the limitations of the tools we use, our finite abilities, experiences, and understanding. We cannot derive a philosophy of life and draw conclusions about its meaning by merely analyzing small fragments of events and experiences. We cannot know the whole by studying a few segments. Until we see the entire room with the lights on, and the painting without the cloth, we will not be able to know the complete meaning of what we are analyzing. So it is with our individual lives.

Given the fact that our lights are feeble, and we cannot put all the tiny pieces of the puzzle of our lives together to see the complete picture and from it derive meaning for our lives, what are we to do? We can combine our feeble lights into a torch. We can use all that we have to the best of our abilities—reason and intuition. We can ask, knock and persist, until the answers appear. We can do what we are capable of right now. We can dare and act expecting that all else will fall in place.

There are three levels from which we can view life and glean an understanding of what it is. The first level is that of the physical manifestation. At this level we experience life as a **product**—a material organization and a physical construction. We can see it, touch it and use our other senses to be aware of it. Just as we see the bricks, shingles and windows of a house, we see the cells, tissues, organs and systems of bodies. These are the vehicles through which life expresses itself as awareness and abilities. Life uses only a few elements to organize and express itself. Some of these are: carbon, hydrogen, oxygen, nitrogen, calcium, magnesium, sodium, potassium, iron, phosphorus, and sulfur. Studying the physical manifestation to comprehend life is important, but the understanding we derive is limited. It is like studying a sealed book for its physical characteristics. We can measure the book, weigh it, analyze its composition, quantify the specifics of its paper and ink, calculate its angle of refraction, and measure its rate of decomposition. We can subject the book to various chemicals, temperatures and pressures. Regardless of how thoroughly we analyze the physical properties of the book, we will never arrive at a complete understanding of the book, its value and meaning. Even though we will get to know the book as a physical entity on an intimate level, we will never know the idea behind the book, or the ideas within the book.

Studying the physical manifestations of life, its products, is limited by the tools we use. Initially, all we could see was what our eyes discerned. It was not until 1665, when Robert Hooke studied the dead cells of cork with a crude microscope that we realized the cellular structure of tissues. In 1674, Antoni van Leeuwenhoek devised double-convex lenses that could magnify objects mounted on pinheads up to 300 times. Leeuwenhoek was the first to accurately describe protozoa, red blood cells and bacteria. In 1677, he described the spermatozoa of both insects and humans. Over time, the light microscope was perfected and objects could be magnified up to the maximum resolution of light. Since the smallest wavelength of visible light is about 4000 angstroms (1 angstrom is .000,000,000,1 meters), any object smaller than 4000 angstroms could never be detected using light as the source of magnification.

With the development of the electron microscope in the 1940s, viruses became visible for the first time. Soon we were able to visualize atoms and through diffraction and other techniques prove the existence of subatomic particles. Yet, with all of our advances, we are still limited in our understanding to the tools we use. Even though we have uncovered and learned a lot, much more lies hidden from our eyes because we lack the appropriate tools to observe them.

The second level at which we can understand life is that of the **blueprint**. Like all well constructed edifices, the physical manifestations of life follow a blueprint. The blueprint of life is the genes. Working with garden peas in the 1860s, Gregor Mendel described the patterns of inheritance. He observed that the traits that appeared in different pea-plant varieties were inherited as separate units, each of which was transmitted independently of the others. He suggested that each parent has pairs of units but contributes only one unit from each pair to its offspring. This unit was later given the name gene. Scientists soon realized that the patterns of inheritance described by Mendel paralleled the action of chromosomes in dividing cells. This led to the conclusion that genes are carried by the chromosomes. Chromosomes reside in the cells of all organisms.

Cells are the fundamental structural unit of all living organisms and they are of two distinct types. In the lower organisms, the genetic material, the genes and the blueprint, are in direct contact with a jelly-like layer of material called the cytoplasm. In higher organisms, the genetic material is contained within a nucleus separated from the cell cytoplasm by a membranous nuclear envelope.

The elements of life, through their specific associations and unique geometry make it possible for life to express its qualities through them. What controls the type of geometry and the associations that form between the elements of life is the genetic code, the blueprint of life. Even though this blueprint is formed from the same basic elements of life, the manner in which these elements are organized into highly complex compounds (nucleotides) enables them to exhibit a high level of complexity, with sophisticated abilities and some degree of awareness. From this blueprint the entire body can be constructed. These blueprints are the libraries that house the life history of the living being and the annals of its race. Yet understanding and tampering with the intelligence in the blueprints (genes) is not the same as understanding and knowing life. Just as we can study the blueprint of any building and once we decode and understand its symbols, we can alter and modify the design, so can we alter the design of a life form once we master its genetic code. This level of knowledge is analogous to our being able to decipher the contents of this page by reading and comprehending the meaning of the words. This gives us an insight into the intelligence carried by the words. We can use this insight to re-write the words to come up with new meaning. This gives us a level of control and mastery of the way words or genes are expressed. For most, being able to alter the genetic makeup, or modify the words in a paragraph, is mastery enough and equates to a sufficient understanding and knowledge of life and literature. However, this is only the second level of intelligence inherent in living beings. Understanding the genetic code of a cell is not the same as knowing the essence of life.

The third level is that of the *architect,* the *author* and the *creator.* Genes in a cell are designed, blueprints are fashioned and words on a page are authored. Who is the architect of the blueprints, creator of the genes and the author of the living words in the form of living entities? Where did the intelligence, awareness and abilities of life that are condensed into blueprints in the form of genes come from? We know that an architect can create several designs and originate an unlimited number of blueprints. If we understand life at the architect's level, then we know life at its deepest dimension. Just as the intelligence on this page is captured by the specific arrangement of the letters forming the words and paragraphs, life is expressed through the particular organization of the elements composing organelles, cells, and highly complex systems. By studying the compounds of life, by deciphering the blueprint in the nucleus, and by understanding the mind of the architect; we get to understand and know life on all three levels. Unfortunately, we have access to the elements and the blueprints only, but not the architect. Even though the architect's handiwork is everywhere, The Architect, The Author and The Creator is nowhere to be seen.

Yet a "bit" of The Architect is in every cell. The life of the cell is an aspect of the life of The Architect. The life of any entity is an image of the life of its creator. Since we can never know The Creator except through the created, by studying all forms of creations we get a glimpse of the omnipotence of the one in whose image we are.

## The Blueprint of Life and It's Architect

While a human being has his or her beginning in one fertilized egg from which the entire body develops, life is a conifer containing an unlimited number of seeds each on its own journey of unfoldment. Just as any fertilized egg proceeds to become the fullness of what its genes hold for it, so it is with life. Life is unfolding as it should based on the intelligence inherent in its genes. These genes are not apparent to us. They are not contained in one nucleus in one cell that we can refer to. The blueprint of life is not even material, yet it is evident everywhere. Its unfoldment is a process of continuing complexity with intertwining relationships between all living entities and nature.

We know where we came from—as seeds from our parents. We know where the seeds of all other life forms came from—as seeds from their parents. Seeds are not the same as their parents. They are a mere mirror image with the potential to differentiate or evolve and unfold into the likeness of the source from which they originated. Mature adults produce seeds that grow and transform into new mature adults producing more seeds. Where did the conifer of seeds of life come from? Who is the mature adult that produced this ultimate conifer of seeds?

The "mature adult" that formed the seed of life is The Architect of Life, or God. Let us take a very brief look at *The Architect* and find out *why* God would want to create the seed of life and initiate evolution and unfoldment.

We know very little about God, but what we know is sufficient to understand the mystery of creating the first seed of life. Most of our knowledge about God comes from religion, philosophy and mysticism (personal experiences). There are those who do not believe in God. For me, it is a forgone conclusion that the architectures and designs that I experience in life must have an architect and a designer behind them. God, for me, is The Architect, The Designer and The Intelligence that causes everything to be, to progress, to unfold, and to evolve.

As far as I am concerned, there are no accidents. The universe is too orderly to be the result of an accident and blind force. All acts are caused by forces covert or overt. Law and order permeate nature. Intelligence is apparent everywhere. Yet, it is also concealed especially in seeds. In order to create the seeds of all life forms, this Architect must have **the ability and the power to create, the knowledge of what and how to create, and the will and the desire to create.** Since this Architect created all, it must be all powerful, or OMNIPOTENT. Since it knows how to create everything, we say that this Architect is all knowing. In other words, this Architect is OMNISCIENT. Since this Architect continues to create, it must be in love with the process of creation. It must love what it is creating else why continue. Since this Architect is the originator of all, it must love all as any parent loves its offspring. In other words, this Architect must be in love with its creation. It is all loving, or it is LOVE.

Hence, this Architect is Omnipotent, Omniscient and Love. Since these are the qualities we attribute to God, or the Cosmic Intelligence, the Architect is the same as God. Hence, God is the Architect of life. Let us imagine a "time" when God was all alone; before God created the world or anything else. Picture a God who is ALL POWERFUL. This means that God has the ability to create anything and everything God desires, wants, or wishes. Imagine also that this God knows how to create anything and everything. All that is left is being moved through love to want to create. Realizing that God is all there is, God's love, knowledge and power could only be directed at Him/Herself. There is nothing else. What would God do with His/Her power, knowledge and love?

Imagine you are full of love, but there is no one else to love. What would you do? *You would love yourself.* Imagine you have the ability and the desire to create anything you want and you also know how to do it, what would you create? Since you are full of love, you would create something that you would love. What would that be? Since you love yourself, *you would create yourself.* So God **reproduced** Himself/Herself. God did not create another fully mature God, for that would have been redundant since God already exists. Instead, God created a seed with the potential to become just like its source. God created the seed and the proper environment for that seed to have a chance to grow, mature and become an adult according to its blueprint.

A seed does not look anything like the source that produced it. A mustard seed is not as a mustard tree. A watermelon seed is not the same as a watermelon. As seeds unfold, grow and mature, they begin to resemble their source more and more. So it is with the seed of life and the seed that we are. To know where we came from and what our source must have been like, all we have to do is look at, not what we are, but rather *what we are becoming.*

To know where this unfoldment is heading, we need to take a closer look at what is happening in life. What we call evolution is the unfolding of the seeds of life in the process of maturation. What differentiation is to the body, evolution is to life. Life began as seeds just as all life forms begin as seeds. Life is now at a certain level of unfoldment just as we and everything else are in a specific stage of progress. As life unfolds, living entities become more complex, sophisticated and gain in awareness and abilities. Currently, we are slowly moving away from power, subjugation and domination. We are, instead, moving toward appreciation for beauty, justice, peace, love and harmony. We are becoming more tolerant of differences, appreciative of the value of diversity, and more concerned with value and meaning than just staying busy and earning a living. We are increasing in our awareness, knowledge and abilities. We are becoming more productive, effective and holistic. We are growing more toward each other, shrinking the distance, time and space that separates us. We are learning to use our diversity for the benefit of all. We are discovering cooperation and moving away from pure competition. We are getting in touch with our inner strength, spirit and source. We are becoming more purpose oriented, appreciative of each other, and caring for our environment. Spirituality is assuming prominence. Humanity is progressing toward becoming an integrated body. We are becoming more and more like Nature and God. Just as looking at the human body we do not see the cells that compose it unless we use a microscope, one day we will look at humanity and see it as an integrated body.

The next question is why did God produce the seed of life to grow and become like Himself/Herself? Is it only because God is loving, or is there another reason? Why was God not satisfied with being alone, all knowing and all powerful? Why share when you can have it all? Why did the ONE, the ALL, decide to become the many? Are there any benefits to multiplicity?

The question of why God produced the seed of life is the same question as to why trees produce seeds, why we reproduce, and why cells divide. If we understand why cells divide and why we reproduce, we get to know why God produced us and what the purpose of life is. **Why do cells divide and why do we reproduce?**

**The Cell**

We know **how** cells divide. Body cells divide by mitosis while sex cells known as gametes (sperms and eggs) divide by meiosis. What we are interested in is not how cells divide and how we reproduce, but **why** do cells divide and **why** do we reproduce. The simple answer: "to perpetuate the species" is not good enough because the question then becomes why? Why should an individual care to perpetuate the species? What advantages are there for the individual to do this? To understand the why of cell division and why we reproduce, we need to look at why cells formed in the first place.

The cell is recognized as the functional unit of life. Hence, before the advent of the cell, there was no life. The cell did not one day simply appear out of nowhere. The cell formed progressively, over eons, starting from a very primitive format that eventually transformed into its current state.

Before we were, there was the cell. Before the cell was, there were organelles. Before the organelles formed, there were the various compounds. Before the compounds formed, there were molecules and atoms. Before the atom was, there were the electrons, protons and neutrons.

Hydrogen is the simplest atom. It has one electron and one proton. These are its subatomic particles. While subatomic particles are "particles," they are the condensed forms of "waves." These waves emanate from an unknown source.

Hydrogen is the progenitor of all the elements. In the sun, through fusion, hydrogen gives rise to helium and subsequently to all the other elements. As more elements are formed, gradually the sun gets transformed from a gas to a progressively more dense material body. Eventually, dense bodies such as planets form. Earth was initially hot and molten. Through heat, radiation, thunder, lightening and rain, simple and complex compounds formed on earth and in its oceans. As these compounds had different affinities and were variously charged, eventually organelles were formed. Each organelle excels at one or two fundamental activities. Some are very good at forming a protective membrane, others are proficient at hydrolytic functions, while still others are very good at extracting energy and building blocks from other sources.

Organelles are extremely primitive and in themselves are not considered alive. They are like viruses that carry on one main function. Just as a virus becomes alive when it invades a cell or a tissue, organelles become alive when two or more of them come together and form a cell. Just as when electrons, protons and neutrons come together they give rise to material expressions in the form of atoms, so too when two or more different organelles come together and integrate their efforts. Something unique and miraculous takes place—a cell with totally new features and characteristics is born. Life manifests.

> *For where two or three are gathered in my name, there am I in the midst of them.*
> *Matthew 18:20*

Anytime two or more atoms, elements, organelles, cells, tissues, organs, systems, individuals, communities, even countries and worlds come together in the spirit of love and unite, something unique and miraculous takes place. **New and unique "features" are born.** In a sense, *the ultimate function of sex and love is to bring individuals together so as new features may manifest.*

When an electron and a proton come together, *hydrogen*—matter is formed. Where did materiality come from? Simply a miracle! When hydrogen and oxygen come together and unite, *water* is formed—wet, liquid, potable water with unique characteristics distinct from either hydrogen or oxygen. Where did the liquidity come from? Simply a miracle! When sodium and chlorine come together and unite, *salt* is formed. Where did the salinity come from? Simply a miracle! When gaseous carbon dioxide, and liquid water meet in the leaves of plants, chlorophyll uses the energy from the sun to split the water molecule into oxygen and hydrogen, uses the hydrogen to combine with the carbon dioxide and forms *carbohydrates*. Chlorophyll then releases the oxygen as gas that we breathe and without which we cannot live. Carbohydrates are food we eat. How can two gases, hydrogen and carbon dioxide, combine to become food? Where does *edibility* come from? Simply a miracle!

When a few organelles came together and united, whether accidentally or because of their nature, a new entity, the cell, was born. The result of the union was far greater than the added sum of the capabilities of the organelles separately. Through union, there was an addition, new features became evident that transformed the separate units and engulfed them in a totally unique "family."

The union of the organelles gave rise to the cell, *a mastermind group* with incredible capabilities and totally unique qualities. The newly formed cell can now protect itself inside its membrane, ingest food and extract energy. It can get rid of waste and defend itself against attacks.

A "speck" of all that we are and can become must have existed as potential, as seed, in the original cell from which we came. Just as from the one fertilized egg cell, all differentiation ensues, all of our capabilities emerge from the qualities of the one original mother cell.

The cell with its life and capabilities came about when the various components gave up their individuality for the sake of collectivity. By giving up their independence, they gained a higher level of independence, new abilities and greater security. By giving up their perceived individuality, they gained the freedom to specialize and share benefits; a feature unattainable on their own.

The cell, in higher orders of life, is composed of cytoplasm and nucleus. The nucleus houses the genetic material while the cytoplasm contains several organelles. A cell is a specific grouping, a *mastermind* of nucleus, cell membrane, mitochondria, both rough and smooth endoplasmic reticulum, Golgi apparatus, lysosomes, vesicles, ribosomes, microtubules, centrioles, cilia, flagella, filaments and fibrils. Each of these components is a complex organization in its own right. Together, they are a formidable mastermind capable of complex functions, intelligence and awareness. Obviously, different cell types have different ratios of cellular components.

Just as the progressive merging together of organelles gave rise to successively more complex cells, cells came together to form tissues, organs, systems and the body. The body is a *mastermind grouping* of its various systems: nervous, immune, digestive, circulatory, skeletal, muscular, respiratory and reproductive. The body is capable of far more than any cell, tissue, organ, or system alone. The body exhibits superior intelligence, keen awareness and impressive abilities.

The next level of organization after the individual is that of the family. The family is a *mastermind group* starting with two individuals and growing to include more. Through the family, two individuals accomplish far more than either could alone. The next level is that of the community. In a community, individuals come together giving up their individual separate existence for the sake of collectivity. The community is a *mastermind group* of the various individuals who specialize and contribute ideas, goods, products and services. Our current level of evolution is at the country level. Once we transcend this level to the world level, we will derive tremendous benefits, increase our awareness of ourselves and each other, and become highly efficient, effective and powerful. We are individually a cell in the process of becoming a body.

The mastermind concept can only work if the individuals concerned are diverse and dedicated to contributing their best by focusing on areas they enjoy and can become experts at. In a mastermind group, individuality exists to the extent of highlighting areas of interest and expertise. Beyond that, every member is equally important and valuable. The fundamental qualities binding all members of a mastermind group are caring for each other, sharing, contributing their best and receiving shared benefits in return. In other words, the binding force of a mastermind group is **love**. In a similar fashion, when we intentionally unite ourselves in love with our source, *rapture* results.

It is love that brings individuals together and propels them to form a larger group, a *mastermind assembly*. Love is the innate realization that whenever two or more come together *in love,* new benefits will be realized by all. This innate realization is the driving force behind cell division and our innate desire to reproduce. This innate force that ever propels us to join and unite manifests as desire, attraction, lust and love. Because of this innate force, life can progress, unfold and mature.

Life progresses from the simple to the more complex, from reactions to abilities and awareness, and from individuality to the mastermind family. **The reason that life is evolving toward more complexity and higher levels of organization and awareness is because through cell division and reproduction ever increasing numbers of individuals become available to interact and form new mastermind groups that can bring forth new and original qualities.**

*Therefore, the purpose of life is to create ever increasing levels of mastermind assemblies united in love.* These mastermind assemblies, whether cells, families, or communities, will give birth to new qualities and abilities which then benefit the entire mastermind assembly. The more the participants love each other, and the stronger the bonds of the mastermind group to which they belong, the better the benefits. Ultimately, the entire universe will become one mastermind group known as The UNIverse. This UNIverse will function as one body composed of an infinite number of cells, individuals, communities and worlds. Hence, our individual purpose should reflect the overall purpose of life. We should live to grow in our abilities, knowledge and relationships. We should strive to form ever mushrooming mastermind groupings. We should master the art of loving and relating, deeply and profoundly. We should strive to specialize and excel giving our best by doing what we love and by loving what we do. Just as by planting one seed, a plant is formed that produces fruit and numerous seeds, by freely giving ourselves to our mastermind assembly, we multiply our power and receive returns several times our original investment.

## Mastering the Art of Living

*My art and profession is to live.*
                              Michel de Montaigne

Living is an art. As we live, we draw on the canvas of space and time. We draw through our thoughts, feelings and acts. What results is a tapestry of experiences and memories.

Not everyone starts life with the same opportunities. As the great parable-teller informs us, we enter the world as seeds that fall in various environments. Some seeds fall on fertile soil, grow and multiply, producing abundance. Other seeds fall on rock with very little soil, produce weak roots and soon wither away. Some seeds fall between thorns and are suffocated. Other seeds get eaten by birds of prey. While seeds in nature have no choice where they fall, we do. Even if we start life in inopportune circumstances, we can change our fate by taking corrective action. Life will lend us a helping hand once we are determined to act. Over time, and through awareness and effort, all circumstances change. Even the seeds that fall on rock eventually get washed away by rain and some manage to grow. Even the seeds that get eaten by birds, eventually get dispersed to far away places with new opportunities for growth. The seeds that fall between thorns remain dormant until they get eaten or the thorns die and then they can begin to grow under new circumstances.

To make the most of our lives, we must maximize the qualities of life in our lives. The American Heritage Dictionary defines life as: *the quality manifested in functions such as metabolism, growth, response to stimulation, and reproduction by which living organisms are distinguished from dead organisms or inanimate matter.* To master the art of living, we must master the functions of life. Specifically, we must excel at:

1. metabolism,
2. growth,
3. response to stimulation, and
4. reproduction.

### 1. Metabolism

*Tell me what you eat, and I will tell you what you are.*
                                        Anthelme Brillat-Savarin

The word metabolism is derived from *metabole,* meaning change. Thus, metabolism is the changes—the physical and chemical processes—that living entities must carry out to maintain life. Two metabolic processes are recognized: constructive and destructive. Through constructive metabolism (anabolism), the body synthesizes what it needs to grow and maintain itself. Through destructive metabolism (catabolism), the body produces the energy it needs, maintains its body temperature and eliminates waste. If the constructive processes exceed the destructive, the organism grows; otherwise, it shrivels.

Mastering metabolism is **the first fundamental of life.** Through metabolism we maintain our life by synthesizing the proper elements into the body, generating the energy we need, and effectively eliminating waste. If we only metabolize air, water, food, vitamins, minerals and light we live. If we also metabolize pleasant memories, we enjoy life. For we are as alive as the quality of our metabolism. To master metabolism, we must master the art of trade and become excellent merchants. For through metabolism, we **exchange** with our environment. We ingest and eliminate. We take in what we need and we give out what we no longer require. If we do not get what we need, we shrivel and die. If we do not get rid of waste, we poison ourselves and die. Breathing, the most fundamental process for maintaining life, itself is a process of exchange. It is a dual metabolic activity of taking in and giving out. We breathe in oxygen and we breathe out carbon dioxide. Thus, we need to exchange, not accumulate and hoard. We need to create a flow and maintain a commerce, not hold on and deny others the opportunity to have what we have.

Metabolic changes do not affect the individual alone, they change the environment. For as we take, we change not only ourselves, but the environment from which we take as well. The best we can exchange with the world is ourselves. If we give our time, skill and love, we acquire knowledge, wisdom and we grow.

## 2. Growth

*What is the most rigorous law of our being? Growth. No smallest atom of our moral, mental, or physical structure can stand still a year. It grows — it must grow; nothing can prevent it.*
Mark Twain

If we want to live, we must want to grow for life is an impetus for growth. We cannot stand still. We either grow, or we regress. ***This is the second fundamental of life.*** The same way that nature produces an abundance of foods to provide for our physical growth, it furnishes us with a plethora of "obstacles," challenges and opportunities for our mental, emotional and spiritual growth.

To grow, we must get involved, fan our interests, and kindle our passions. Being passionate creates a potential difference which we can use to act. If one passion is quenched, we must discover or create a new one. We can transform our wants, needs and desires into passions through vivid imagination. Thus, we should neither extinguish nor unnecessarily suppress our desires for these are our impetus for growth.

People grow differently. Some grow quickly and then stop. Others grow so slowly that for all practical purposes they are standing still. Some grow despite adverse circumstances, while others do not grow even in the best of environments.

The extent of our growth is a function of our comfort zone. To grow properly, we must understand our styles and comfort zones. We must be comfortable with the pace and the methods we employ to grow. Just as we maintain the temperature in our homes within comfort levels, we live our lives within "comfort zones." If our comfort zone is dynamic and changes with our circumstances, we progress, otherwise we stagnate on that level. Comfort zones are limits we set for ourselves and accept as real boundaries. They become like the borders between countries which we zealously guard. Comfort zones, however, are only real if we make them so. When we do, we build ourselves a psychological jail that keeps us from extending and applying ourselves. Once we get used to our comfort zones, they form cocoons about us. It requires effort to break out of them. Confined to our comfort zones, we become like a fly in a jar that is free to fly away, but does not having been confined to a closed container for too long. If we keep ourselves caged, we will not grow beyond the walls of our prison.

We are told that a human being has the capacity to easily learn the contents of several encyclopedias, master forty languages and acquire several doctorate degrees in a variety of fields. These are by no means the limits. No one has as yet tested the outer reaches of human capabilities. Our world and universe are spherical. These spheres are capable of limitless expansion. In the laws of mathematics, each degree of increase along the radius increases the volume of that sphere three fold: $V = 4/3 \Pi r^3$. So it is with us. With each degree of extension in our reach, the new volume of our world and the sphere of our opportunities is also increased three fold. We extend our "radius" when we acquire additional knowledge, increase our skills and when we either establish new relationships or deepen existing ones. We grow with the expansion of the circle of our relationships beginning with our family and friends. As our relationships expand, our world grows, while the world at large shrinks for us. Our actions assume more importance and their impact multiplies.

We are traders in the stock market of life. We must earn dividends as we trade. How much dividend or growth is enough? This is a personal matter. However, the giver of life, "money" and our talents expects us to be active. We cannot be idle. We must invest and, at a minimum, double our assets in each cycle.

> "For it will be as when a man going on a journey called his servants and entrusted to them his property; to one he gave five talents, to another two, to another one, to each according to his ability. Then he went away. He who had received the five talents went at once and traded with them; and he made five talents more. So also, he who had the two talents made two talents more. But he who had received the one talent went and dug in the ground and hid his master's money. Now after a long time the master of those servants came and settled accounts with them. And he who had received the five talents came forward, bringing five talents more, saying, 'Master, you delivered to me five talents; here I have made five talents more.' His master said to him, 'Well done, good and faithful servant; you have been faithful over a little, I will set you over much; enter into the joy of your master.' And he also who had the two talents came forward, saying, 'Master, you delivered to me two talents; here I have made two talents more.' His master said to him, 'Well done, good and faithful servant; you have been faithful over a little, I will set you over much; enter into the joy of your mas-

ter.' He also who had received the one talent came forward, saying, 'Master, I knew you to be a hard man, reaping where you did not sow, and gathering where you did not winnow; so I was afraid, and I went and hid your talent in the ground. Here you have what is yours.' But his master answered him, 'You wicked and slothful servant! You knew that I reap where I have not sowed, and gather where I have not winnowed? Then you ought to have invested my money with the bankers, and at my coming I should have received what was my own with interest. So take the talent from him, and give it to him who has the ten talents. For to every one who has will more be given, and he will have abundance; but from him who has not, even what he has will be taken away. And cast the worthless servant into the outer darkness; there men will weep and gnash their teeth.'
*Matthew 25:14–30*

We are entrusted with the resources of time, abilities and environment. We are expected to apply our abilities within the given time frame and transform ourselves and our environment. We invest best when we grow the most. We grow most when we seize each moment and take advantage of its opportunities.

*Lose this day loitering, it will be the same story tomorrow, and the rest more dilatory. Thus indecision brings its own delays and days are lost tormenting over days. Are you in earnest? Seize this very minute; what you can do, or dream you can, begin it. Boldness has genius, power, and magic in it. Only engage and then the mind grows heated. Begin and then the work will be completed.*
*Goethe*

### 3. Response to Stimulation

*My mind rebels at stagnation. Give me problems, give me work, give me the most abstruse cryptogram, or the most intricate* analysis, and I am in my own proper atmosphere. I can dispense then with artificial stimulants. But I abhor the dull routine of existence. I crave for mental exaltation.

Sir Arthur Conan Doyle

Life is based on a few elements out of the more than one hundred elements available on earth. Of these, carbon plays the central role. In fact, compounds containing carbon are termed *organic* in that they are in the composition of all living matter.

What is so special about carbon that gives it such a vital role in the process of life? **Carbon has a very low heat capacity.** Heat capacity (amount of heat required to raise the temperature of a substance by 1 degree C.) is a measure of the sensitivity of an element and its readiness to undergo change. It is the degree of responsiveness of a substance to stimulation and hence is a measure of its "aliveness." By definition, *the more heat (energy or effort) an element requires to undergo change, the less "alive" that element is.* Carbon's low heat capacity makes it very "alive". Substances of low heat capacity have low resistance and a correspondingly high degree of wave nature (consciousness and sociability). Because of this, carbon is heavily distributed into a huge variety of organic compounds.

If carbon is the vehicle of organic life because of its sensitivity and low resistance to stimulation and change, we must be likewise. To maintain our aliveness, we must have a low "heat capacity" and we must be sensitive to our environment. We must remain alert and ready to respond to positive stimulation. Hence, *to the degree that we are sensitive, flexible and responsive to that degree we are alive.* **This is the third fundamental of life.**

One of the outstanding features that babies possess is their flexibility. It is amazing how they manage to fit themselves in the contours of the birth canal and emerge onto center stage through such a small opening. It is only as they "grow up" that they begin to lose their flexibility and become rigid "adults."

The more sensitive we are to our surroundings, the better we are able to "read" our environment. Since most of what we achieve in life comes to us from others, the more sensitive we are to people's needs, the more responsive we will be to them and the better service we can render. As our services improve, the quality of our lives is enhanced.

By developing our sensitivity to the needs of others, we develop empathy and our inner self grows. As our inner self expands, our identity mushrooms and our individuality blossoms. We acquire power and dominion, not over others, but over our circumstances.

The barometer of our flexibility is the state of our mind, our emotional aliveness, behavior and our physical resilience and endurance. Mental flexibility manifests itself as openness to new ideas, willingness to listen to varying and opposing opinions, and to be tolerant. Since our minds create the atmosphere through which we view and experience life, we must keep our minds open, ever questioning and inquisitive.

Emotional flexibility is openness, responsiveness, the absence of possessiveness and the ability to freely express and receive emotions such as empathy, praise and love, and to cry and laugh heartily. Experiencing life is mostly experiencing emotions. We must experience thrills, deep joys and be moved by the happiness and misery of others. The more flexible we are emotionally, the more open, receptive and responsive to life we are. Our emotional flexibility manifests mostly through our behavior. Behavioral flexibility is indicative of our ease with uncertainty, comfort with newness, and rapid adjustment to change. Our behavior must match the circumstances and the environment, and change as these do. We must remain responsive to our inner and outer environments.

Physical flexibility is being able to bend and be pliable.

Even though we require strength and stamina, it is equally important to be flexible. Since rigidity sets in naturally over time, remaining flexible requires effort and awareness.

## 4. Reproduction

*Life is a flame that is always burning itself out. But it catches fire again every time a child is born.*
George Bernard Shaw

Of all the systems in the human body—the immune, skeletal, digestive, circulatory, nervous, respiratory and muscular—only the reproductive system is directly concerned with the survival of the species rather than with the survival of the individual. Why should the individual be concerned with the survival of its species? Is reproduction merely for the benefit of the species, or are there other advantages to reproduction, especially in humans, than what is at first apparent?

Reproduction is an essential aspect of life. Through reproduction, life ensures its immortality. Through children, humanity climbs the rungs of eternity. Watching salmon die after spawning makes us believe that our primary function in life is to reproduce. Reproduction is only one aspect of our lives for we reproduce for only a short period. The rest of the time, we must produce instead of reproduce, for ***productivity is the fourth fundamental of life.***

Life is not just change and exchange, it is ***interchange*** as well. Interchange requires a means for it to take place. Sex is the means for interchange in life. That is why we do not simply reproduce, we have sex to reproduce. Sex is the means for interchange in higher life forms. Sex can be routine and boring, or alluring, enjoyable and most of all, profound. Sex is essential for it is the means of physical creation—reproduction. Sex, like all essential functions, is incorporated into the subconscious as *instinct*. However, in humans, it should be anything but instinct. It should involve awareness, clear intent and a readiness to give and receive physically, emotionally, mentally and spiritually.

The deeper the layer involved in an interchange, the more lasting and profound the effects. Exchanges take place at "sites." These sites have the quality of getting "psyched" and excited for the exchange. In the human body these specific sites are termed the *erogenous zones*. Erogenous zones are like markets where merchants gather for the specific purpose of interchange and exchange. The merchants in the human body are the neurons (nerve cells). Neurons are well suited for being merchants because they are experts in dealing with electrons. Electrons are the carriers of charge—the currency of exchange in the body.

Neurons are excellent transmitters and receivers of electrical charge. They gather in erogenous zones and wait for the opportunity to participate in exchanges. When enticed through excitement, electrons flow freely and generate electricity. Where there is electricity, there is excitement. Excitement is the measure of the availability of "cash" to consummate an exchange. Excitement leads to expansion by causing electrons to move farther from the center of the atom to higher orbits or quanta. The higher the quanta of an electron, the more its potential energy and its readiness to take part in the exchange.

Excitement is important, not only in sex, but in our everyday activities as well. If life is a process of exchange and interchange, and if excitement is the cash of the interaction, the more excited we are about life, the more cash we have to exchange and interchange, touch and be touched, impact and be impacted, and in the process experience life more fully and abundantly.

Desire is fundamental to excitement, but desire alone is not enough to bring about activity. There must also be the willingness to carry out the desire—to give in and fully consent to the activity. The degree of this consent is directly related to the participants' awareness, and the absence of any mental or emotional reservations.

Sex is an innate desire to merge with, to melt into, and to unite with another to replace our separateness with wholeness. Sex is an enactment of our true nature. Just as the salmon yearns to return to its spawning place, we yearn to return to our source. We were originally *one,* both male and female. We were united with our source. Now we feel separate and apart. We behave as if we are either male or female. We attempt to deny our duality of both maleness and femaleness. Our "femininity" comes from Earth the source of our body, while our "masculinity" comes from Heaven the source of our *breath, life and soul.* By denying half of our complete being, we feel unfulfilled and lacking. To fill this void, we desperately seek to intimately join with another who has complementary features. Through this joining, we vicariously feel united once more with our source, God, and Heaven.

Life is a drama and sex is its main theme. This is so because sex provides us the means to experience life as fully and completely as possible. Through it we can experience the four general qualities of life: metabolism, growth, response to stimulation and reproduction. Through touch, taste, smell, sight, sound and the immersion of ourselves with the being of another, we can **metabolize** the essence of another into our own being. By giving ourselves wholly and in complete abandon, we can share and **grow**. By being aware, awake and alive, we can stimulate and **respond to stimulation**. Finally, through sex we can **reproduce**.

## Personalizing Life

*Each man must look to himself to teach him the meaning of life. It is not something discovered: it is something moulded.*
                                            Antoine de Saint-Exupéry

Metabolism, growth, response to stimulation and reproduction are general functions of life. They enable us to live. Being alive, however, does not necessarily mean living a life of meaning, joy and self-actualization. It could be a mere survival. We must be more than simply alive. We must live our dreams and make them our realities. We must live the life that actualizes our potential and realizes our purpose. We must not only be content with what we are given like our "name" or what comes our way. We must lend nature a helping hand by causing things to happen the way we want them to progress. We can create and write a new "name" for ourselves. We can live to leave behind memories that are the inheritance we wish to have and bequeath.

We can personalize life. To do this, we must customize life by adding to the four general functions of life the particular qualities we deem necessary to make living worthwhile for us. God could have created the world in four "days." Instead, God, took seven days. We also need seven "days," functions, or fundamentals to make life personally meaningful and rewarding. To personalize life, we require three additional functions:

5. quality,
6. diversity, and
7. a journey of self-discovery.

### 5. Life as Quality

> *From time to time there appear on the face of the earth men of rare and consummate excellence, who dazzle us by their virtue, and whose outstanding qualities shed a stupendous light. Like those extraordinary stars of whose origins we are ignorant, and of whose fate, once they have vanished, we know even less, such men have neither forebears nor descendants: they are the whole of their race.*
>
> Jean de La Bruyère

The type of life we live and its quality is mostly a matter of choice. How aware we are of these choices is a matter of how awake we are. Life is impersonal. What we make of our lives determines its quality.

## Decipher the Meaning of Life

In my work place, a sign reads: *"Quality only happens when you care enough to do your best."* Quality in business involves customer satisfaction. It centers around identifying the business processes, measuring their effectiveness and attempting to improve the essential ones. In the business of our lives, we are our own customers. We must be satisfied with our lives. Quality in our lives involves identifying how we are currently living, measuring its impact and striving to progress toward the meaningful and abundant life as we understand it to be. We can simply exist by metabolizing, growing, responding to stimuli and reproducing—a simple cycle of birth, existence and death. We can, on the other hand, choose to fully participate in life by immersing ourselves in relationships and activities, by enjoying what we do, and doing the things we value most.

When we are born, we enter the world in its own relative and somewhat chaotic state. There are wars, hatred, intolerance, injustice, ignorance, and above all, a "low" level of existence. When we eventually die, we must leave the world behind with an improved state of being. There must be fewer wars, a little less hatred, intolerance, injustice and ignorance. We must make a difference by adding to the quality of life by the mere fact that we have lived on this earth with quality. Our impact can be small or great. With billions of people on earth, every contribution matters.

We all start with twenty-four hours every day. What we do in these hours is what sets us apart. Since there is so much to do and so little precious time, we must know what is important and what is not. Many of us are aware of the Pareto principle which states that 20% of what we do accounts for 80% of the results we get. A variation of this principle is that 80% of our activities are trivial while only the remaining 20% are critical. What really matters is the critical 20%. So, we should spend 80% of our effort chasing the critical few and ignoring the trivial many. We must train ourselves to do the critical things first.

We must take good care of ourselves. We must exercise our bodies, emotions and minds properly. We must keep on learning since the more we know, the more interesting we become. We must also take time to help others. Service is critical to happiness. Without unselfish service, there can be no happiness.

We create quality when we live the life we choose with enthusiasm and joy for we come alive through our excitement. This generates a spark and causes our lives to become charged. As with any spark, we must maintain a "gap" through which "electricity," or excitement can jump.

We maintain a gap as long as we have a lack, a want, an unfulfilled dream and a hunger for something that is a challenge to attain. We must have an inextinguishable fire within us that nothing completely satisfies or puts out. For when all desires are satisfied, we stop functioning and die. Separating birth from death is a major gap. Within this primary gap there are several secondary ones the number of which we determine. Living is filling these gaps with the memories of exciting experiences, or the ashes of a sad and boring life.

We maintain gaps in our lives for as long as we never fully grow up. When we are children, we create gaps easily. This is because there is a tremendous potential difference between what we are as "children" and what we can become as adults. As children, we are mere seeds. The gap between the seed and fully grown plant is enormous. As we "grow up" and lose some of the qualities of childhood, the gaps begin to fill up and disappear. When all the gaps occlude, the spark extinguishes and we have nothing left to live for. We die.

As long as we remain children at heart, we will always have gaps for the spark of life. Children have a lot going for them. They are active, inquisitive and flexible. They have a tremendous potential for growth; physically, emotionally and mentally. Because of these qualities, children are imbued with much life. However, not all the qualities of childhood are desirable. Even though children are curious, spontaneous and playful they are also dependent, insecure and have a limited grasp of the world. It is the first set of qualities that we need to maintain. The second set, comprised of lacks, is negative. We can fill these lacks and acquire independence, security and a comprehensive grasp of the world. At the same time, we need to maintain our curiosity, spontaneity and playfulness.

We cannot live quality lives unless we have quality relationships. This involves our family, community and the world. We can start making a difference right now by focusing on service. By providing what others need instead of dwelling on what we want, by claiming ownership of our emotions, thoughts and actions, and by acting instead of reacting we can improve the quality of life for everyone. Additionally, we can train ourselves to look at things as if we have never seen them before, for we have not. We can touch things as if we will never experience them again, for we will not. Value is not in the events and activities, but rather in what we *bring* to the events and activities. We can choose to bring love, passion, joy, humor and a deep sense of appreciation. For these are some of the quality acts we can use to spark and enliven ourselves and others.

The world begins with us. To improve the world, we must improve ourselves. We can stop our personal wars, reduce our ignorance, intolerance, hatred and injustice. We can add to the quality of our world by improving the qualities of our lives. We must exhibit and live the qualities that we seek in others and in the world.

### 6. Life as Diversity

*Variety's the very spice of life, that gives it all its flavor.*
William Cowper

To know life as diversity is to know ourselves with incomparable possibilities and states that we can assume and experience. One of the best ways to live is to mirror the diversity of life by living a diverse life ourselves. We must strive for diversity in our interests, activities, the foods we eat, the clothes we wear, what we enjoy and the people we associate with. Since each individual or event is unique, there is no end to the varieties we can experience. By appreciating and enjoying these varieties, we never get bored. We remain enthused and live creative, happy and exciting lives.

How would our lives be if we ate the same food day after day? How would we feel if all we had was one type of car, only one sport and the same unchanging weather? The antidote for boredom is diversity. Because the benefits of diverse individuals working together as a harmonious unity far exceed the abilities of similar individuals, everyone in the diverse group reaps greater benefits.

The success of life is mainly due to its abundance and diversity. We should live reflecting the abundance and diversity of life. We can achieve grater diversity by having diverse friends, reading books on different subjects, learning about the various arts and sciences, traveling to diverse locations, developing many interests and hobbies and by appreciating change and variety.

One evening I picked a cucumber from my garden, sat on my porch, and slowly began to eat it. It tasted sweeter and felt more alive than the cucumbers I buy at the store. The skin was softer and I could actually eat it without peeling it first because it was not covered with wax. This cucumber is mostly from the earth that is in my garden, I thought to myself. I can definitely eat and enjoy this cucumber. I cannot eat the earth that is in the garden. This cucumber is not only soil, but soil mixed with elements from air, water and sunlight. I cannot eat these by themselves and say I have eaten a cucumber. These elements must combine in a specific way to form the cucumber before I can eat and enjoy it.

When diverse elements contribute their separate qualities to form a new coalition, the new entity manifests qualities not found in any of the contributing elements alone. When a cucumber seed is planted in the soil, it draws to itself diverse elements and combines them into a unique entity, a plant that produces cucumbers. All "seeds" have the ability to bring together diverse elements and form new alliances. We are seeds in the garden of life. If we reflect the capacity of seeds in our lives, then we can attract diverse elements together and through them give rise to new capabilities as well.

## 7. Life as a Journey of Self-Discovery

*No two human beings have made, or ever will make, exactly the same journey in life.*

Sir Arthur Keith

Life is a journey and we are sojourners on the fairways of life. However, we should not live as if life is a journey to go through and arrive at our destination as quickly as possible. Instead, we should live life as a journey through which we discover ourselves, learn and contribute. As the journey progresses, we are exposed to a variety of situations from which we can learn and through which we can contribute. Journeys can be fun, or they can be a drain. Any journey we take in life, and the journey of life, have a lot in common.

Is it possible that our birth into this world is the start of a journey, and this start is like the start of any journey we undertake while here on Earth? When we are born, we are thrust forth like a guided missile seeking the fulfillment of our potential. We search throughout life trying to find out what it is that we can grow into. We have an inner urge to do, to accomplish great things, to make a difference and to leave a name behind that we can be proud of.

Some journeys are short, direct and exciting. The destination is quickly arrived at. Other journeys are long and tiresome. Some are eventful, others are not. Some journeys are through side roads and strange terrain, and we, at times, get lost and feel very frustrated. So are the journeys of our lives.

Some go through life quickly, doing what they came to do and then just as quickly, they leave. Others tarry along taking side roads and the scenic route. Some get lost along the way and end up with the feeling that they do not belong, that they do not know where they are going or even why they are on the road. Still others travel in luxury, act as if they own the road and seem very sure of where they are going and when they will get there.

One January my wife had to travel to Atlanta, Georgia, on a business trip. I was left behind with our two very young children. At first, I was overwhelmed. There was a lot to do. I had to feed and clean them, wash their clothes, stay awake with them through most of the night, get up early and prepare their food, take one to preschool and the other to the baby sitter. Initially, it took a lot of time to do very little. In a few days, I adjusted and a routine set in. My efficiency slowly increased and I could do the work in much less time and with much less effort and frustration.

Is this how we feel when we first start the journey of life? As inexperienced babies we are clumsy, inefficient and easily frustrated with inability. Soon we learn how to walk, talk, think and accomplish a great deal with comparatively little effort. We gain knowledge, develop abilities and establish relationships but these mostly remain separate and ineffective. We seldom add all of our resources together and use them like an orchestra to produce the symphony we desire in life. If we learn to utilize all of our resources, create a harmonious unity of purpose out of our diverse capabilities, interests, and relationships, we can give birth to excellence.

Before we start a road journey, we might look at a map or mentally decide on the routes we can take. We visualize the destination, getting and being there. This mental journey does not take any time that we are aware of. We simply see in our minds where we want to end up. This prepares us for undertaking the physical journey.

The physical journey, however, does not start as soon as

the mental journey is visualized. The actualization of the mental journey must await the proper time and other conditions must be met before it can begin. We usually wait for what we consider the appropriate conditions before we start a journey. There are always more details to the journey than are apparent initially.

Accidents can happen while on a journey. Our journey through life can be fraught with accidents as well. While on a journey, we may encounter distractions. We stop for rest, food and fuel. As we travel, we become aware of all the other travelers along the way. Our private journey is, all of a sudden, in a public world. It takes time and effort. We must avoid other cars and remain alert. Unlike the mental journey, the physical journey is in time and through space. It takes many hours, perhaps even days to get to our destination. There is the weather to contend with. We might have to spend some nights in hotels. We must be equipped to handle all of our needs and requirements.

Being on a journey makes us responsible for ourselves, our resources and getting where we want to go. We must be aware of our fellow travelers. They too, have a right to the road. Since we are all on the highway of life together, instead of collecting speeding tickets along the way, let us endeavor to collect good will and appreciation for each other. Let us learn to cooperate and make each other's journey a more pleasant one.

Since there is no final destination to reach in life, we do not need to rush to get to our destination. For when we reach the end of one journey we rest for a while and then start another. Why not, then, take the time to enjoy each trip? Even if life provides us diversions along our route, we can still relax and use them to recharge ourselves. After all, we have a very long journey ahead, and time is not a factor. If all we concern ourselves with is reaching our destination as quickly as possible, we will miss out on all the wonderful things along the way. We will also experience stress. Living a stressful life can and often does lead to sickness and premature aging and death. One way to alleviate this is to live life as if we are on vacation. We can afford to take the time and shop for the little things we enjoy. These will be our memorabilia and a reminder of the journey.

As we continue our journey of life, we are constantly bombarded with the changes that are taking place around us and in us. We are reminded that the pace of change is accelerating and that our inability to cope with change leads to stress. If we live life as if we are on vacation and in an exciting place, we can ignore most of the changes. We can even anticipate change as the source of new experiences. If we expect change, we will not be stressed by it when it arrives. It will be an adventure. Adventures are fun and exhilarating. They are the antidote for stress and fear of change.

It behooves us to travel light. We will have less to worry about and take care of. The lighter we travel, the freer we feel. We can simplify our lives by getting rid of garbage. By getting rid of junk, we make room for quality. We tend to carry physical, emotional and mental "garbage." Carrying heavy loads requires us to expend a large amount of energy that we can use for constructive purposes. Let us be aware of the habits, attitudes and beliefs we have and carry within us. Unless they serve us by enhancing our lives, they should be discarded, or replaced. To fly high, we must carry only the few essentials and throw away the heavy loads that drag us down and hamper our ascension.

We pack our luggage based on where we are going and how long we intend on staying. If we are on a journey of awakening, what do we need to carry with us on such a trip? We need only seven items:

1. A keen vision to distinguish between what is essential and what is trivial. We must concentrate on the essential few and ignore the trivial many;

2. A strong desire to grow and keep on growing;
3. Curiosity, interest and the flexibility to respond to the challenges of life;
4. Creativity to combine the right elements to produce ever-improving products and services;
5. The infectious disease of quality to infect whomever we encounter and whatever we undertake;
6. Sense of humor and appreciation of diversity in self, nature and everyone else;
7. The ability to make life a never-ending vacation where pleasure and satisfaction are derived from the process of living rather than the promises of the destination.

We are currently somewhere en route along our life-long journey. Let us take a rest, stop and evaluate our progress. Are we where we want to be? Are we on the right highway heading in the right direction? How well are we collaborating with the other travelers on the highway of life? Where are we going and what do we expect to find once we get there? How well are we enjoying our traveling (living)?

Living is the journey to unfoldment. We are not alone on this journey. The entire universe is on a similar journey. The Milky Way Galaxy is on the move, and so is our sun and all the planets. Where they are all heading, no one knows. It must be toward a much more powerful source of light; a much larger Sun, perhaps a white hole (SUN) that draws all to itself. The light of this larger Sun will wake us up and infuse our being with radiant **light** (awareness and knowledge), magical **life** (vigor, enthusiasm and growth) and magnetic **love** (deep appreciation and profound relationships).

STAGE 5

# *Understand Why We Age and Die*

*Nothing is so firmly believed as what we least know.*
                                        Michel De Montaigne

Charles Darwin in *The Origin of Species* (1859) presented the theory of the origin and evolution of the species. Darwin viewed life as a constant competitive struggle in which some members of the species possessed certain advantageous traits. These traits were passed down through generations by a process termed "natural selection," strengthening the species and enabling survival of the fittest. Natural selection is the tendency for only the best adapted organisms to survive and reproduce.

Present-day evolutionary theory is derived from Darwin's work and maintains that in any population of a gene pool, there are random mutations in genetic forms and characteristics. When mutated characteristics provide survival advantages, mutants persist to pass on these new traits. In this way a species effects gradual changes to adapt and survive in a competitive, and often changing, environment.

Aging and death are an aspect of evolution and a part of our make-up selected by nature for the vital role they play in the survival of the species. Even though evolution appears to have begun as a blind process, blind in so far as the individual is concerned, the purpose of evolution is anything but blind.

We are the descendants of a very long and successful line of evolution. All the qualities that we have, have been naturally selected for a good reason—they provide survival advantages. Since aging and death are fundamental characteristics of our species, they must, by the mere fact that they have been selected through evolution, play a critical role and provide survival benefits. The question then is not whether aging and death have any merit, for they must. Rather the question is, why did they get selected in the first place? What benefits do aging and death provide?

Aging prepares individuals to leave the stage of life, while death ensures it. This allows the species to progress and evolve. Thus, the benefits of aging and death are more for the species than the individual. Evolution is for the advancement of the species. Individuals are merely the means of the advancement. To allow the species to advance, individuals, especially the weaker ones, are sacrificed. Hence, if we as individuals are to avoid being a sacrificial lamb, we must wake up and actively direct the course of our evolution through awareness and proper action.

We age and die because we are individuals. We belong to a tribe and we must pay our tribal dues. We do this by reproducing, aging and dying. Like the cells of the body that must die and make way for new cells so the body may continue to live, so it is with us. We must die so the species lives. As the cells age and die, they pass their skills and knowledge to the next generation and the body evolves.

Once an individual reaches sexual maturity, aging begins in earnest. Even though we can interfere and alter the course of events if we are aware and act appropriately, we do not for we lack the knowledge of what to do. We allow our genes and inertia to take hold and direct our lives. The balance tips, aging spreads its fangs and soon death devours us.

It is imperative that we age and eventually die, for we are given a limited time here on earth to experience, learn and make a contribution. However, we do not have to age a day sooner than we have to and we do not have to die one day earlier than we need to and no one knows the limits of our lives. Not everyone ages at the same rate, or dies at the same age. Through awareness and action we can influence not only the rate at which we age, but how and when we die. Even though the specific instructions for aging are in our genes; the timing, rate and manner in which these are expressed is due to our environment which, to a large extent, we can control.

Life is characterized by balance. We see this in nature and the human body. Balance in nature is not the same as total equality. Rather, it is a process of maintaining equilibrium while undergoing change and evolution. Tipping the balance a little to one side is a desired activity. It creates movement and progress. Tipping the balance too far in one direction leads to catastrophe. We see this in the relationship between predator and prey, parasite and host, government and industry, freedom and security, poverty and wealth.

Aging is the process of progressively tilting the balance in favor of death. Death occurs when the balance tips completely and unalterably. Aging and death are a trademark of our living pointing us to the purpose of our individual lives—contributing links in the long and complex chain of life. We are a cell in the flowing body of life. Being a cell in the body of life is significant for without the cells there can be no body. We connect the past to the future, participate in the knowledge transfer and contribute to the health and vitality of the body.

## Why We Age

*If wrinkles must be written upon our brows, let them not be written upon the heart. The spirit should never grow old.*
James A. Garfield

Instinct, habit and inertia will rule nature unless interfered with. An apple will fall to the ground once ripe. A seed planted and provided for, will grow, mature and then die. Once conceived, we will grow and age. What is born must inevitably die. Left alone, all organized and orderly systems will move towards more entropy or disorder. This is inertia, the path of least resistance, and is one of the main reasons we age. All natural events will take place as they normally do unless the process is interfered with. Interference changes predictable outcomes and renders them unpredictable.

We start life with nature at the helm. Fertilization, pre-birth development and the few years after birth are governed by nature. The various systems of the body form and function without our conscious effort. Soon we begin to develop our consciousness of self and the environment. We progress from unconscious to conscious living.

The more conscious we are of our lives, the less we follow the script that is in our genes—inertia. We are not, however, accustomed to think that we have a role to play in our aging and eventual death. We are not in the habit of being responsible for our experiences. We mostly live as victims of circumstances. Hence, to guard against entropy, we must willfully and conscientiously convert disorder into order, the dull into the exciting, struggle into challenge, work into play and obstacles into opportunities. We do this through enthusiastic engagement. One of the easiest ways to remain enthusiastic is to live life as if it is a hobby. According to H. W. Arnold, *"The worst bankrupt in the world is the man who has lost his enthusiasm."* Enthusiasm is the force that counteracts the impact of entropy.

Aging is due to entropy. It starts in our minds with our thoughts. It then progresses to our emotions and finally manifests in the body. Our essence does not age nor do our atoms. What ages is the way we see and feel about ourselves. Staying youthful requires energy, constant attention and vigilant awareness. Aging, on the other hand, does not require energy for it is movement toward more entropy. If our lives are like a garden and we are the gardeners, it takes effort to feed the desirable and weed the undesirable factors and maintain a lush garden. If we stop tending the plants that we want, weeds grow in the garden and sap them of their energy. Weeds transform an orderly organization into a haphazard and disorderly system. To stay youthful requires an eternal vigilance against all sorts of "weeds" that find their way into our garden, invading our bodies, clogging our arteries and veins, fatiguing and aging our organs and systems.

William Evans and Brian Rosenberg in their book *Biomarkers* outlined the changes the body goes through as it ages. The following areas are negatively impacted with age: lean body mass, strength, basal metabolic rate, body fat, aerobic capacity, blood pressure, blood-sugar tolerance, cholesterol/HDL ratio, bone density and body temperature regulation. Biomarkers, however, are the symptoms of aging, not the causes. They are the memories of what we metabolized etched in our tissues, organs and psyche. These markings are as permanent as we allow them to be. We can erase past negative marks by writing new positive ones to replace them.

We exist in an environment. This environment engulfs us like a fish in the ocean or a bird in the atmosphere. Being engulfed in our environment, we are exposed to the elements and are bombarded with impressions. Even though we have some freedom in choosing our environment and with it the type of impressions we are exposed to, we are subjected to undesirable impressions never-the-less. More important than the impressions that we receive is our response to them. We can choose our response regardless of the nature of the stimulus. Our choice lies in whether we ignore, react, or act. If each time we receive a stimulus we immediately react, we are not in charge of our lives. We live and age based on the conditions we face. On the other hand, pausing to evaluate the stimulus and then responding in a manner consistent with our best interests, puts us in charge. By acting with awareness, we achieve the results we seek.

There is a direct relationship between aging and retiring from living. We age to the extent that we retire from living. Retiring from life is becoming passive about the qualities of life and is the surest way to accelerate aging and prepare for death. As mentioned earlier, there are four general and three specific factors that characterize our lives: metabolism, growth, response to stimuli and reproduction are the general factors while quality, diversity and the journey of self-discovery are the specific factors. When these are positive and we are actively pursuing them, they are life-enhancing. When these same qualities become negative and disruptive, they become life-depleting. What used to sustain us turns sour and begins to devour and age us. Without our conscious interference to alter the course of events, we have no chance to restrain aging and avert premature death. Thus, the same factors that make life possible, if allowed to reverse course, will cause aging and lead to premature death. Since natural processes are cyclical, they will reverse course at mid-cycle.

**Metabolism** is building up through anabolism and breaking down through catabolism. Even though some catabolism is natural, excessive catabolism is not. This is usually due to ***improper metabolism, disease, neglect and abuse.*** Therefore, these are the negative conditions of metabolism.

**Growth** is selective assimilation into self. It is slow, orderly, coordinated, holistic and proportionate. As children, we grow because we have a lot to learn and assimilate. As we mature, we slow down, or even stop assimilating into self. Continued growth demands that we remain challenged. On the other hand, unchecked growth is cancerous. It is rapid, uncontrolled, selfish and destructive. When a group of cells grow without regard to the welfare of the entire organization, cancer ensues. Cancer is the selfish expansion of the interest of individuals at the expense of the larger community. Cancer is disregard for the welfare of the community. Therefore, *lack of controlled growth, cancer and the absence of a sense of community* are the negative conditions of growth.

**Response to stimuli** is sensitivity to the environment. It is a measure of our flexibility and aliveness. When we find our environment stimulating and we respond easily in a positive way, we remain youthful. We age when the stimuli decrease in their effectiveness—we either cease to respond to them appropriately, or we require increasingly intense stimuli before we respond. This is usually due to boredom, stiffness and sclerosis. Therefore, *boredom and rigidity* are the negative conditions of response to stimuli.

**Reproduction** is creation. It is union with another to bring forth new life. When the fabric of this synergy weakens through withdrawal from engagement, aging manifests. Even though we do not reproduce throughout our lives, we must not cease to produce and create. Therefore, *withdrawal from engagement and lack of creativity* are the negative conditions of reproduction.

**Quality** personalizes life. It separates our life from life in general. Even though we live in a community, we remain individuals. The type and quality of life we choose for ourselves sets us apart and declares our values to the world. Even though we must produce, it is up to us to decide what to produce and their quality. The quality of our lives depends on the type of "fruits" we produce daily. These are the lettering that when strung together will spell the name by which we are known and which we will leave behind.

Quality is what sets us apart. Ultimately, the quality we reflect is a direct result of our inner motive to live. Therefore, **indifference, or** *lack of a positive personal motive to live* is the negative condition of quality.

**Diversity** is variety. Positive diversity is when collectivity functions as individuality. It is symbiotic and synergistic. Positive diversity is the acknowledgment that the power of the group is far more than the added powers of the individuals in that group. Yet all individualities remain intact. Negative diversity is when individuality is sacrificed at the altar of collectivity. It is when the group shapes and molds every individual. Therefore, *tyranny of the group and lack of individuality* are the negative conditions of diversity.

For the **journey of self-discovery** to continue, there cannot be a final destination. The process must be as important as the destination. The journey must continue and the process must remain challenging. The luggage we carry along is vital, but as we add other pieces to our luggage; over time, our luggage turns into baggage. Eventually, as we carry this baggage along, the burden of the weight becomes too heavy. We get tired of carrying the load. We give up our sense of joy in the journey and replace it with an expectant attitude to arrive and rest. We age from carrying the heavy load. We long for respite. Therefore, *lack of joy in the process of living and the increasing burden of the baggage we carry along* are the negative conditions of the journey of self-discovery.

Thus, the seven causes of aging are:

1. improper metabolism, disease, neglect and abuse;
2. lack of growth, cancer, or absence of a community sense;
3. boredom and rigidity;
4. withdrawal from engagement and lack of creativity;
5. indifference, or lack of a positive personal motive to live;
6. tyranny of the group and lack of individuality; and
7. lack of joyful living and the increase of burdens.

## 1. Improper Metabolism, Disease, Neglect and Abuse

*Our body is a well-set clock, which keeps good time, but if it be too much or indiscreetly tampered with, the alarm runs out before the hour.*

*Joseph Hall*

We are what we have metabolized. Individual variations are largely due to what each metabolizes daily. If we are not happy with what we are, we need to change our metabolism. Improper metabolism is due to taking in items of poor quality, inadequate quantity, or incorrect mixture. Improper metabolism results in denying the body what it needs. What the body needs is more than food. It requires nourishment, proper life style and appropriate mental, emotional and spiritual states. We do not only metabolize food, water and air; we also process impressions of events, time, space and the associated thoughts and feelings. If what we internalize is positive, we anabolize and rejuvenate the body. Otherwise, we catabolize and age the body. Just as we can control the qualities of food, water and air that we ingest, we can control the character of the impressions, feelings and thoughts that we process. Positive thoughts and emotions are creative and expansive. They are vitamins that take the form of love, peace, joy, sympathy, hope, trust and harmony. Negative thoughts and emotions are destructive and constrictive. They take the form of fear, guilt, worry, anger, jealousy, envy, blame, frustration and hate. What we metabolize can lead to stimulation and youthfulness, or to stress and aging.

We can influence our metabolism through awareness. The more aware we are of what we process, the more in charge we are of whether we build or break down. We can slow down our rate of metabolism or we can speed it up. We can even spice up our metabolism by adding laughter, music and good company to change the nature of what we metabolize. The better we metabolize, the less we require to metabolize, the less the debris that we must get rid of, the healthier we get and the slower we age.

Metabolism is both ingestion and elimination. We cannot only be concerned with ingestion, we must equally be interested in elimination. If we keep on consuming without proper elimination, we poison ourselves. This applies not only to the food that we eat, but to the elements that we process as well. We must rid ourselves of the emotions, thoughts and beliefs that we no longer need for a healthy and harmonious life. We must eliminate these along with the excrement that we find no use for. Harboring harmful emotions, thoughts and beliefs will poison us as effectively as old and putrefied excrement that we do not get rid of. Effective metabolism is extracting what we need to maintain and rejuvenate our bodies and then quickly eliminating the refuse.

Caring for the body is our responsibility. Our bodies require proper nutrients, sleep, rest, play, stimulation, cleanliness, use and challenge. We crave nurturing, laughter, pleasure, value and meaning. When the body has all it needs, it is vibrant and healthy. Otherwise, it is in a state of disease.

Disease is an imbalance in the internal environment of a living system. It can result from lack, excess, drastic change, ineffective metabolism and the introduction of disease agents. Its onset can be quick or slow, mild or severe. What causes the imbalance is not only what we ingest or leave out, but what we keep for too long that we no longer need as well.

We need to use our bodies, not abuse them. Abuse takes the form of repeated excessiveness. This can be physical, emotional and mental. Abuse results in disproportionate wear and tear, accumulation of toxins and premature aging. We must learn to use our bodies properly, or prepare to lose them prematurely.

Since the body functions best when it is fine tuned and all of its parts are working harmoniously together, we must exercise the body to stimulate, not to exhaust. While stimulation leads to health, vigor and youthfulness, exhaustion causes us to deteriorate.

## 2. Lack of Growth, Cancer, or Absence of Community Sense

### Lack of Growth

*Anyone who stops learning is old, whether at 20 or 80. Anyone who keeps learning stays young. The greatest thing in life is to keep your mind young.*

*Henry Ford*

There are many factors that contribute to lack of growth: improper nutrition, hormonal imbalance, genes and lack of the desire to grow. Growth, like metabolism, is not merely physical. It is emotional, mental and spiritual as well. Even though our physical growth is limited and controlled by our genetics and environment, our growth in awareness, skills, knowledge, understanding, relationships and the building of our character and personality are unlimited and are up to us.

Growth must be balanced, controlled and proportionate or else it can cause disease and lead to cancer. We must maintain both internal and external balance as we grow. Internally, we must maintain a balance between the various hormones, enzymes and elements. We can not have too much acidity at the expense of alkalinity, excessive sodium at the expense of potassium, disproportionate amount of calcium at the expense of magnesium, or steep levels of copper at the expense of iron. We must maintain our bodies in equilibrium. We can do this by remaining attuned to our bodies and the cycles of nature.

We must continue to grow in our relationships with our family, friends and community. We must grow in our ability to laugh and cry, work and play, belong and maintain our individuality. We grow to the extent that we get involved, give of ourselves, experience and learn. Just as the more we use our muscles the less they atrophy, so it is with our brains, abilities and skills. The more we use them, the sharper they get.

To grow, we must extend. To extend, we must risk and experience. Many stop growing because of fear, anxiety and a false sense of security. Many fear making mistakes. Instead, we should expect to make mistakes if we want to grow for without mistakes, we cannot adequately evaluate our progress, improve and gain mastery. What is important is that when we make a mistake, we learn from it, adjust and go on with life. As we learn, we realize our options and the steps we can take to reduce future risks. We are at the mercy of fate to the extent that we are ignorant of our choices and are powerless to act.

One of the greatest lessons we can learn is that we are responsible for our experiences. Experiences are the infrastructure upon which we build our next level of growth. They are the emotional, mental and spiritual food we need to grow.

## Cancer, or Absence of Community Sense

*Man is a special being, and if left to himself, in an isolated condition, would be one of the weakest creatures; but associated with his kind, he works wonders.*

Daniel Webster

Cancer is related to lack of a sense of community. Cancerous cells are like individuals who disregard the welfare of the community. They do not feel they are a part of the community in which they exist. Hence, they feel free to exploit it. Cancerous cells or individuals, if aggressive enough, live short and miserable lives. Their speedy growth at the expense of the community does not last, or go very far. Ultimately, they destroy themselves and the community.

Living an opportunistic life, without a sense of belonging to family, friends or a community, renders an individual weak and prone to disease. For without a sense of belonging, an individual has no deep connections, can be easily uprooted and is at the mercy of the elements. Life is arduous to be faced alone. Like birds that flock together, connecting with others and the community confers the strength of the group to the individual. Individuals in a community who care, share and love derive strength, meaning and long life from their association. Developing a sense of community strengthens our desire to live by giving us a motive. It fortifies our immune system, provides us the medium through which we can serve and receive abundant returns.

## 3. Boredom and Rigidity

### Boredom

> *Boredom is the dream bird that hatches the egg of experience. A rustling in the leaves drives him away.*
> 
> Walter Benjamin

A couple in love will find each other interesting and exciting. Often, this same couple after years of association, undergoes a reversal in their relationship. What was once exciting becomes boring, what was life-enhancing is now life-depleting. Why? What causes the change? Familiarity.

Familiarity can breed contempt if it induces us to withdraw from engagement. However, this same familiarity, if used properly, can lead to understanding, love and communion. We store our experiences as memories. Memories can be a burden or a stimulant. If we learn to use our memories as allies, we maintain our youthfulness, otherwise, we grow old and atrophy.

To prevent premature aging, we must prevent boredom by cultivating our ability to eagerly anticipate, experience excitement and maintain our enthusiasm. To do this, we must remain young at heart. We must think, act and live as the young do; maintaining such qualities as playfulness, curiosity, spontaneity and open-mindedness. The main culprit for losing these youthful qualities in adults is often *memory*. The first few times we perform an act, it is easy to find it exciting. As we repeat an act, we realize that we already have a memory of this act. With the accumulation of familiar memories, excitement wanes. Furthermore, the more we perform an act, the more habitual that act becomes. The more habitual an act, the less intention we put into that act. Unintentional acts do not carry much energy content and value. To reverse this trend, we must become aware of our acts and infuse them with excitement, enthusiasm and importance. As we become interested in our acts, we overcome boredom.

We hold the key to the lock that is memory. We can use memory to give continuity and meaning to our activities, or we can use it to lose interest in our endeavors. We can either grow by adding new and exciting memories, or we can shrink, wither and age as we block out exciting experiences and focus on the old memories instead. Memories can fill life with the ashes of boredom and slowly squelch the spark that is life, or they can create sparks through anticipation, excitement and joyful remembrances.

We age when our lives become saturated with lifeless memories. These act like deposits that obstruct the flow of life—biosclerosis. If these obstructions persist and increase, they constrict the gaps through which the spark of life flows. Life slows to a trickle and soon stops flowing altogether. Rapid aging ensues. The antidote to this is excitement, anticipation and joyous engagements. Even though we cannot manipulate our minds to find everything exciting all the time, we can find at least one thing at a time that is enticing. Excitement keeps our life lines clean and open. Life flows in the channels created by our interests. The more interests we have, the more life we exhibit and the more healthy, vibrant and youthful we are.

It would be wonderful if there were a gene for newness and by keeping it "turned on" we could experience any act as new. Since there is no such gene, or until we discover one, we must do it manually. By *"pretending"* that something is exciting, we can fool our bodies into excitement and overcome boredom.

## Rigidity

*The weather-cock on the church spire, though made of iron, would soon be broken by the storm-wind if it . . . did not understand the noble art of turning to every wind.*

Heinrich Heine

As we grow up, we tend to exchange our youthful flexibility with adulthood rigidity. We trade our sense of adventure, discovery and inquisitiveness with the responsibilities of adult life. Most often this happens when we get married, have children and acquire many responsibilities. Feeling responsible, we become serious. Being serious, we turn rigid. As we exchange our sense of play with work, we acquire tension and a host of other life-depleting burdens. As our obligations increase, our control over our time, money and life diminishes. We have no time for fun. At times we rebel, but our rebellion is not a mutiny to get rid of our burdens and live a simpler and less burdensome life. Instead, we become more rigid in our ways. Rigidity can be physical, behavioral, mental, or emotional. Ashley Montague used the term *psychosclerosis* to describe mental rigidity, while Wilhelm Reich wrote about character armoring where our psychic stiffness manifests in various body parts as physical rigidity and ailment.

Physical rigidity is stiffness—a quality of death. As we

grow up and exchange our flexibility with rigidity, we give up life for death. At the last exchange, we give up all flexibility and *rigor mortis,* complete rigidity, sets in. Even though we require some rigidity for strength and stamina, it is even more important to be flexible. Since rigidity sets in naturally over time, remaining flexible requires effort and awareness.

Emotional rigidity is the inability to freely experience emotions. It is to lack the capacity to cry and laugh heartily. Since experiencing life is equivalent to experiencing emotions, if we are emotionally rigid, we are unable to experience thrills, deep joys and be moved by the happiness and misery of others. The more emotionally rigid we are, the less responsive to life we are.

Behavioral rigidity manifests as inability to cope and adjust to uncertainty, newness, and change. Since our behavior must match our circumstances, being rigid we cannot adequately respond to our changing circumstances.

Growing up does not have to mean giving up our childhood. We can maintain the desired qualities of childhood and add to them the preferred capabilities of adulthood. It is not an either/or case. We can have both. The desired qualities of childhood are: inquisitiveness, curiosity, playfulness, purity of heart, simplicity and spontaneity. The preferred qualities of adulthood are: accountability, reasoning, wisdom, understanding, adventure, calculated risk, deep and abiding relationships and lasting love.

In certain ways, we must be like Peter Pan—never grow up. To do this, we must learn to take charge of our thoughts, actions and memories. We must forget our ages, change our expectations about growing old and completely disregard what is expected of us as to how we should behave based on our age. We can maintain our positive childhood qualities at any age. Since we are born with these qualities, there is no reason to ever give them up for they are vital to our health, happiness, and survival.

Expectations play a major role in the way we act and the qualities we exhibit. When we are young, we do not give much thought to acting like a child. We are not as self-conscious. We do not usually fear ridicule. We simply play, have fun, laugh and abandon ourselves into the intricacies of the simplest of things. It is easy to get interested, excited and passionate. As we grow older, our expectations of ourselves and other's expectations of us change. We give up playfulness to be responsible, spontaneity to live by the clock, inquisitiveness to passively watch television. When we give up these qualities of childhood, we give up much more than we realize. We give up our ability to remain young. We grow old and age. If we want to give up any of our childhood qualities, let it be these: irresponsibility, ignorance, weakness and dependency.

We can use the cycles of life to our advantage and remain young. Even though we grow up and mature, we have other chances to remain young. We can immerse ourselves in the world of the young as presented to us through children—our own or other people's children. We can spend time playing with them and seeing the world as they do. We can volunteer to lead children's groups. We can become Boy or Girl Scout Leaders, Coaches and Assistants to youth organizations. As our children grow up, we are presented with another opportunity in the form of grandchildren. By immersing ourselves in their world, we get yet another chance to see the world as new, exciting and adventurous.

## 4. Withdrawal from Engagement, and Lack of Creativity

### Withdrawal from Engagement

> *To say yes, you have to sweat and roll up your sleeves and plunge both hands into life up to the elbows. It's easy to say no, even if it means dying.*
>
> Jean Anouilh

People use many excuses to withdraw from life. Some withdraw from engagement because of previous disappointments and "failures." Others are beset with fears. Some are not sure of themselves; they compare, judge and hold back. Whatever the reason, withdrawal from life is a retreat from the source of our sustenance. Withdrawing from life is like a plant that withdraws from the soil and sunshine. It is giving up life. To live, we must engage, plow forth and remain involved. Obviously, we will face some obstacles and setbacks. These are the challenges of life and the price tag for receiving all the benefits that come from living. Disappointments and failures are mere events. We can turn them into obstacles or opportunities.

There is a universe outside and inside of us waiting to be discovered. Our world does not lack challenges and opportunities. Life is full of "problems" that are begging to be solved. Society has many perceived shortages. What we often lack is not material goods and resources; rather courage, ambition, curiosity and the desire to get involved, do something worthwhile and make a difference. It is not only beauty that is in the eyes of the beholder, so is excitement, challenge and opportunity. We create our world by the decisions we make. We can live like the gods of our own universe ever creating and transforming, or we can confine ourselves and exist as the prisoners of our self-imposed limitations.

## Lack of Creativity

*Make visible what, without you, might perhaps never have been seen.*

*Robert Bresson*

Creativity is an aspect of growth. It is an extension into new and uncharted territory. Creativity introduces change, excitement and energy into our lives. If biological success is determined by an organism's ability to reproduce, creativity is the means to give birth to new ideas, products and services. While reproduction plays a critical role in the survival of the species, creativity plays an essential role in the survival of the individual.

Our productivity is an outflow of our creativity and our products are the rent we pay for being alive. What we create (produce) takes many forms based on our assets, passions and the environment we find ourselves in. As depicted in the movie *Mr. Holland's Opus,* our entire life is a series of productions. What we produce are tangibles and intangibles and both are equally important. Many aim to produce one grand magnum opus. It is better to view life as an orchestra; with each moment we have the opportunity to add another note. Even though to live is to produce, this must not be construed as an obligation. It is our nature to produce just as it is the nature of the sun to shine. We can produce words that aid, comfort and encourage. We can help bring about a smile on someone's face. We can create art and technology. We can live an exemplary life. This, too, is a production for through our lives we influence the activities of others—what they produce.

## 5. Indifference, or Lack of a Positive Personal Motive to Live

> *In these years we are witnessing the gigantic spectacle of innumerable human lives wandering about lost in their own labyrinths, through not having anything to which to give themselves.*
>
> José Ortega y Gasset

Desire is synonymous with life. Without desire we have no incentive to act and without motive we have no enticement to live and experience. We stagnate and become prone to disease, aging and premature death. Through desire, we keep our bodies, emotions and minds active and engaged.

Desire is energy. It transforms our lives from a stagnant pond to a running stream.

Our desire to live is our motive to live and this does not have to be of cosmic importance. It can be simple, personal and change with our changing needs. Expressing our nature through work, play and creativity is a good enough motive to live. Having fun and extracting pleasure from our engagements are vital for sustaining life.

We are born to achieve the purpose for which we entered this world. We are not here to live as long as we possibly can. We are here to live long enough to complete whatever we wish to accomplish. To achieve our purpose, we must have and know our motives, for we live and we die based on the motives we harbor in our hearts. The more powerful our motives are, the stronger is our will to live. We live for as long as we find pleasure in what we do. What we do is the meaning we ascribe to our lives and is our motive for being.

## 6. Tyranny of the Group, and Lack of Individuality

*The nail that sticks up will be hammered down.*

*Japanese Proverb*

We derive great benefits from the communities we live in because of the contributions each member makes. However, we do not live for the community. Rather, we live through the community. Community, like life, is a complex chain. It is as healthy, strong and prosperous as its strongest links and it is as diseased, weak and poor as its weakest links. All are intricately connected in a community.

In some communities, the will of the majority is the law. In others, the will of the powerful few is the law. Communism advocates the sacrifice of individuality for the sake of collectivity, while capitalism exalts profit and individuality at the expense of the community. A community should function like a healthy body where participants contribute and receive benefits, give up some individual freedoms to acquire collective security. The human body is collectivity functioning as individuality and individuality harmoniously blended into the larger collectivity of the community.

Totally abandoning individuality for the sake of collectivity creates resentment, anger and frustration. It diminishes the will to create and the motive to excel. It deprives the individual and robs the community. Even though individuality should not be sacrificed for the sake of the community, enlightened individuals willingly give of themselves for the good of all. Balance must be maintained at all times. Extreme individuality is as dangerous as no individuality. One leads to tyranny, selfishness and cancer, while the other snuffs innovation, reduces intellectual diversity and stifles creativity.

Each person in society occupies a niche as a member of this larger "body." Societies offer tremendous benefits, that is why we form them. However, not all the contributions of society are positive. One of the major negative influences of society on the individual is that the standards and expectations of society often become the standards and expectations of the individual. Society becomes to an adult what peer pressure is to a child. We behave as society expects us to behave. We fit the statistics, the norm and the culture of the society we belong to. We learn through imitation, indoctrination and "education." Our community sets the norm and we live accordingly. Since we like to belong and be accepted by the group, we strive to fit by fulfilling expectations. *Eric Hoffer* said: *"When people are free to do as they please, they usually imitate each other."*

We imitate each other in health, wealth and sickness. We influence each other in how we live, how we age and when we die. We grow old or stay young based on what we feel is needed and expected of us by the community. Being surrounded by people who are constantly aging and dying, we believe it to be our fate and we do likewise. Imitation is not only the best form of flattery, it is the trademark of any society. If fifty or sixty year old people in our community are considered old and treated accordingly, when we are fifty or sixty years old, we usually consider ourselves to be old and treat ourselves accordingly as well. We are human. Therefore, we behave the way humans are expected to behave. We are social. So we emphasize belonging and we imitate. If the only examples we ever see of how humans are or can be are the ones surrounding us, how are we to break the norms of society and transcend our humanity? We can break these norms by escaping the tyranny of the group and by emphasizing our individuality. We can break the impact of "community pressure" by being in the community, but not of it. We can take the benefits of a community, but not its handicaps. We do not have to be one of the statistics. General statistics of health, wealth and mortality apply to the general population and to the common people. If we distinguish ourselves, then we are no longer common and the statistics have no relevance to us. If we believe we are common, then the common rules apply to us as well. We live, age and die by the laws we accept and internalize. Our community provides us the free software (freeware) that gets loaded into our minds and runs the hardware that is our body. To live individual lives, we require customized software.

Living a normal life, our experiences will only be normal. Normal people live, age and die like normal people are supposed to. If all we see and experience is a reminder of what the normal is, we seldom experience the possible life. Our environment shapes and molds us. We assume its characteristics. It requires extra effort to be different, stand out and attain escape velocity. It is easier to succumb to "peer pressure" and give in. It is the natural thing to do. Or, so we assume.

Assuming is a two edged sword. It can empower us, or it can disable us. If we assume that we are getting old, we are. If we assume that because our children are growing we must be getting old, we are. If we assume that we no longer are young, for our friends are not, then we are not. If we assume that our interests, activities and behavior reflect the fact that we are old, they do. If we retire and act like we are old, we are. If we believe that we are old by the way we are treated by the young, then we are. If all the assumptions and reasoning, conscious and subconscious, and the "realities" engulfing us lead us to one conclusion: we are old, getting older and there is no escaping our fate, then that is our reality and fate. We assume our expected roles.

Members of a society influence each other whether they are aware of it or not. Lord Alfred Tennyson said: *"I am a part of all that I have met."* We take part in forming and shaping each other. We are, in fact, one gigantic body with each of us being a cell in this body. This body acts as our environment. It shapes and molds us into the being that we end up becoming.

To guard against the tremendous weight of "society pressure," we must learn to detach ourselves, mentally, emotionally and sometimes physically, from society. We can do this through psychological detachment, or by physically breaking away. We can detach via meditation, vacations, mental and physical retreats, deep and creative thinking and communion with our ideals and nature. By practicing detachment, we can disengage ourselves from what is taking place around us. Even though we are in the world, we do not have to be of the world. Thus, even though our peers age and our children grow up, we do not have to get old (weak, sick and disabled). Just as we do not have to give up our childhood to grow up, we do not have to give up our individuality to belong to society. We can have both. We can choose to take what we want and leave the rest behind. We were born individuals and we can live, age and die as individuals.

It is not easy being different for we stand out, are alone and even lonely. It is not easy going beyond our apparent barriers for these have become our boundaries. To break loose, we must free ourselves, open our eyes and see ourselves not as we are, but as we want to be.

Individuality is the special creative window through which God gazes at nature and displays Himself/Herself as diversity. Individuality is the means of introducing variety, change, breakthroughs and leadership into an otherwise common, ordinary and drab world. There can be no creativity, or a God, unless there is individuality. For to create is to make something that is brand new, unique and original. When God created, He saw that it was good. We are each the product of that creation. We are good. Let us express and celebrate our individuality and goodness.

## 7. Lack of Joyful Living and the Increase of Burdens

### Lack of Joy

> *Sorrow is the mere rust of the soul. Activity will cleanse and brighten it.*
>
> *Samuel Johnson*

Pleasure and joy are the most fundamental of human values. We engage in activities to derive pleasure or to avoid pain. There is no sense in living if we cannot derive joy out of life. Pleasure is as much in the activity as it is in our outlook, attitude and expectations. The mind can make a heaven of hell and a hell of heaven. What we often lack is not pleasure, but the ability to use our minds constructively. A child, for example, can derive pleasure from the simplest of activities, while an adult may receive no pleasure from the deepest engagements. To enjoy life, we must carry our sense of joy along like a spice and add it to all that we take part in. The pleasures life has to offer are far too many. All we need to do is to get out of our shells, engage, expect pleasure, provide it whenever we can and enjoy ourselves. To make life interesting and meaningful, we must encounter adversity once in a while. These are our challenges that we can transcend and transform. When faced with pain, we can counter it by engaging in pleasurable activities. When faced with struggle, we can offset it by looking for new opportunities. When faced with misfortune, we can defy it by creating fortune. If our environment is dull, boring and stressful, we can provide the counterparts and make it colorful, exciting and challenging.

The more we enjoy life, the less we concern ourselves with our age, how long we live and whether that is enough. Life is long enough for those who fully live it and too short for those who squander it away.

Play is a major source for pleasure. We do not have to learn how to play. We are born playful. We do not have to labor as we work either if we never forget how to play and be creative. Growing up does not mean giving up play for work, freedom for responsibility and stress. We do not have to abandon our nature. We can play through work and work through play. We can be free and responsible. All we have to change is our attitude. One of the most beautiful passages ever written about work is by Kahlil Gibran:

> You work that you may keep pace with the earth and the soul of the earth. For to be idle is to become a stranger unto the seasons, and to step out of life's procession, that marches in majesty and proud submission towards the infinite.
> When you work you are a flute through whose heart the whispering of the hours turns to music.
> Which of you would be a reed, dumb and silent, when all else sings together in unison?
> Always you have been told that work is a curse and labor a misfortune.
> But I say to you that when you work you fulfill a part of earth's furthest dream, assigned to you when the dream was born, and in keeping yourself with labor you are in

*truth loving life, And to love life through labor is to be intimate with life's inmost secret.*

## Increase of Burdens

*Simplicity is making the journey of this life with just baggage enough.*

Charles Dudley Warner

As we journey through life, we accumulate and carry along increasing loads of baggage. Even though we might have needed each piece at some point as luggage, we never seem to discard them once they serve their purpose. We tend to accumulate and hoard. Soon the luggage becomes baggage and instead of enjoying the expedition, we are instead caring for the baggage. Our baggage is all of our "possessions" and negative feelings such as guilt, resentment and fear. Our baggage is our outdated beliefs. These are a burden to carry along. If the burden is allowed to increase, it soon becomes like the national debt. We spend more time caring for the burden than enjoying the fruit of our labor. These burdens become the focus of our lives.

The best thing we can do for the journey of life is to travel light and not accumulate baggage. If we need a piece of luggage for a particular reason, we can get it. As soon as the purpose is served, we must discard that luggage, or it turns into baggage and becomes a burden. Periodically we need to examine all the pieces we carry along to determine whether or not they are needed. By lightening our burden, we conserve our energy. We use our resources constructively. We live happier, healthier and more abundant lives.

Carrying heavy baggage makes life a struggle, tiring and stressful. Many live life as if it is a struggle to survive. We even consider evolution to be survival of the fittest. This causes anxiety and leads to stress and disease ultimately shortening our lives. We can change this by altering our attitudes toward life. Additionally, we must distinguish between our wants and needs. There is no end to what we can want. What we *need* to live healthy, happy and meaningful lives are few—*something to live on, someone to live with and something to live for.*

## Why We Die

> *To die is poignantly bitter, but the idea of having to die without having lived is unbearable.*
> Erich Fromm

The answer to the question of why we die is intricately intertwined with the question of why we live. To understand the mysteries of life and death, we do not have to look further than our own life and experiences. The events of our lives are great learning tools. Looking at our lives, we quickly realize that, in the final analysis, all of our experiences have been exclusively for us. All, that is, except for the last one—death. We do not die for ourselves, rather for our species—humanity.

We saw earlier how all of our bodily systems are for the benefit of the individual except for one—the reproductive system which is for the benefit of the species. So it is with our experiences. They are all for us except for death. We are born from our species, we live to enhance our individuality, contribute to our species and then we die for the express benefit of our species.

Birth into this world is not unlike my immigration to the United States. I had to leave my old world behind, apply and be accepted prior to my actual move. I had to have sufficient reasons for coming here. Once here, I required some time to adjust. When I came to the United States, it was as if I was born anew. I began a new life, in a new country, with a new language, culture, challenges and opportunities. The United States is a huge country. I had to select where I wanted to live. I decided to make Maryland my home state. It took me a while to adjust to life in Maryland and in the United States. After a while, I settled down, got comfortable and felt at home.

Prior to moving to the United States, I lived in Lebanon as a student at the American University of Beirut. A university is an institution for higher learning. It normally houses several colleges. One must apply, be accepted and enroll prior to becoming a student. So it is with life. Earth is a learning institution with several schools, colleges and universities. We apply, are admitted and we enroll into this institution. We choose which school, college, or university we attend based on the "major" we select and the skills we want to acquire.

All students are on a temporary status. They may stay in school for as long as they are students. Some drop out early. Others stay for many years. Eventually every student must graduate and leave. Similarly, our stay here on earth is temporary. Once we gain the skills we need, we graduate and must leave. Our stay on earth varies based on the skills we need to develop. Some require more time than others.

In the institution of earth we learn practical skills and applied knowledge, not theories. Our teachers are our circumstances and our lessons are our experiences. We have one book and that is nature. Opening the book of nature, we soon realize that we are governed by laws. These laws apply equally to all. We are to use these laws to live healthy, joyous and abundant lives. We can also see that permanence is not an aspect of this world. It is nowhere to be found. We are engulfed by change. This change, however, is not random and haphazard. Even if it appears chaotic, order is it's underpinning. Recurrence governs most changes. As nature evolves by going through cycles, it unfolds just like a seed in soil, or a fertilized egg in a womb.

Every spring, grass grows, birds lay eggs and the pear tree in my back yard adorns itself with flowers. Each flower soon withers away leaving behind a bud that is the start of a pear fruit. The pears slowly grow, mature, ripen and if not picked, fall off. Life also proceeds through cycles. Even business, society and earth go through cycles. Cycles are in the atmosphere, land and sea. There are cycles in our bodies such as menstruation and the Krebs Cycle. Even the elements undergo cycles. We know of the Nitrogen, Citric Acid and Carbon Cycles. The ancients were also familiar with cycles. Some cultures even established mysteries such as the Eleusinian Mysteries which were held at Eleusis, Greece to celebrate the abduction of Persephone and her return to her mother Demeter, symbolizing the annual cycle of death and rebirth in nature, as well as the immortality of the soul. In Buddhism, Jainism and Hinduism there is the cycle of birth, death and Nirvana, a state of supreme bliss. Nirvana is attained only after the liberation from suffering, extinction of all attachments, and one's deliverance from the bondage of ignorance and desire which bring about the repeating cycles of death and rebirth.

Going through cycles is a fundamental aspect of living. Just as it is the nature of seeds to slowly transform into mature plants, bring forth flowers, fruit and more seeds and then die; it is our nature to go through cycles, wake up and gain mastery.

Each cycle can have several stages within it. Seeds in nature go through several stages to complete their cycle. They start as dormant seeds; get planted; shed their protective coats and begin underground growth; break the surface; grow to maturity; produce flowers, fruit and more seeds; and then they die. Embryos exhibit similar "stages" in their development. They seem to recount the story of the evolution of the species and the various stages of unfoldment. Even individual cells, while undergoing division, clearly exhibit "stages" in the process of "creating" additional cells. The cell starts from a state of rest or interphase and undergoes prophase, metaphase and telophase before the cell finally divides, grows and reaches a new stage of interphase as two distinct cells. Even the story of creation in the Bible alludes to creation being, not an act, but a process proceeding through stages of increasing complexity and organization. Each stage of development is the outgrowth of the preceding one. Hence, each current stage rests squarely on the stage preceding it while it supports the one just ahead. We, too, are in a process of unfoldment. We are going through cycles, each with several stages. Where we are now, is our present. This present is rooted in our past and stretches into the future. As a species, we go through several cycles and stages as well. We are giants because we rest on so many great shoulders that preceded us.

Why do we go through cycles? What controls the duration of each stage? George Santayana said that *"those who cannot remember the past are condemned to repeat it."* Buddhism teaches that we cannot attain Nirvana, the absence of cyclic birth and death, until we overcome our attachments and ignorance. In other words, until we learn. Is it possible that we undergo cycles in order that we have a variety of experiences and learn from a multiplicity of circumstances? Is it possible that we stay in a stage for as long as we need to in order to develop the necessary skills and once we do, we move on? Cycles afford us the opportunity to digest what we learn, incrementally add to our knowledge and gradually spiral up the "ladder" of evolution. Cycles and stages are the rungs we can use to unfold. They are a fundamental aspect of the overall plan of the universe.

The universe is too orderly to lack a grand plan. I believe that it is the plan for us to go through stages and experience cycles until we finally wake up and take control of our lives. We see this plan everywhere especially in the development of our consciousness. Initially, our progress is relegated to the genes, the subconscious and our environment. Slowly, we develop self awareness and begin to take charge of our lives while at the same time we continue to rely on our subconscious for all matters that should be automated such as breathing, digestion, circulation, . . . Life on earth is ideal for what we need. It provides us a variety of opportunities to experience a medley of phases, stages and cycles; encounter an abundance of obstacles and opportunities; and through these experience, grow and unfold. Through cycles we develop mastery under a variety of circumstances. This is the only way lasting mastery can be gained.

Even though we must go through cycles, how many and how long we spend in each stage is up to us. How long we dwell in a state is based on how quickly we learn and demonstrate mastery. We can do this rapidly through awareness, or we can learn slowly through pain, struggle and suffering. As we mature, we direct our evolution, become partners with God as co-creators and help transform our earth into a heaven of our choosing.

We can divide each cycle of existence into three main stages: an entrance through birth, living and evolution, and an exit through death. The two stages we are least comfortable with are the first and the last—birth and death. We seem unable to control these or know much about them with certainty. Birth and death, for most, are big unknowns. We do not feel comfortable with unknowns. We like to know and be in control. This is why many fear death. It is inevitable and there is nothing anyone can do about it.

## Birth

> *Our birth is but a sleep and a forgetting;*
> *The soul that rises with us, our life's star,*
> *Hath had elsewhere its setting,*
> *And cometh from afar:*
> *Not in entire forgetfulness,*
> *And not in utter nakedness,*
> *But trailing clouds of glory do we come*
> *From God, who is our home.*
> William Wordsworth

We enter the world through the portals of birth. We exit the world through the gateway of death. If there is birth, there must also be death. When we are born, time starts for us. The clock begins to tick. Once we have a beginning in space and time, we must have an ending.

Like all beginnings and endings, birth and death are merely apparent beginnings and endings. They are only relative starts and ends. Since everything is interdependent, there are no absolute beginnings or endings.

Even though birth is a beginning, it is not THE BEGINNING. Even though it appears that we had our beginning in a sperm and an egg, these had to exist prior to their meeting. For the sperms and eggs to form, our parents had to exist. For our parents to exist, their parents had to exist and so forth. We are a mere link in the immensely complex and interconnected chain of life. Without a true beginning, we cannot have a true ending.

For some, birth is pain and agony. For others, birth is a joyous celebration. The birth of Christ exemplifies the nature of birth in the cosmic sense. It is an occasion where the heavens and earth rejoice. It is a miracle where angels sing, humans marvel and the wise give gifts of thankfulness and appreciation.

Birth is a dual process. As we are born here, we die where we came from. Birth is a mere journey from one dimension into another, a change in phase.

Being born is like entering a new school. We feel awkward initially. It is the start of a new phase for discovery, learning and eventual mastery. To lessen the impact of this experience, we form relationships with others who are in the same predicament. We form friendships, families and communities.

We have the same choices in birth as the ones we have in choosing a new school. Our freedom is limited by what is available, our needs and circumstances. We always enroll in the grade for which we are eligible.

We choose to come to earth the same way we choose to go to any college or university—for what it has to offer, location, environment and cost. We come expecting to leave as soon as we graduate.

When we begin our education, we are freshmen. Our environment is new and we feel out of place until we adjust. We begin at the institution of earth as babies. We feel lost and it takes us a while to adapt and feel at home.

Our potential is so vast that we can only develop a small fraction of it each time and under any one circumstance. We require unlimited cycles to transform our potential into actual. That is why we must undergo several births and deaths until we are fully aware, awake and actualized. Once we are, we no longer need this environment, we graduate.

## Living

*The best use of life is to spend it for something that outlasts life.*
*William James*

We are not on earth by accident. There are no accidents, only ignorance of causes. We live and die according to a masterful plan. We live to learn, grow and unfold. This is what we have been doing ever since we were conceived. The best way to learn is by experiencing. As we experience, our eyes open and we get to know our deeper reality. By experiencing a variety of challenges, we develop more aspects of ourselves.

There are two ways to live—in accordance with the law or in grace. Living in accordance with the law, we are subject to all the forces of nature. We struggle, sink or swim. We react to every event that comes our way and we learn through trial and pain. We are governed by karma. To live in grace is to know who we are, why we are here and to feel our connection to our source. It is to live with awareness and power. For we are always connected to our source. This source dwells passively in our depths. To activate the contact with our source, we must want it, reach in and touch our source through our awareness and intent. If we live separate from our source, we are weak, at the mercy of circumstances and we experience fear and insecurity. If we live as an expression of our source, we have nothing to fear. If our source, God, is with us, whom and what shall we fear?

Being in touch with our source does not mean that we will not face difficulties. These are for our education. We need challenges to build our character, strengthen our personality and demonstrate mastery. Many of our abilities would not be developed, or we would not even know that we had them, if we did not face challenges. Challenge adds to the value and meaning of our lives. If we live a completely easy life without ever facing any challenges, life would lose its excitement and value. For if we are not challenged, how can we appreciate ease? If we never get tired, how can we enjoy rest? If we never cry, how can we value laughter? It is through the variety of our experiences that we glimpse ourselves. We would never know what type of a husband or wife we are until we get married, what sort of a father or mother we would be until we have children, what kind of a student, teacher, soldier, actor, scientist, artist, priest, or coach we would be until we actually engage in the activities, experience and discover ourselves through them. How can we know how we act in the face of stress unless we face some stressful situations? Or react to calamity unless we face it? How can we know how strong we are unless we have an opportunity to test our strength? I wonder how much we do not know about ourselves simply because we lack the specific experiences that reveal us to ourselves.

An infant that does not struggle several times in its attempt to stand up, fall a few times, get up and try again having learned from the previous experience, will not walk and run. A bird that does not face the discomfort of leaving its nest, and trusting the wind to take off, will not learn to fly. Individuals who do not risk, err, learn and improve will not prosper and live up to their potential. We are designed to attempt, and through several trials, learn and gain mastery. This is the nature of life. Through engagement, we gain mastery. We are problem solvers, and our challenges give us the opportunities we need to solve these "problems."

Discovering ourselves through our experiences is like studying, not always easy or fun. Often, we require an incentive to exert the required effort. The best incentive is the onset of the examinations that we must take and pass in order to graduate. Without tests, we might not prepare adequately. As in school, without set dates for tests and quizzes, we might ignore studying. We might procrastinate. Having to pass to graduate, is often incentive enough to study, prepare and pay attention in class. If we are tested and we pass, we go on to the next higher level. If we fail, we will require more opportunities to learn. This is not punishment; rather, it is for our learning and growth.

In the school of life, we do not have to pass our tests the very first time we face them. It is all right to err and learn from our mistakes. In fact, we are expected to fail often before we finally succeed. While in the school of life, we learn at our own pace. We learn to the degree that we are aware and apply ourselves.

Some people equate making mistakes with sinning. Hence, they fear death because they believe that once they die God will punish them. We can rest assured that God does not judge or punish, only we do. Punishment is not in the nature of God. We should remove it from our own. It is in us as a reflection of our immaturity. God can only love. So must we—ourselves, God and everyone else. Hence, we do not have to fear "sinning" and falling short of what we could be. God created us perfect only in potential. God expects us to make mistakes, learn from them and **strive** for perfection. God does not expect us to be perfect—only He is perfect. We can forgive ourselves and each other for failing.

Just as our children attempt, fall and bruise themselves several times before they master the art of running, jumping and playing sports so it is with us.

It will require us several life-times or cycles of rebirth to complete our education and receive our diploma. As we progress from one level to the next, we advance and unfold. Eventually, we face the ultimate graduation, from school to real life, from learning to using what we learned. This is when we become full time partners with God as co-creators.

## Death

*Do not go gentle into that good night,*
*Old age should burn and rave at close of day;*
*Rage, rage, against the dying of the light.*

*Dylan Thomas*

Death is the other side of birth. By dying from one side, we are born into another. By dying from darkness, we are born into the light. Death and birth are the rites of passage from one phase to the next. Even Christ had to die before He could be resurrected (reborn). No one can "ascend" into Nirvana or Heaven until one is reborn into a body of light and knowing. No one can go to God, who is spirit, while in the physical body. When we die, we leave the body behind. We revert back to our pure nature—spirit, essence and intelligence. In that state, we are more like our source.

Unlike schools, colleges and universities where students take their examinations together and at a specified time and place, in the school of life, we choose to take our final examination privately and sometimes with a small group. Death is a personal and an intimate experience. While many leave through normal graduation, some encounter accidents and drop out. Some leave early through disease or suicide, while others are forced to leave through violence or disciplinary action. Eventually all must leave. The results of our final examination determine whether we have learned and can move on, or we must come back to complete our education.

We have a limited time to prepare for our final examination. If we had limitless time, we would not take our lives seriously and act. Having finite time is our incentive to act. Life is like a game of soccer, basketball, or football. All games are played for a certain duration. Life is lived for a limited duration as well. If we invest ourselves and at least double what we started with in any given life time, we are allowed to graduate and move on to the next level.

Just as the students who prepare for their final examination are not intimidated by it, we need not fear death if we prepare and are ready for it. Death is not a curse. It is a very important motivator. It is a friend and an ally that helps us get the most that life has to offer. With the shadow of death constantly hovering over us, we should do what is important. Not knowing when we will face our final examination, we must be ready at all times. We can rest assured that there is no escaping our final examination. It is the only way we can leave this school. Death is our gateway to the other worlds. It is our passport and visa.

Graduation from school is a happy event for those who have done well. It is a time for reflection for those who could have done better. It is also a sober time having to enter a world we are not accustomed to. Graduation from the institution of earth is similar. It is a time for rejoicing for it is a release from limitations and bondage. It is a time for reflection on how we did and how we could have done. It is also a somber time for we know not what to expect in the new world we are about to face.

The more ignorant we are of why we live and die, the easier it is to be controlled by the power-hungry and the unscrupulous. Fearing death is like fearing to open a door to see what is behind it. Quite often the thought of an experience is worse than the experience itself. We know much more about death than we care to admit, for we have died many times before. We also know of many who have had close encounters with death—near-death experiences. Their experiences were of light, beauty, compassion and joy; not of fear and punishment. Each came back realizing that they had a mission to fulfill and a service to render.

Fear of death is an unnecessary burden to carry around. By replacing ignorance with knowledge, we gain the light we need to see clearly and move through life with confidence and peace. We are taught many untruths about death and what happens afterwards. What we learn from others is often their opinions and beliefs. We can learn a lot from others if we listen to their experiences instead of their beliefs. We should always start our search for answers by examining our own experiences. If we do not find what we want within us, we seek others who have had experiences in areas we are interested in. I am fortunate to have had my own encounter with death, an encounter which left its indelible marks on my consciousness and from which I learned a great deal.

## *A Personal Experience*

March 24 is a special day for me. It is the birthday of one of my favorite personalities, Wilhelm Reich, a psychologist and scientist. I learned a great deal from him and consider him to be a giant among men. He is a man for whom I have great love and respect. It was my habit to quietly and privately celebrate his birthday.

It was March 24, 1982. That morning, I stopped at a pastry shop and picked up a fresh strawberry pie and brought it to work to celebrate the special occasion.

There, through a phone call, I learned that Rudy Howard, a friend, had passed away. He had a heart attack the day before and died on the way to the hospital. Rudy was thirty-six and the father of two little girls, ages 4 and 7.

Rudy and I had known each other for many years. We had

just finished serving together as officers of the local lodge of the Ancient and Mystical Order of the Rosy Cross; the Rosicrucian Order, AMORC.[1] Two days earlier he expressed his appreciation for the chance to serve and work with me. The news of his passing away left me dumbfounded.

A few days later, a friend and I took a taxi to the church where the funeral was being held. The services were religious, Masonic and Rosicrucian. Rudy had been a Freemason in addition to being a Rosicrucian. As I sat quietly observing the Masonic ritual for Rudy, I underwent an experience that is very difficult to describe. I felt intensely emotional. These emotions began deep inside me, welled up and erupted explosively like a volcano immersing all. Suddenly, I was transformed. I lost awareness of my current surroundings. Instead of attending Rudy's funeral services, I was witnessing *my own funeral.*

The state I found myself in was intensely real, emotionally charged and vividly detailed. It was like being in a theater totally absorbed watching a three-dimensional rendition of my life. I saw the faces of the people. I heard every word that was uttered. I was surprised to see some of the people and was equally surprised not to see others. It was moving to hear what people had to say about me. Yet, some of the particulars of the service unnerved me, especially the readings from the Bible. I definitely did not want a religious service or any passages from the Old Testament read at my funeral. I did not want any priest to consign my soul to a heaven of their understanding.

I wanted to object to what I was witnessing. I could not utter a word or move. I could not interfere or protest. I was a

---

1. The Rosicrucian Order exists throughout the world as a nonsectarian body of men and women devoted to the investigation, study, and practical application of natural and spiritual laws. The purpose of the organization is to enable everyone to live in harmony with the creative, constructive cosmic forces for the attainment of health, happiness and peace.

mere passive witness. This situation reminded me when I was out of my body and could not move any part of it. As I continued to witness my funeral, I became more unhappy with what I saw. The intensity of my emotions rose. Since there was not much I could do, I had no choice but to continue to observe what I was witnessing. I was like Scrooge being shown my "graduation" ceremony.

Finally it was over and I returned to Rudy's funeral. The service was almost over. I was so emotionally charged that I dared not look anyone in the eyes, for I knew that I would burst into tears. To avoid looking at or talking to anyone, I quickly left the church and took a taxi back to work.

On my way to work, a distinct voice surged from deep within and urged me to write down exactly how I wanted my funeral to be. I attempted to ignore this voice and the urge. I was not prepared to deal with the imminence of my mortality.

Over the next few days the urge to write down instructions on how I wanted my funeral to be persisted. I woke up several times at night with the strong impulse to get up, go to my desk and write down my final instructions before it was too late. I was reluctant to comply and kept on resisting.

It was very clear to me how I wanted my funeral to be—a Rosicrucian service followed by a quick and inexpensive cremation with no prior viewing of the body. I wanted to be remembered as qualities and the memories I left behind in the hearts and minds of those I came in touch with. I did not want to be associated with a religion, or a final resting place. In my eulogy, I would urge people to question and trust their own experiences. I would ask them to seek the truth instead of blindly following doctrines and teachings that glorify systems rather than empower individuals. I would encourage people to overcome fear and to place more trust in the sacredness of their being. I would ask people to become more compassionate, tolerant and peace loving. The details of my funeral service were clear in my mind. All I had to do was write them down. The inner urge to write my final instructions persisted and got stronger. I sensed the urgency of the prompting and became aware of the warning that if I kept on refusing to write down my instructions, things were going to happen contrary to my wishes and out of necessity. The message was clear: write the instructions, or accept the consequences. Still, I resisted. I was afraid to comply. Somehow, I was reluctant to admit to myself that I was to die. I did not feel ready to let go of my life. I was gripped with fear.

\* \* \* \* \*

After watching the 7 p.m. evening news the night of March 31, 1982, I got myself a glass of white wine and relaxed in a bathtub of hot water. All at once I knew, completely and beyond any shadow of doubt, that I had come to the end of my life. *I was dying.* Instantly, two things happened at once. First, I sensed a sudden and complete contraction. This contraction was not physical; rather, the essence that was me, all at once, shrank and collapsed into a "point," located below my navel. It was like the bursting of a balloon, but in reverse. Simultaneously, I felt the "warmth of being alive" suddenly leave me. My heart stopped beating, my physical body went into convulsions and turned cold. Concurrently, my awareness of space and time collapsed. "I" was aware but not of space or time. Instantly, pictures from my past flashed in front of me like scenes from a movie filmed for me and about me. In one of these scenes, I saw the doctor pronouncing the cause of my death as a heart attack. As I saw this, I knew that the heart attack was not the cause of my death. It was more a result of the contraction as "the warmth" left my body. In another scene, I saw Sylvia, Rudy's wife, in the funeral home. She was saying to a group of mourners: "First Rudy, now Shahan; and both were so young. If calamities come in threes, I wonder who is going to be next."

I saw my brother John talking to my brothers, "I do not care what people say. It does not matter what you eat or what you do to yourself. When it is time to go, you go. Shahan always took good care of himself and look what happened to him. He was the first to go. Look at me, I smoke and seldom take care of myself and I am still here."

I saw myself talking to two young ladies in Beirut, Lebanon. I was saying: "I want to die young. Once I finish doing all that I want to do, let me go. Why wait until I am old and decrepit. It is best to die while I am young and fully functional. The key is doing what you want quickly and once done, leave quickly as well." One of the girls said sadly: "That is fine for you. What about your wife and children? How will they feel and how will they manage after you are gone?"

This scene, more than any other, made me realize that I either had something to do with the timing of my death, or at least was aware of it on a subconscious level. Right then the thought occurred to me that perhaps I can do something, even now, to change the outcome. Perhaps I could alter my status and live for a while longer. I attempted to visualize my daughter Olivia as grown up and me with her. I had no success. I struggled to visualize her about to get married and see myself at the wedding. Again, I failed. As hard as I tried, I could not visualize anything in the future. There was no longer any future left for me. Somehow the ability to project my consciousness into the future had forsaken me. Instantly, I was back with more scenes from my life.

I felt as if I had lived in a maze. I had come to the end. I was at a wall that I could not go beyond. It became evident to me that my life was like a computer program that had run its course, or completed its execution. While living, I had the option of writing my own programs or choosing from among several pre-written ones that I could adopt and use as my own. Once I made a choice, I had to live out those programs. These programs allowed modifications but only prior to the end of their execution. It became clear to me that while living, I was executing a set of instructions stored in my genes and mind. These instructions were like the "scent of food" for an animal in a maze to follow. The scent of food I was pursuing was the set of instructions engraved within me. The realization dawned upon me that I always had the freedom to change the course and follow a different "scent." I also realized that I had actually done this a few times during the course of my life, thus living several small "lives" within the one life.

Suddenly, I wondered how my family would feel after my departure and the hardships that this might cause. I immediately discerned that my life was primarily my own, lived by me and for me. Even though I had a family, my life was a private journey. The paths I used for the journey of my life intersect with and run parallel with others. Even when it merges with another, it is only for a while. Each highway always maintains its identity and course. While my path and the paths of my family members mingled and intersected, each remains intact and clearly individual. Ultimately, we are each on our own journeys traveling our own paths. We have our individual lessons to learn, contributions to make and relationships to consummate.

Instantly, I became aware of three "beings" who knew who I was and what I was going through. At no time did I see them in detail. I became aware that they were discussing my case and that there was some ambiguity concerning the next steps. Even though my time was up, I was resisting to leave. I "saw" a discussion taking place. I felt anxious. Soon, I vaguely sensed that there was more that I could do while still in the body. What exactly I was to do was not clear to me.

I do not know how long I remained in that state, or what transpired next. I do know that I had many more insights and realizations about my life and the nature of reality. Unfortunately, I forgot these as soon as my consciousness returned. Somehow, and without any effort on my part, I was back in my body. Slowly vitality crept back into my limbs and organs. I became aware of my body in the bathtub. I was thankful that I was alive once more.

As I regained awareness of my body and surroundings, I realized that I was extremely cold and began to shiver uncontrollably. My solar plexus area was highly sensitive and inflamed. Additionally, I had the strange feeling that my status was only temporary. No long term decision was made. I had only an interim lease on life. Regardless, I was glad to be back in my body. I decided to go to bed and get under the covers to warm up. The shivering was intense, persistent and uncontrollable. I struggled to get out of the bath tub. I made it to my bed, but continued to shiver. I wanted to get more blankets to cover myself, I could not. I felt too weak to go anywhere. I did not even have enough energy to call for my wife who was in the living room. After a while, I decided that I could not stay in bed. I had to get up and get more blankets. I was simply too cold. I struggled to get up and as quickly as I could covered myself with more blankets. Even with four additional blankets, I was still very cold and the shivering continued for a long time.

Additionally, during the next several days, I had diarrhea and could not keep down any food. My solar plexus area remained highly sensitive, as if inflamed. However, the shivering stopped. I did not relate my experience to anyone as yet. My wife was aware that something out of the ordinary had taken place. She was in a heightened emotional state and wept on several occasions. Two close friends called the next day and told me they had a distinct feeling that something unusual had happened to me. They could not fully explain or understand their feelings.

For the next six days, I remained in an in-between state—in limbo. My awareness was focused on death and dying. When I looked at people, I saw how they would look when they were dead. I was aware of the stench of death wherever

I went. People looked hollow. I saw them like they were wearing masks of death. My body felt hollow as well. I did not sense my body as a solid object. It felt like I was a mere guest in this body instead of living there. The meaning of the word *Zombie* became an experienced reality for me.

On the seventh day, I went to work and at lunch time, went walking on the Mall in Washington, D.C. with my wife. As we walked and talked, I was still seeing and smelling death everywhere. I was aware how hollow my voice sounded, when all of a sudden I felt that something landed on me, permeating my entire being. Instantly, death and its aspects left me and life with its attributes took hold. I felt that I had just been given another life and with it another opportunity to live and experience.

## Eight Reasons We Decide to Die

*A physician can sometimes parry the scythe of death, but has no power over the sand in the hourglass.*
Hester Piozzi

Even though we might not be able to extend our lives beyond their physical limits, we can shorten our lives and die prematurely. The same factors that cause aging will ultimately lead to death. Death like taxes, is a certainty. Just as we need not pay a penny more than we are legally obligated, we need not die one day short of what our physical limits entitle us. We are responsible for how we live, and how and when we die. Whether we actually assume these responsibilities or abrogate them is a different matter. Unless we leave a will behind, the prevailing laws will take effect. Unless we make the decisions of our lives, our environment, genes, or subconscious will take over.

We cannot remain students in the school of life forever. We cannot postpone our graduation indefinitely. Eventually, we must graduate and leave. As we near the end of our education for this cycle, the call of death becomes progressively louder inviting us to give in and rest in peace. Like sleep, which we cannot resist indefinitely, eventually we succumb. Sleep and death are similar in many ways. Just as we cannot alter the fact that we must sleep, but can choose when and how to sleep, so it is with death. If we know why we sleep, we will understand why we choose to die. The same laws govern both.

Recently when I asked a group of people why they went to sleep the night before, they gave the following reasons:

1. I felt tired and needed to rest.
2. It was time to go to bed.
3. I had to get up early the next morning.
4. I did all I could for today—I did not feel like doing anything else.
5. I was bored.
6. It was an accident—I was reading in bed and I just fell asleep.
7. I wanted to sleep and dream.

While the above are reasons we go to sleep, there is one more reason that is specific to death. We decide to die to dissociate an association we no longer care to keep. We die to dissolve the corporation—the body.

8. Dissolving the Corporation.

## 1. I Felt Tired And Needed To Rest

*Rest: the sweet sauce of labor.*

*Plutarch*

We have limits to our endurance. Eventually, and this varies from one individual to another, we get tired and we need to rest. The best way to rest is to quiet the body and preserve its energy. This is accomplished through sleep.

Living for many years is like running a marathon. It is tiring. This is felt by the body, the emotions and the mind. Eventually, we all need time to rest. As with our daily labors, the best way to rest is to allow the body to sleep. At the end of our journey on earth, we undertake the long sleep. We choose to die.

Feeling tired does not necessarily mean that we really are tired. We are familiar with second winds. Additionally, we will stay up longer to do something we enjoy than we would to do something we find boring. While boring activities tire us, interesting activities enliven and energize us.

Even God had to rest after the long process of creation. On the seventh day, God rested. Death is our seventh and last stage in this cycle of birth. It is our day of rest. Just as the body requires rest after exertion, we require rest after activity. Just as we lie down to rest from a busy day, we lie down to rest from a busy life. To rest from activity, we sleep. To rest from living, we die.

We go to sleep every night without any guarantees that we will actually wake up the next morning. Yet, we are not alarmed. Similarly, we die without any knowledge of what we will experience after we let go. Just as we trust that we will wake up from our sleep, we trust that we will wake up from our "death." Just as we wake up from every sleep until one day we do not, we are reborn after every death until one day we graduate from this school and this plane of existence. No one knows what is in store for us after that. Whatever it is will be part of the overall plan and intelligence that guided us so far.

Individuals vary greatly in their endurance, energy level and need for rest. Some have an abundance of energy and require very little rest. Others are the opposite. Whatever our type, we know when we are tired and need to rest. When we do, we act. Some more willingly than others.

### *Personal Experience*
### *My Mother*

My mother died prematurely at the age of thirty-seven. I believe that my mother got tired and needed to rest. She had a very rough and tiring life. By the time she was thirty-four, she had six children and many miscarriages. She struggled a lot and was greatly abused. She seldom had a happy day. Eventually, the burden of her misfortunes got her down. She saw no light at the end of her tunnel. The future held more of the same. She gave up on life, succumbed to her condition and went to sleep for the final time.

Her death, however, was not all for naught. By dying, my mother gave her children her most precious gift: the freedom to leave their current circumstances and seek a better way of life. Even though this was not easy, it became an option none-the-less. Without her death, none of her six children would have left home in Syria. Had my father died early instead, my mother would have kept us together as a family. Soon after she died my father decided to re-marry. To do that, he got his children out of the way thus setting them free. This diaspora gave us the opportunity to break loose and have a taste of the possible life. Eventually, we all came to the United States, became citizens and began to live better lives. Without my mother's death none of this would have been possible. Many of us perhaps would have been killed in the Middle East wars since service in the military is mandatory. By going to sleep, my mother enabled us to gain our freedom and an opportunity at a better life.

## 2. It Was Time To Go To Bed

*For everything there is a season, and a time for every matter under heaven: a time to be born, and a time to die; a time to plant, and a time to pluck up what is planted; a time to kill, and a time to heal; a time to break down, and a time to build up; a time to weep, and a time to laugh; a time to mourn, and a time to*

> dance; a time to cast away stones, and a time to gather stones together; a time to embrace, and a time to refrain from embracing; a time to seek, and a time to lose; a time to keep, and a time to cast away; a time to rend, and a time to sew; a time to keep silence, and a time to speak; a time to love, and a time to hate; a time for war, and a time for peace.
>
> Ecclesiastes 3:1–8

There is a time and a season (stage and cycle) for everything under the sun and we are in tune with these stages and cycles. There is a cycle for activity and another for rest. There is a cycle for focusing on self and another for establishing relationships and developing interest in others. There is a cycle to earn and another to spend and enjoy. There is a cycle to venture forth and another to take it easy and appreciate what is at hand. Just as we know it is time to eat when we get hungry, to sleep when we are drowsy, we know it is time to die at the end of our journey. Just as simply as we eat and fall asleep, we die.

Our decision to die could be conscious or subconscious, resulting from contentment, or as a release from pain, suffering, senility and disease. This decision should be based on awareness and not mere instinct. For often, even though it might appear that it is time for something, it might not really be time for that thing. Just as getting drowsy could be the signal that it is time for sleep, it could also be an indication of boredom or the need for more oxygen. Thus, when it feels like it is time to die, it might be time to die, or it could be time to die from something old and worn out and start something new.

What does *"it is time"* mean anyway? Reality is multifaceted and we only know some aspects of it. According to what we learn in school, there are at least two systems under which we can experience space and time. One is the Newtonian system; the other is the relativistic system of Einstein. Under the Newtonian system, a day is a day, an hour is an hour and a yard is a yard. Under the relativistic concepts of Einstein, a day is not necessarily a day and a yard is not necessarily a yard. It is all relative and due to position and speed. Some can experience a day as a century, while others can experience the same day as a moment. That is why a day in the eyes of the Lord might mean centuries. Equally, a day in our eyes might mean centuries in the eyes of a subatomic particle.

We are familiar with the many instances in which people die soon after they retire or after their spouse dies. It is clear that these people must play a role in determining the onset of their deaths. They decide that it is time to die. They do this by having nothing worthwhile to live for. At times people lose interest in life, or find that the pain of losing a spouse is greater than the joy of living alone. Whatever the reason, they decide to let go and die. They decide it is time not because there is a time set for them, but because they do not want to continue in their present state. These people, through their action or inaction, decide when it is time. Once they decide it is time, then it is time for them.

### *Personal Experiences*
### *Mary*

We celebrated Mary's seventy-fifth birthday together. She was healthy, happy and vital. She lived by herself, joined clubs, danced, traveled and had a wonderful time. When Mary turned eighty-seven, she decided to live with her only daughter, who was married to a military officer. While they were stationed in San Francisco, Mary had a wonderful time. Then the daughter and her family moved to a small town in Georgia. The mother went along, but she was unhappy, for there was little she could do in a small town.

We met Mary and her daughter's family at the beach for a week in North Carolina. Mary looked fine, but was on medication. She told me that there was nothing for her to do where she was and that she was getting very bored. Mary began getting sick. Her boredom was translating into disease. She was in and out of the hospital many times.

As I talked and listened to Mary, I realized that she was employing words that she never used before. She reminded me several times that she was old. Whenever we talked about a future event, she kept saying, "If I am still around, I am getting old, you know." I realized that she was preparing for her death.

On the way home, I told my daughters that this might be the last time they would see Mary. I explained that Mary had given up on life. She felt it was time to go.

Four months later we received a Christmas card from her daughter informing us that her mother was very sick and in the hospital. She was battling with disease and struggling for her life.

It is not too late to reverse a decision. If we change our environment and take new, bold and life enhancing actions, we can "buy" ourselves more time. Instead of reacting to a negative situation by changing our outlook toward life, we can either change the situation, or find something good about it and dwell on that. Unfortunately for Mary, even though her family was on the move again, she did not take advantage of her new opportunity to delve into life with renewed interest and vigor. She got progressively more sick. She fought death for a long time. Eventually, she decided it was time to let go. She gave in and passed away.

### Cole Bunny

On September 9, 1988 my wife bought two dwarf bunnies for Olivia's 8'th and Emily's 5'th birthdays. Olivia picked a black one while Emily chose a brown one. No one was concerned with the sex of the bunnies at the time. Everything was great until both of the bunnies matured and we realized that both were males and very territorial. The bunnies began to attack each other savagely. They attempted to injure each other. Our attempts to keep them separated failed. Begrudgingly, we decided to give one of the bunnies away. After an emotional process of selecting which bunny to keep and which to give up, we gave up the brown one.

The girls had named the remaining black bunny Cole. From the beginning I had litter trained the bunny so Cole was free to roam around the basement. We lavished Cole with our love and attention. In summer and on nice days, we kept Cole outside in our yard in a large fenced area. We fed the bunny pellets, carrots and special treats consisting of yogurt drops. When Emily brought a turtle home one day, we discovered that the bunny loved to eat the apples we gave the turtle.

For 8 years the bunny did great. We discovered that he was much more aware and intelligent than we attributed to bunnies previously. We communicated well. He let us know when he wanted to go outside and when he preferred to remain indoors. When we held him too long and he wanted to visit his litter, he let us know by getting restless and, on occasion, by giving us a slight bite.

I often held him in my arms while I watched the evening news. He would lay there content licking my arm. One day, when it was time to let him go downstairs, I took him to the stairs and let him go down. He would normally hop down the stairs and quickly go to his area in the basement. This time, he fell while going down the stairs. He had never fallen going down the stairs before. After making sure that he was all right, I let him be.

A few days later, I observed an unusual behavior. Normally, when I offered Cole a treat, he got very excited, located the treat instantly and started eating it while still in my hand. This time, it took him a few seconds to locate the treat. Somehow his sense of smell was not as acute.

Over the next several days, I noticed other unusual behaviors. When I went downstairs to check on the bunny, I began to find water mixed in with his food. I would get upset and tell the bunny not to do that again. I then would take the food and water bowls, clean them and give him fresh water and food. The next day, I would find the same thing, water mixed in with the food. After several days of this, I placed the water far away from the food and in a container that the bunny could not tip over into his food bin. That put an end to having water mixed in with his food. However, this led to yet another unusual behavior. The bunny stopped using the litter pan. He began leaving his pellets everywhere. After a week or two of this, I confined him to one room in the basement by placing a barrier at the door. A few days later I realized that the bunny was not eating. He was losing weight fast. In a matter of days, he was on the verge of dying. I reasoned that he must be old, very old and near his limit.

When my wife came down to visit with Cole Bunny, she got the bright idea that perhaps instead of giving him a whole carrot, she would shred it for him. That was a brilliant idea. The bunny began to eat once more and improved. Suddenly, I remembered how I would find water mixed in with the bunny's food. I realized that the bunny was attempting to soften his dry food. He was wiser than I imagined. I began to give him shredded apples, carrots and potatoes. I also poured water in his regular food. Additionally, I gave him lettuce, bananas and tomatoes just to find out what he would eat. He ate his wet food, the shredded apples and carrots.

A couple of weeks later, all he would eat was shredded apples. He was still underweight and would lose his balance if he moved fast. He was also getting very dirty. For the first time in over 8 years, I began to give him baths.

One evening, I went downstairs to visit the bunny. I found him laying on his side with his feet up in the air. I thought he was dead. Observing him closely, I saw that he was still breathing. I went upstairs and informed my family that the bunny might not make it through the night. My wife and daughters went downstairs and visited the bunny for over an hour. When they came up, Olivia informed me that the bunny's predicted demise was slightly exaggerated. In fact, he was doing fine after they attended to him. Olivia was right. The bunny began to eat once more and improved.

Slowly, Cole Bunny began to lose more of his abilities. It became exceedingly difficult for him to eat and move about. Cole Bunny refused to go outside, or even let us hold him. He felt too old to do anything. He appeared to give up on life. He was not enjoying life anymore. For Cole Bunny, it was time to go to bed and rest.

On Sunday, January 12, 1997 Cole Bunny died. After a simple ritual, we buried him in the corner lot where he spent most of his time while outside. Olivia painted the picture of a bunny and a heart on a stone with the words: Cole Bunny, 1988–1997.

I have learned a lot from our bunny. I learned about aging and eventual death. I learned about the role care, attention and love plays in the will to live. I also learned about the role we play in each others desire and decision to live or die. From our bunny, I learned about myself. How I will age and how I will eventually die.

## 3. I Had To Get Up Early The Next Day

*Early to bed, early to rise makes a man healthy, wealthy and wise.*

*Benjamin Franklin*

We willingly, and at times, gladly go to sleep because we know that sleep is only temporary and, come morning, we will wake up. We live a cyclic life of day and night followed by other days and nights. Our going to sleep is an indication of the deep and subconscious trust we have that somehow this is not our last sleep and that there will be another day. We know the laws of life on the subconscious level far better than we accept them on the conscious level. This is understandable, since our objective thinking is clouded by our culture, biases and beliefs.

Fortunately, subconscious knowledge is deeply implanted in the soil of our being and its roots are well established. Subconscious knowledge guides our innate decisions and keeps us more in tune with the laws of life. That is why we do not live every day as if it is our last. We know, from deep within, that we will wake up once more. Similarly, we do not live our current life as if it is the last or the only one. We know that we will wake up once more into another life and start a new cycle just as we have been doing over eons of cyclic existence.

We are aware of an unspoken law: *we know not whence we came, yet we are here. If we were born once without our **conscious** knowledge and volition, there is nothing to prevent us from being born once more. If we came once, we can return, again and again. We remember not why we were born and we remember not why we die.* It all seems to happen based on an intelligence and a will higher than our conscious awareness. This intelligence and will we attribute to God. We must, however, realize that we are part of this intelligence, connected to it through our individual intelligence.

If we have to get up early the next day, we go to bed earlier than usual so we can wake up fresh and start our activities with energy and vitality. Similarly, when we let our bodies age and we still have major plans for our lives that require an abundance of energy, we decide "to go to bed early." We die knowing that we will wake up again at the beginning of another day or cycle. When it is time to wake up once more, it will happen simply, naturally and miraculously. We wake up rested and ready.

### *Personal Experience*
### Sam

When I left the monastery in Zahle, Lebanon, to continue my high school education, I enrolled at the Girard Institute in Sidon, Lebanon. There I met my two best friends, Sam and Elias.

Sam and I became friends instantly. We did almost everything together. We had a lot in common. While I had a father who was in Syria, Sam had a father who traveled a lot for business. Neither of us had much of a family life. Sam would visit his aunt in Beirut, Lebanon, during the summer between school years. I, on the other hand, would attempt to find a job somewhere. If I worked in Beirut, I would stay with my Aunt Faith.

After nine years in Lebanon I emigrated to the United States. Shortly after, I joined the United States Army and established my residency. In the summer of 1974, my brother Joseph, who was in the United States Navy, and I took a military hop back to the Middle East.

It was late evening when we arrived in Beirut. After checking into a downtown hotel, I called my friend Sam. We talked for a while and I told him that I would come and visit him the next day. He insisted on coming down to the hotel to see me that night instead. I refused because it was late and I was tired. We agreed to meet the next day in a place familiar to us both.

We met early the next day and spent the day together. Late in the afternoon, we stopped at a restaurant which I used to frequent. The restaurant was not crowded so we took our time eating and talking. On several occasions I asked Sam to come to the United States. I described in detail life in the United States. Sam never answered me. All he did was look at me and smile. I asked him repeatedly why he was noncommittal. Again, he simply looked at me and smiled. He kept insisting on just enjoying the moment and leaving the future alone.

The next two days I did not see Sam. Since I was going to stay in Lebanon for just a few days, I decided to locate and visit some of my other friends and relatives. Thus, my brother and I spent the next day visiting. On the third day, we decided to be tour guides to some Canadian tourists whom we met on our way from Turkey to Lebanon.

The next day, around 2:30 p.m., I called Sam. A stranger

answered the phone. I asked the lady if I could please speak to Sam. She asked me who I was. I told her that I was Sam's friend. She then told me that I obviously did not know what had happened to Sam. I was alarmed and answered that I did not. She then told me that Sam had died three days ago and they had just come back from his funeral.

How could this be? Sam was with me three days ago. He did not look sick enough to die within a few hours. He did not tell me that he was even sick. Besides, why was I not informed of the funeral? He was my best friend, after all, and why such a quick burial?

I was dazed as I approached the house where Sam used to live. A woman I had never seen before opened the door. When I walked in, I saw many of my friends, the same friends that I had been trying to locate and visit. When Albert, Sam's father, saw me, he burst into tears. He came over, hugged and kissed me. He told me that Sam had Hodgkin's disease. He fought the disease as best as he could, but eventually got tired of fighting. The last few months he was not doing well at all. When Sam received my letter that I would be visiting Lebanon soon, he got better and was anxiously awaiting my visit. On the day I was to arrive in Lebanon, Sam was glued to the telephone waiting for my call. When I finally did call, he wanted to come downtown to see me that same night, but it was too late and I would not let him because I was tired. The next day when we got together, he was the happiest and healthiest he had been for a long time. The next morning he passed away. They could not contact me because they had no idea where I was staying and whether or not I was still around. They tried, but in vain. Since he had been sick for some time and they were expecting his death, they decided not to delay the funeral.

I could not comprehend what was being said to me. All I could see was Sam's face smiling whenever I mentioned anything about the future. He knew that there was not going to be any future for him. His smile was the smile of *knowing* that he was going to die soon. Sam was in his twenties when he died. I never found out if Sam was buried or cremated. I never saw Sam sick, or dead. In a way, that is how I want it. I remember him the way I saw him last, with a knowing smile on his face.

Sam went to bed early. Even though there was a lot he wanted to do, the circumstances were not right. He opted to go to bed early and rest. There will be another day for him. He will sleep and rest and when he wakes up next, he will find himself in the appropriate environment to do whatever he chooses to undertake.

## 4. I Did All I Could For Today—I Did Not Feel Like Doing Anything Else

*And God saw everything that he had made, and behold, it was very good. And there was evening and there was morning, a sixth day. Thus the heavens and the earth were finished, and all the host of them. And on the seventh day God finished his work which he had done, and he rested on the seventh day from all his work which he had done. So God blessed the seventh day and hallowed it, because on it God rested from all his work which he had done in creation.*

*Genesis 1:31–2:3*

There is a lot we can do in one day. Some do more in a couple of hours than others do in an entire day. Either way, once we feel and know that we have done all we want to do for that one day, we cease our activities. Similarly, we do a lot in a lifetime. Some, like Princess Diana, with a mere few years of living, impact society more than others who live for a century. Individually, we measure our deeds by our own yard sticks. When we feel that we have done all we set out to do, we know that we have come to the end of our journey. We then take a long rest. We die.

People who belong to the "Hemlock Society" induce their death willingly once they decide that they have lived enough. They reason that it is best to pass away voluntarily while able, than have to endure suffering, disease and old age.

We are more ready to let go and die once we feel we have fulfilled our mission as we consciously or subconsciously accept it. When we know that we have a strong reason to postpone our death, we do so until we feel that that reason is satisfied. It was shown in a study that more people die after long weekends, holidays and good seasons than before. This is yet another indication that we have some control as to when we die. Once we do all that we set out to do, we do the only thing left for us to do. We die.

### *Personal Experience*
### *My Father*

My father died of a broken heart. He had six children from his first marriage but none to enjoy. Even though he remarried and had one more son, he was never content. Since he was very abusive as we were growing up, we left home soon after my mother died never to return to a family life that included my father. As far as we were concerned, we did not have one. My father, on the other hand, grew fonder of us the longer we were away from him. He wove stories in his imagination and lived in a fanciful world. He believed that one day we would send for him and have him live with us. He waited and waited and waited.

I stayed in touch with my father because I knew he was in dire financial need. I wrote him for over fifteen years monthly to send him money. My letters to him were very terse: "We are all doing fine. I hope all of you are doing fine as well. Enclosed with this letter is money to help you out. Let me know when you receive it." Every time I received a letter back, he told me that he got the money, but he wanted more. Thank you was not part of his vocabulary.

I was concerned that he might save some of the money and take a flight from Syria to the United States. To prevent this, for my return address, I used a post office box instead of my home address. One summer while my sister-in-law was visiting her family in Syria, my father stopped by to see her and inquire about us. He asked for our addresses and she gave him my brother John's address in Massachusetts. When I received a phone call from my brother John saying that our father was in the U.S., I was troubled and dismayed. My worst apprehension had materialized.

My father's surprise visit was, as expected, a complete disaster. None of us were prepared to receive him. He, on the other hand, imagined that he could simply come to the United States and live with us. So when he saw us, he was eager to hug and kiss us. We, on the other hand, had no feelings for him.

My father had his most civil visit in Massachusetts with my brother John and other relatives. When he visited the rest of us in Maryland, he was in for a surprise. He tried to hug and kiss my sister. She did not respond. In fact, she pushed him away when he tried to hang on too long. How could she feel anything for him? He had given her up for adoption when she was about four years old. She was now married and with a child of her own. She could hardly even remember him. When he tried to hug and kiss me and my other three brothers we could not respond either. We were not intentionally cold. We simply had no feelings for him and could not feign any.

My wife was very polite and did her best to serve and attend to him. In an effort to let bygones be bygones, I avoided all discussions of the past. However, I still could not force any warm feelings toward him. I treated him as well as I would treat any human being. After a few days he insisted on knowing why he was getting such a cold treatment after all that he had done for us. I simply could not restrain myself. I had to know what exactly he had done for us.

He looked surprised and puzzled that I would even ask for an explanation. The more he tried to tell me about the past, the angrier I became. He was fabricating stories. He must have told himself these stories for so long that he actually believed them. I then began confronting him with the facts as I lived them. I told him that all of my memories of him were of beatings and abuses. I asked him why he never held us, kissed us, or played with us when we were young. I asked him why he came to visit us here in the United States, but would not visit my brothers when they were in an orphanage in his own city. I reminded him of the savagery we all endured under him; how he tried to pull my mother's tongue out with a pair of pliers because she dared to talk back at him; how he got everybody out and locked me in a room and savagely attacked me, beating me with a whip and trampling over me with his boots. I ended by telling him that as far as I was concerned he was simply responsible for my birth and for that I was thankful. But, he had not been a father to me. Therefore, I had none.

I felt terrible for having confronted my father. It must have hurt his pride and feelings so badly that he fell sick. In a couple of days we had to take him to the hospital. It cost us thousands of dollars to take care of him. Soon afterwards, he flew back to Syria.

My father's hopes of establishing a relationship with us failed. He could not hold onto false hopes any longer. Even though he had a new family, he did not feel like doing anything anymore. He felt that he did all he could for that day and this life. The situation was too broken to be repaired. He gave up and died.

## 5. I Was Bored

*Against boredom the gods themselves fight in vain.*
                                              Friedrich Nietzsche

Boredom is "a condition of mental weariness, listlessness and discontent." It is a state we can only tolerate for a short duration, after which we must do something to introduce change. Boredom is the lack of excitement for and the absence of value and meaning in what we do. Just because we are doing something does not necessarily mean that we are not bored. Even though boredom is not always apparent, it is powerful enough to cause us to eat when we are not hungry, go to bed when we are not sleepy, it can even lead us to sickness and premature death. Boredom can take its toll quickly or slowly. We can have boring days, weeks, or even lives. This boredom, if not remedied, will turn into hemlock and slowly devour us. We first lose our senses of interest, excitement and pleasure. Once these are gone, our other faculties begin to atrophy. According to Georges Bernanos: *"The world is eaten up by boredom.... You can't see it all at once. It is like dust. You go about and never notice, you breathe it in, you eat and drink it. It is sifted so fine, it doesn't even grit on your teeth. But stand still for an instant and there it is, coating your face and hands. To shake off this drizzle of ashes you must be for ever on the go."*

Boredom is not our enemy, even though it can be. Boredom is an ally meant to spur and lead us to meaningful activity. It is the biological means for introducing change into our otherwise drab lives. If we are aware, we interpret the body's messages as inducement to introduce change and act constructively. If we are asleep, we allow boredom to drive us to harmful activities, age and die prematurely.

### *Personal Experience*
### *A Day at Work*

I went to bed around 10:30 p.m. I was fully awake at 1:30 a.m. I knew I should get up and write. Finally, after resisting, I got up. I walked around the house and checked on our two daughters. I went to my work room and stayed there for a short while doing nothing in particular. I decided that I wanted to get back in bed. I lay awake until around 4:00 a.m. The alarm clock woke me at 5:30 a.m. I was in deep sleep and struggled to get up. It was Friday morning and while I thought about staying home, I went to work.

I did uninteresting but necessary activities most of the day with numerous interruptions. Finally, it was time to go home. Suddenly, I felt a surge of energy. I was free. I was all done with work - until next Monday.

Why would anyone care to lengthen their lives for the sake of doing menial, boring and meaningless work? Most people who go to work wish their lives away. They cannot wait to go home. They cannot wait until it is the weekend. They cannot wait until they retire. It seems that we are wasting our lives away, waiting from one activity to the next. I will really start living after work, we say to ourselves. By then we are too tired and drained to do much. Besides, we have other obligations. There are the children and their activities and demands. There are friends and family with their needs. There is the house with its maintenance. There is the garden, the yard. . . .

Perhaps we can really live when it is the weekend. By then we feel like taking it easy. We worked very hard during the week, we reason. It is time now for rest and relaxation. So, we mostly "rest" doing nothing in particular. But how can we rest and enjoy ourselves unless we first engage in activities that get us tired? Resting *after* we get tired from active involvement makes sense. Resting from boring activities that mentally drain us is not relaxing. Mental boredom requires active relaxation—play. Not being too good at play since we are adults now, we do not live and enjoy ourselves over the weekend either.

We can really start living when we retire, we reason. There will be no alarm clocks to wake us up. There will be no bosses to deal with, no organizations or family dependents that demand our energy and time. But even then, we will find reasons and excuses as to why we cannot fully enjoy ourselves. If we have been making excuses all these years, what is to stop us then? The habit of postponing our enjoyment of life will have taken hold, with roots as deep as our many years of procrastination. At this stage, change is almost impossible. There is only one course left. We take the plunge and go through the Mother of All Changes—death.

This pattern of waiting, always waiting, like Samuel Beckett's *Waiting for Godot,* is one of the main reasons people do not live long, healthy and passionate lives. As Richard Bach wrote in *Jonathan Livingston Seagull:*

> *Jonathan Seagull discovered that boredom and fear and anger are the reasons that a gull's life is so short, and with these gone from his thought, he lived a long fine life indeed.*

To live better and longer, we must want it. To want something, it must appeal to our senses. It is meaningless to remain alive for the sake of adding years to our age. We must live to add life to our years by engaging in meaningful activities from which we derive pleasure, meaning and joy. To live longer and better, we must never let a job get in the way of our living.

For most, work is a necessary, but unwelcome activity. The term work engenders visions of labor, effort and drudgery. Work does not have to be any of these. Work can be *love made visible,* as Kahlil Gibran writes in *The Prophet.* This cannot happen unless we find meaning in what we do and make work be our play.

There is a direct relationship between aging and the meaning we attribute to what we do, between how much we appreciate life and how well and long we live. To be motivated to live a long, healthy and meaningful life, we must change our beliefs about work and ourselves. We must live a life we truly want to promulgate. We must keep on craving playfulness, excitement, challenge, novelty, adventure and discovery. These are the true exterminators of boredom and the elixir of youth, health and longevity. We live best when we live the life we enjoy and love.

## 6. It Was An Accident—I Was Reading In Bed And I Just Fell Asleep

> *I don't believe in accidents. There are only encounters in history. There are no accidents.*
>
> Elie Wiesel

Some people read in bed and fall asleep. Others watch TV and fall asleep. Still others drift into sleep after making love. If these people wanted to ease into sleep, it was a conscious decision on their part to end up asleep. One way or another, these people prepared for sleep by setting up the appropriate environment and by being in bed. Similarly, during our last days, we prepare for death, whether this preparation is intentional and conscious, or subconscious.

Falling asleep, just as getting killed, may seem accidental. However, accidents do not happen as often as we think they do. Most accidents can be prevented. In fact, we often prepare the way for accidents to happen. If we are more aware of causes and the role we play in our experiences, perhaps our experiences will be different and the rate of our accidents will fall sharply.

Proper planning goes a long way in preventing accidents. Just as if we know we have a long journey ahead, we make sure we have enough gasoline in the car, if we do not want to fall asleep accidentally while reading in bed, we should not read in bed. All accidents are caused. While many die as a result of accidents, most are due to carelessness and negligence. Running out of gas is not by accident. Crashing a car through speeding, or while driving under the influence of alcohol is not an accident. Neither is being hit by a car. Things only happen if we are ignorant of the forces at play and we do not prevent them from happening. We can interfere and change outcomes. Unfortunately, we do not exercise our will adequately and our level of awareness is limited. We do not attempt to see beyond the immediate.

The first step in preventing a premature death is to be aware of what we are doing, everyday. Examining our daily life is the beginning of wisdom. What we do today is the foundation of what we end up with tomorrow. If we want to overcome death tomorrow, we must express more life today. We must examine our attitudes, expectations, beliefs, habits, thoughts and feelings for these determine our experiences. It is far better to prevent problems than to deal with them later. Prevention is work up front to conserve time, effort and resources later.

There is much we can do to prevent accidents and ensure that we do not have an untimely death. We can keep ourselves awake, alert and fit. We can examine the tools and implements we use. We can stop abusing our bodies through excessive eating, drinking, drugs and inappropriate behavior.

We know that if we ate the right foods in lesser quantities; ingested all the required vitamins; kept our immune system strong through merriment, laughter and positive expectations; avoided quick and massive changes to our system; and stayed healthy through moderation, exercise, cleanliness, rest and play, we would have a much better chance at living a long and healthy life. Why, then, do so many people avoid these activities and die prematurely? Why do we not do what we are able to do to enhance our chances to live as well as we possibly can? Why do we knowingly shorten our lives?

Few die a natural death. We mostly kill ourselves. We kill ourselves through what we eat, how we eat, when and how much we eat. We kill ourselves through drugs; lack of hygiene, exercise, pleasure, laughter, play and creativity. We kill ourselves by abandoning our purpose and ideals and by building mounds of stress and swamps of fears, guilt and ignorance. We kill ourselves, actively or passively, slowly or quickly, with our own commissions or omissions. Finally, we kill ourselves by creating and fulfilling our own prophesies, by assuming that we have lived long enough and that it is time to die. We are not the victims of circumstances that we think we are. We are not as helpless as we make ourselves appear. We frequently permit events to overtake us. We participate in these events, even painful ones, for one reason or another. We are responsible for our lives and our deaths. Just as we killed Christ and claimed that He came to die, we kill ourselves and claim that it was time to die anyway.

### *Related Experiences*

Accidents seem to have a life of their own. People appear to get killed in what seems "unavoidable accidents." People die in plane crashes, train wrecks and car collisions. Princess Diana got killed in a car wreck. She was 36 years old. The son of a friend of ours was recently riding his bike when he had a flat tire, ran into a post, fell unconscious and drowned in a puddle of rain. He was thirty-one years old.

From the looks of it, we appear to be helpless in the face of accidents. I believe that there is more to it than what at first is apparent. Like reading in bed and falling asleep, to encounter an accident, we must first be there. This is a matter of choice. Thus, most accidents are potentially preventable. However, we do not attempt to prevent something whose outcome we do not know at the time. I believe that on the subconscious level we are much more in tune with events than what we are conscious of. We prevent far more accidents than we are aware of. For we only know of accidents after they take place. We have no idea how many we prevent and avoid. We have heard of many cases where individuals, for one reason or another, avoid an almost certain calamity. Additionally, even though many seem to die of accidents, many more are saved from the same accidents. It is my belief that we do not even get sick accidentally let alone die from it. One way or another, we play a role in our lives. Ignorance is acquiescence and not an excuse.

We tend to make too many excuses and lay blame where it does not belong. Irresponsibility and lack of accountability are prevalent. We routinely give up our power of choice and action to the professionals for they know more than we do. We abdicate the responsibility of caring for our bodies, minds and souls. We live and die irresponsibly. This is our choice. There is an alternative. We can take back our lives and live responsibly and with awareness. If a hair does not fall off our heads without the knowledge of our Father, nothing happens to us without our consent. If we are connected to the Father within, we can be aware of what we need to know and do.

One day when I got sick, I wondered if there was anything I could have done to prevent it. I was told that I got sick because of the germs that I had. I am exposed to germs all the time. Why do I fight them off successfully often, but at certain times, I fail and get sick? What role do I play in the outcome? I soon discovered numerous reasons why I allow myself to get sick. If I do not want to face another boring day at work, then I wish sickness upon myself as a way to get out of going to work. If I am working too hard and do not allow myself rest, then I invite sickness to force myself to rest. Sometimes when there is a disease going around and I am exposed to people who have it, I let myself get sick in the spirit of community. Obviously, I do not get sick every time I am exposed to disease. I select not only the time of illness, but how long it lasts as well. At times I get sick to get attention, to cleanse my body, to strengthen my immune system, or to be like everyone else who gets sick. One way or another, I play a role in my health and sickness.

Disease is a dis-ease, a state of imbalance. We get sick to announce the imbalance and as a way to restore balance. Germs on their own however, do not make the body sick. There are animals that eat carrion, gorge themselves on cadaver and drink from dirty streams. These animals do not get sick from the germs that can kill us. We get sick, not necessarily because of the bacteria, but because of what we have adapted to. We get sick because we feel dis-ease at what we are eating. We feel dis-ease because our established culture does not allow for certain conditions to coexist with its own. Our bodies, emotions and minds constitute a specific culture. They form the "soil", the womb, that nurtures or rejects the different "seeds" we plant, or find their way there. If what we take in, be it food, germs, thoughts, ideas, or feelings, does not fit our already established culture, it is considered an intruder. The body tries to get rid of the intruder one way or another. A battle ensues and sickness can manifest.

Certain thoughts and beliefs act as germs. They weaken our defenses and actually prepare us for disease. If we believe that we can deal with any situation and trust our bodies and give them all they need to do their part, then we are in control of our lives. If we feel that we are victims and anything can invade us, then we are helping the invaders. We have read how Genghis Khan conquered nations by spreading rumors about the invincibility of his army. We also know of the placebo effect and how people get well thinking that they have received medicine when, in fact, all they were administered was sugar water. The reverse is also true. If beliefs can make us well, they can also make us sick.

## 7. I Wanted to Sleep and Dream

*To those who are awake, there is one world in common, but, of those who are asleep, each is withdrawn into a private world of his own.*

Heraclitus

We choose few things in life. We inherit most of what we end up with. Most of us do not select the country or the political system under which we live. Few of us consciously formulate our beliefs. We end up inheriting the beliefs of our parents and tribe. Even though it appears that we select our careers, we mostly settle for what is available and take jobs out of necessity. There are those who live the life they love, but the vast majority merely manage to survive. Most live and die as a result of "natural selection" and by accident. Few grab life by the horns and tame it to comply with what they want and decide upon. Even though we believe we are endowed with choice and free will, we seldom exercise them.

Choice is a tremendous power, but only if we practice it. We can choose when to go to bed, sleep and with practice experience the dreams we want. Equally, we can decide when to undertake the long sleep and what kind of "dreams" we will have. We can choose to go to bed willingly and free ourselves of our bodies and allow our true nature, our inner self, to roam and express itself in unencumbered creativity. We can choose to do the same when we die. We can experience death as a "freedom song."

If sleep is akin to death, then dreams are what we experience after we die. We enter a new dimension where we engage in cycles of creativity, rehearsal and preparation. We go through several of these until we are ready to wake up once more in a new body. Then, we forget most of the preparations and get immersed in our physical reality. Once in a while we remember some of our dreams and the experiences from one state bleed through to the other side. Our "wakeful" and "dream" states are connected and influence each other. We are awake or dreaming based on which side of the fence we find ourselves.

Just as we dream several dreams in one sleep cycle, we live many lives within one life time. Equally, we die many small deaths before we undertake the big one. With each life and death, we outgrow our older limiting shells, don new and more brilliant apparel and become more awake. As we wake up, we become more aware of our choices, actions and their impacts.

The ancients considered dreams as communications from the gods. They trusted their dreams, sought interpretations and then acted upon them. In modern times, we seldom take our dreams seriously. Yet dreams can be therapeutic, creative and highly enjoyable. They can provide us insight into our fears, fantasies, or deep rooted beliefs. Dreams can give us the answers we seek, lead to breakthroughs in our understanding and can even provide us a glimpse of the future. They can engender peace, excitement, release and act as an escape mechanism.

We dream because we exist on more than one plane. We are multi-dimensional. Just as easily as we drift from one reality into the next through dreaming and wakefulness, we move from one life to the next through death and rebirth. Each dream has a life of its own and is analogous to a "real" life. We live two lives and in two worlds: awake in the physical and asleep in our dreams. Dreams are creative acts and in their own state are as real as wakeful events. We do not label a dream as "unreal"—we do not even know that we are dreaming while we are dreaming. If we never woke up, would we ever know that the experiences we had while dreaming were only dreams?

## 8. Dissolving the Corporation-

> *. . . you are dust, and to dust you shall return.*
>
> *Gen. 3:19*

To thrive, a corporation must fulfill a purpose by providing goods or services that satisfy the needs of its customers. Since we are a corporation we, too, must have a need to fulfill and a service to render. This is our motive for being and the reason behind forming our corporation, the body.

The first and foremost activity we undertake immediately after conception is the formation of our corporation—the body. We do this for one obvious reason: to experience physical reality. We build our bodies to experience the joys, the sorrows, the agonies and the glories of being alive in a physical body here and now in this world. If this is the primary reason for forming the body, then we must experience life as fully as possible. We must train our eyes to see with a sense of marvel, our ears to hear with amazement, our skins to feel with titillation, our taste buds to savor and our nostrils to be intoxicated with fragrances and perfumes. If experiencing physical reality is not the motive for being here on earth, why else did we form the body?

Obviously, something is responsible for holding and keeping the body together. What is it? **It is we who hold the body together through our motives, intentions, desires, dreams, hopes and aspirations. As long as our bodies serve our purpose, we maintain and sustain them. As the reasons for living are slowly depleted, we give up on life, age, dissolve the corporation and die.**

It is we, as the executive officers and the board of trustees for our corporation, (the body), that make the decisions about our life, aging and death. Unfortunately, we are seldom aware that we are the decision makers. We mostly live and function in a passive state, a state of oblivion, unaware of our responsibilities and the subconscious decisions we make. Whether we function from the conscious or the subconscious, it is we who decide the fate of our bodies. Ultimately, it is we who decide to accelerate or slow down our aging, to maintain or dissolve the corporation. *Whose life is it anyway?*

We dissolve our corporation, the body, for one of two reasons; either to satisfy our own need, or to serve the needs of humanity. When we dissolve our corporation through death, we sever our link not only to our body, the "corpus", but to our larger corporation—humanity, as well. We do this consciously or subconsciously. This is obvious when we undertake dangerous and heroic acts. We sacrifice ourselves because deep down we know that life is a process and we are part of this process and as such do not die. We know that we are a mere cell in the body of humanity. This knowledge is not always conscious. Yet, we carry the memory of this knowledge in our genes, psyche and soul. Just as we carry the memory of many dreams in our bodies, we carry the memory of many lives in our personality even though our ability to recall these memories is rudimentary. We are a living library. We are oblivious to a lot contained within us.

We receive many benefits from our family, race, and the nation into which we are born. We receive security, the knowledge we start with and the boundaries to function within. In return, we are expected to give back to our family, race and nation when the need arises. At times, we do this by dissolving our corporation. When we do, we give up everything we inherited from our tribe. This includes the rules, laws and traditions of our tribe; our sex, race, skin color and the country of our birth. What we inherit is like the garments we wear. We must change these periodically, for our size and needs change as we grow up. These garments are incidental to the self. They provide the environment that we need for certain experiences. Just as our clothes provide us protection, our inheritance from our race provides us the boundaries within which we can experience and grow *for a while.*

As infants we require diapers and baby clothes. As adults we need larger clothes. If we live in the desert, we need different clothes than if we lived in the arctic. As our needs for garments vary, so does our need for various experiences. One set of circumstances is not enough. We cannot know what it is like to be a woman, unless we live as one. To know what it is like to be red, black, white, or yellow we must walk in their shoes. To have the chance to experience many nationalities, genders and bodily characteristics, we must be able to break loose of the hold each one has over us. Death enables us to let go of these peripherals and to shed our garments. Through death, we can be free of all that we identify with. By letting go of these, we have an opportunity to try something else—enter a new school, under a different set of circumstances and with a brand new set of accouterments.

Life is unlike any school in that it has an unlimited number of classrooms and grades. Yet, we are not required to go from one grade to the next. We can skip grades or we can quit altogether. There is no one to force us to stay in school. We learn for ourselves. After being in a school for many years, we get fed up with school and learning. We yearn for a break. We cry out for rest, for a moment of peace that recharges us, a moment of separateness that allows our soul respite and time to reflect and digest the past experiences. We decide to dissolve the body as a corporation in favor of a new enterprise starting fresh using a brand new body that is unencumbered with unnecessary burdens. After a long and full life, we begin to lose our zest for living. We cease dreaming of adventure. We allow the quality of our lives to deteriorate. We no longer cope with change easily. We are no longer challenged by the opportunities presented to us. Our memories are full. We do not wish for more experiences. Contentment sets in. Activities which excited us when we were younger no longer grab our interest. Life loses its appeal. It does not hold the value for us that it once did.

We have come to the end of our day and just as surely as night follows day, the "night" of our lives descends upon us. The lights are out and the curtains are drawn. We are ready for sleep and dreaming. The corporation we formed and cared for has served its purpose. We are at our self-appointed destination. We have arrived. This day has ended. The corporation is dissolved.

As we close our eyes and abandon ourselves to sweet sleep and creative dreams, we bid our farewell and with the *Prophet* by Kahlil Gibran[2] say:

*"Fare you well, people of Orphalese.*
*This day has ended.*
*It is closing upon us even as the water-lily upon its own tomorrow.*
*What was given us here we shall keep,*
*And if it suffices not, then again must we come together and together stretch*
*our hands unto the giver.*
*Forget not that I shall come back to you.*

*A little while, and my longing shall gather dust and foam for another body.*
*A little while, a moment of rest upon the wind, and another woman shall bear me."*

---

2. Gibran, Kahlil. *The Prophet.* Alfred A. Knopf, New York: 1973 page

STAGE 6

# *Release Your Brakes*

*The history of the world is none other than the progress of the consciousness of freedom.*
Georg Hegel

As we journey through life, we follow a path guided by our interests, needs and circumstances. Our path could be narrow and tortuous, or it could be wide and paved like a super highway. Most follow a pre-existing path. Some create their own paths as pioneers and entrepreneurs. We are not accustomed to search and find out what available paths are best suited for our needs, or what we can build. We tend to travel on any road we happen to find ourselves on or just take the first road we encounter that satisfies our needs. Once we are on a path, we are like vehicles moving on the highways, or the byways of life. We can enjoy the drive best if we feel comfortable with ourselves, our vehicles and have an idea as to why we are on the road and where do we intend to go. It is easiest to travel if we pick a well-paved road and use a highly functional vehicle. Just like any vehicle in motion, how well we fare in life depends on several factors:

1. the condition of the vehicle—the body, its emotions and mind;
2. the road—our jobs, careers, hobbies and interests;
3. the weather—our environment and circumstances;
4. availability of fuel—our energy, wants, needs, hopes, aspirations and passions;
5. how well we know the vehicle and the roads—our skills and abilities;
6. how clear we are about our destination, or how well is the trip mapped out—our goals and plans and how ready and prepared we are;
7. traffic—our relationships; and
8. our skills as drivers—how well we use our circumstances and the qualities we develop and use.

Skilled drivers follow a map, change lanes when appropriate, vary their speed, fuel up, stay alert and take a break when necessary. They adapt and drive based on the vehicle they have and the other vehicles around them. They look out for pertinent signals to slow down, speed up, yield, stop, change course, or take a detour.

We can choose to be skilled drivers on the highway of life by mastering our vehicle, mapping out the trip, choosing the best highways, waiting for or creating the proper circumstances and by being ready and prepared. We can glide with the least effort toward our destination. We can also choose to move about aimlessly hoping that eventually we will arrive. We can hinder, not only our progress, but the traffic as well. We can even cause accidents and endanger lives.

Whatever we decide to do, we reap accordingly. As we give, we receive, and as we plant, we harvest. The fact remains that we are already in a vehicle and on the road. What we must decide is where we want to go, how to best proceed, and how we feel about the trip.

## Release Your Brakes

One of the main features of a good vehicle are reliable brakes. Good brakes are critical to our journey on the highway of life. Yet brakes should be used sparingly—only when necessary to slow down or stop. During normal driving, the brakes must be fully released. Whereas a vehicle has few brakes, we can have many. These brakes not only slow us down, but can completely stop our progress toward the abundant life that is ours to claim. Our brakes take the form of ignorance, fear, pain, suffering, guilt, shame, resentment, envy, jealousy, hate and a host of other negative emotions, habits, attitudes, expectations and beliefs. Some of these we have had for so long that we do not even know that we have them. If we live with something long enough, we adapt to it and it becomes like a second nature. We cannot move very fast or go far in life if we live with our brakes frequently applied. If we are serious about living the possible life, we must release our brakes and glide freely. Even though brakes come in many forms and shapes, they all have one thing in common: they are restraints. To restrain is to hold back. If we want to be held back, then we should keep our brakes applied. Otherwise, we must release them like we would a burnt match.

To release our brakes, we must know what brakes we have on and why we applied them in the first place. There are good reasons for applying brakes once in a while. We have brakes because they are needed. Keeping brakes on after their purpose is served is the problem. We tend to forget to release our brakes. Over time these applied brakes (buried negative emotions) become compacted and heavy. They turn into a burden which we carry along and a malaise that infests the body, mind and soul. We get so used to carrying these burdens that we seldom know that we have them. Yet they are there, hidden like a virus, covertly sapping us of our vitality.

I have had many opportunities to feel the effects of brakes

in my life. For instance, when my daughter wanted to stop at the Seven-Eleven store after soccer practice one evening because she was thirsty, I gladly drove her to the store. When she spent five dollars buying snacks, I felt compelled to tell her that spending that much money on snacks was wasteful. I felt an uncontrollable urge to lecture her about the wise use of money. Even though I knew my daughter rarely wastes money, I lectured her never-the-less. Why did I do it even though I felt stupid later for doing it? We can certainly afford to waste the money. Besides, how could that be a waste if my daughter wanted the snacks? Why the fuss?

Childhood memories. As a child and through my teenage years, I rarely had enough money for necessities so I applied my brakes on all of my spending. I had to use the little money I had wisely. Since it was a struggle for me to get money for school supplies and I had to ask my father several times and give him a few days advanced notice before he would give me a dime or a quarter for a pencil or a notebook, I became seared with poverty consciousness. Thus, lodged deep within me is a fear—fear of not having enough. This fear clouds my awareness and tinges my consciousness. The memories from my childhood are still a force in my life. Unless I release these brakes, I will not have the relationships I want with my children. I will not teach them how to live life abundantly. My behavior is certainly not consistent with what I want them to learn. I must rid myself of my poverty consciousness.

Just as the best way to eliminate a bad habit is to replace it with a good one, so it is with these negative conditions. Most are simple to release. All we need to do is to let go of what is no longer needed and focus on what we want instead and practice it repeatedly until a new habit forms. If, for example, we are infested with poverty consciousness, guilt, shame, resentment, envy, jealousy and hate, we can let go of these by focusing on their complementary emotions and by taking the appropriate actions. If these are the poi-

## Release Your Brakes

sons then, we can inoculate ourselves with their antidotes: prosperity consciousness, praise, esteem, compassion, forgiveness, contentment, admiration and love. Since applying brakes consumes energy, releasing our brakes avails us with energy. With an abundance of energy, we can take action, propel ourselves and achieve.

Releasing a brake is letting go of resistance. Yet resistance has survival benefits. However, misused resistance can deny us much pleasure, adventure and growth. When my boss asked me to take an Assembly Language Coding (ALC) class recently, my immediate response was resistance. I did not want to take the class. Not having a good reason to refuse, I agreed to do it. The class was six weeks long, five days a week and required the use of a great deal of my personal time for studying. To pass, I was required to write three programs that executed error-free and take three three-hour tests with 70% being the passing grade. When I started class on the second day having missed the first day, my stress level was very high. It did not help knowing that only 4 out of the 18 students from the previous class had passed. In a couple of days, I realized that I was getting sick. My throat was sore and my ears were congested. Subconsciously, I was trying to find a way to get out of having to take this course. A couple of days later, while studying at night, my wife stopped by and watched me struggle through conversion problems. "This is fun," she said. "I took ALC years ago and I really enjoyed it." It was shocking to hear her say that. For me, the class was anything but fun. It was stressful, demanding and long. I tried to brush off what my wife said, but could not. Her statement kept playing back in my head. Initially, I attempted to resist the implications. But the thought kept coming back to me. What if I *make* this training fun? What if I *pretend* that it is fun? I felt that I should give this option a chance. I began to view my experiences with ALC as fun. I kept saying to myself and meaning it: *this is fun. This is really lots of fun.* Soon everything changed. Instead of being a difficult subject, it became fun and easy. I took my first test and did very well. Everything had changed. The stress was gone. I was healthy once more.

What caused the change? By transforming resistance into an opportunity for challenge and fun, I was able to release my brakes and change a situation where I might have failed into one where I did well and enjoyed myself in the process. We succeed when we recognize our brakes, understand why we apply them and learn when and how to release them.

We live with too many restraints. We apply many brakes unnecessarily. These squelch our ability to live and experience joy, creativity and abundance. Some of these restraints are minor while others are major. Some are temporary while others last for a long time. Some are easy to identify, while others are difficult to detect. Unless we release our major brakes, we cannot live happy and meaningful lives. No life can be rich and no vehicle can move freely on the highway of life with these restraints constantly hovering over us and preventing us from enjoying life. Humanity cannot progress far if it is blinded by ignorance, gripped with fears, held captive by pain and tormented by suffering. These are some of our major brakes. If we want to stop these thieves from plundering us, we must eliminate them from our lives. **Ignorance, Fear, Pain and Suffering** must go first.

### Ignorance

*Everybody is ignorant, only on different subjects.*
Will Rogers

Ignorance is like an uncultivated field. Mostly useless weeds grow in neglected fields. The weeds of ignorance that grow in the mind act like a multi-layered veil. This veil blocks our view, limits our understanding and causes us grief, pain and suffering. To live life in ignorance is to live wasteful and potentially dangerous lives since ignorance can lead to fanaticism, war and destruction.

Ignorance is a multifaceted brake that remains applied until we release it through education and learning. If ignorance governs our lives, it will not only hinder our progress, it might even lead to the demise of our entire species. Admitting that we are ignorant on several fronts is the first step toward gaining the knowledge we need. We must then seek knowledge, gain it and share it freely, sincerely and with love.

It is easy to know when we have fears, are in pain, or suffering. It is more difficult to know if we are ignorant. For unless we open our eyes and see, we do not know that we dwell in darkness. Just as we cannot know we are dreaming until we wake up, we cannot know that we are ignorant until we gain knowledge. We think that we know a lot because of all the advances we have made. In reality however, compared to how much there is to know and how much we can know, we know very little indeed.

Not knowing that we do not know, we live pretending that we do. If we pretend long enough we become convinced that we actually do know. We remain, not only ignorant, but sincerely so. As Martin Luther King, Jr. stated: *"Nothing in the world is more dangerous than sincere ignorance and conscientious stupidity."*

The reason that our lives are filled with violence, disease and poverty is because we are ignorant of so many things. We are oblivious to the true nature of our bodies, minds and souls. We are not cognizant of our responsibilities for ourselves and each other. We are ill informed of the nature of life and death.

Education is the cultivation of the mind with the proper seeds that blossom into happy, healthy and a well adjusted life. It is a process of gradual increase in awareness, understanding and expertise. As we add to our knowledge, we push the walls of our ignorance further away from us. We begin to gain freedom and lasting power.

### Personal Experience

One of the areas I am ignorant of, is electronics—how it works and why it works. I use a Walkman to listen to educational tapes on a routine basis as I ride the metro to and from work. The other day I was listening to a tape by Stuart Wilde entitled: *Infinite Self, 33 Steps to Reclaiming Your Inner Power*. I was on tape six, side A when I stopped listening for that day. The next day, I pressed the start button to continue listening to the remainder of the tape. Somehow, unbeknown to me, the auto reverse button was accidentally pushed and side B began to play. Instead of the voice I expected to hear, I got a beeping noise. I stopped and started the tape player several times and each time I got the same beep. I reasoned that the batteries must be weak. At home that evening, I replaced the batteries and tried the tape player again. Once more all I got was beeps. I reasoned that these batteries must be old and drained. I went to the store and purchased new batteries. I tried the tape player and once more all I got was an intermittent beep. I was baffled, but did not give up. I reasoned that perhaps the tape player head was dirty, so I attempted to clean it. I went back to the store and purchased a head cleaning cassette and fluid. After cleaning the player head, I reached into the stack of cassettes I had on my shelf and inserted a randomly selected tape into the player. Success at last. What I heard was voice and not beep. I proclaimed my success to my wife and felt good about what I achieved.

The next day while on route to work, I inserted the *Stuart Wilde* cassette into the player and pressed the play button. Shockingly, there was that beep again. I was puzzled. I thought I had taken care of this problem. I had tested the player the day before and it was playing fine. What happened? I opened the player and took the cassette out. I examined it carefully and stuck it back in. I pressed the play button and listened. Beep, beep and more beeps—one every four seconds. I reasoned that perhaps side B of the tape was defective. I opened the player once more and took the cassette out. I turned it over and stuck it back in. I pressed the play button and listened. This time, I heard a voice. I was glad. At least it was not the player. Believing that side B was defective, I resolved to call the company and request a replacement. To use my remaining time constructively in the metro, I decided to listen to the good side of the tape—side A.

As I neared the end of the tape, I heard Stuart Wilde say: "On the next side of this tape I have prepared for you a theta metronome that is a special 4 second beep to help you relax, clear your mind and deepen your meditation. The entire second side of the tape is the beeping theta metronome." The tape was fine after all and so were the player and the batteries.

Just as darkness persists until dispelled by light, ignorance endures until replaced with knowledge. Where light shines darkness cannot exist. If ignorance is the antigen, education and enlightenment are the antibody. As soon as we know, ignorance is vanquished.

**Fear**

*Fear Fear is the darkroom where negatives are developed.*

E. L.

Fear is an attitude of fright, dread, or alarmed concern. It is an awareness of an actual or imagined danger. It is a feeling that something may happen contrary to one's desires. Fear is a powerful emotion. This emotion may be temporary or may last for a long time. It may be conscious or unconscious.

There is a whole spectrum of feelings associated with fear ranging from natural anxieties to irrational phobias. There are also many kinds of fears. People fear public speaking, the dark, high altitudes, or closed places. Some fear the devil, others God. Some fear death, others full conscious living. Some fear success, others failure. Some fear being by themselves, others being in crowds.

Fear can be induced by ignorance, superstition, authority, natural phenomenon and learned behavior such as guilt. The underlying cause of all fears is a feeling of helplessness in the face of an undesired experience. Fear is based on the notion that we might not be able to handle what may come our way. Fear has its origins in the early stages of humanity's evolution. Faced with violent natural phenomenon such as thunder, lightening and volcanic eruptions, or attempting to escape the jaws of a wild beast, it was natural to experience fear and dread.

Fear is a natural emotion. It prepares us for fight or flight. However, fear in the absence of eminent danger is a heavy burden to carry around. It stifles our effort and paralyzes our initiative. This can lead to frustration, procrastination, depression, disease, pain, lack of will and blocked creativity. Fear can shorten our lives. Needless fear is a pernicious weed that must be plucked out or deprived of nourishment so it may die a natural death.

We can get rid of our fears if we:

- want to be free of fear;
- learn what to do to replace fear with its opposite emotion, confidence; and
- act according to the new emotion, repeating it until it takes root and replaces the old habit of fear.

Like all realities, fear is represented in the mind as images with associated sounds, movements and feelings. The more the "life" of these representations, the more real they seem. The "life" of an image, or a mental representation, is based on its energy content. The bigger, brighter, more detailed and colorful an image is, the more real it is. Hence, the image of what we consider real has a high energy content. It is bright, sharp, detailed, focused, colorful and stable, while the image of what we consider as fictitious is fuzzy, dull, black and white, dim and unstable.

We can overcome our fears by mastering the art of image manipulation in our minds. Since the mind is the laboratory where all negatives (images) are developed and experienced as realities, we can effect a change through directed visualization. We can take the life out of a fearful image and drain its energy. We do this by rendering it small, fuzzy, dull, black and white, dim and unstable. Additionally, we can replace the representation of a fearful event by confidence in our ability to handle anything life brings our way. To replace a fearful image such as that of a snake, instead of seeing in our minds a large, poisonous, colorful, lively, sharply focused snake, we can see a small, friendly, black and white snake that is not well defined. Once this act is repeated vividly several times, the old image with its undesired effects is replaced with the new image and its preferred effects. Additionally, we can focus on the positive aspects we desire instead of the negative ones we want to avoid. Snakes have many admirable features, are useful and have their place in the natural order of things. Most are harmless and play an important role in pest control.

Snakes are the symbol of wisdom. We can personalize this symbol by imagining a friendly snake and using it as the gateway to our inner and wiser self. This symbolic snake can act as our protector, guardian and our resource for knowledge. We can imagine this snake as a pet living in our magical lamp. We rub the lamp and our friendly pet snake bows to us and says: "Your bidding is my wish, what is your command of me today, master?" We can then ask the snake any question we have and rest assured that the answer will come to us at the appropriate time.

In the above example, we need to visualize ourselves as self-assured, relaxed and confident. We must see ourselves as the master, while the snake is our obedient pet and servant. We feel a surge of power within us. We know that nothing can touch us for we are protected. We know that we can handle any situation that presents itself to us. We visualize this a few times with an intense feeling, giving life to the images we form in our minds. We then let go of the images resting assured that the desired results have already taken place and will soon materialize in physical reality.

For added confidence, we can add self-talk to our visualization. We can create a message specific for the occasion, or we can use a passage from an inspirational source. One such passage familiar to many is the 23rd Psalm:

> The LORD is my shepherd, I shall not want; he makes me lie down in green pastures. He leads me beside still waters; he restores my soul. He leads me in paths of righteousness for his name's sake. Even though I walk through the valley of the shadow of death, I fear no evil; for thou art with me; thy rod and thy staff, they comfort me. Thou preparest a table before me in the presence of my enemies; thou anointest my head with oil, my cup overflows. Surely goodness and mercy shall follow me all the days of my life; and I shall dwell in the house of the LORD for ever.
>
> Psalm 23:1–6

It is always helpful to know why we have a fear in the first place. Where, when and how was the first seed planted in the fertile soil of our minds? We can then relive that original event, changing the outcome to suit our needs. Instead of the fearful event that we ended up with, we can change it into a harmless or humorous event. By repeating this visualization, enhanced with positive feelings and self-talk, we can replace the old mental habit of fear with a new program more compatible with what we want for our lives. Just because something happened in the past does not mean that we must live with it forever. We are as powerless as we choose to be, and are as capable as we are knowledgeable and willing to act. We can change our past just as easily as we can shape our future.

*Personal Experience*

Living in the United States availed me with tremendous opportunities. I took advantage of only a few. Like an element in a centrifuge, I found my comfort zone and resting position in life. This state, though much higher than where I started from, was nevertheless far below my potential. After several years of attempting to advance in my career, improve my finances, expand my social contacts and increase my enjoyment of life, I met only limited success. It was as if I had reached a ceiling beyond which I could not progress. At this point, the harder I tried, the more I struggled, and the more difficult the obstacles that got in the way became. I began to question myself in earnest.

Why am I stuck in a groove from which I cannot seem to escape? Why am I frozen at a current level far below my capacity? Why am I not gaining financial independence? What is stopping me? If I clearly know what I want to do with my life, why am I not doing it? If I love to write, speak and publish, why am I procrastinating? What brakes am I applying that are slowing me down? Why am I not releasing them to live more abundantly?

After persistent questioning for a couple of years, I realized that I was the cause of my own limitations. I had no one to blame but myself. I seemed to have created a glass ceiling and allowed it to stop me every time I could have moved beyond a level that I found comfortable. I had a well established comfort zone beyond which I dared not venture. Where did this comfort zone come from and why is it so limiting?

The answer startled me. I am gripped by a fear lodged deep within me that allows me to progress only so far before I sabotage my own advancement. This fear had crippled and slowed me down every time I was ready to take off. *I was afraid of success*—to succeed beyond my artificial comfort zone.

Success to a great extent is establishing an equilibrium between the expectations we have of ourselves and our actual reality. If our expectations and experiences of reality match, we will be content and happy. If these two are out of synch, we will feel out of place, stressed and unhappy. We will attempt to change our expectations, or reality, until a balance is established.

Because of my earlier experiences in life, I did not feel that I deserved much. I suffered from low self-esteem. I stored these childhood feelings as images in my mind, which acted as a barometer indicating to me the level to which I could comfortably rise. I had a value attached to my worth and I made sure that I remained within the boundaries of that value. Once I attained the level I expected of myself, subconsciously, I made sure that I maintained that level.

We are often prisoners of our own expectations. We tend to float in life at levels consistent with these expectations, guided by the images we house, and the barometers we set for ourselves as to what is normal for us. What is normal for us, is what we feel comfortable with. If we grow up in a clean home we cannot be comfortable with mess and filth. If we grow up in a messy home we feel at home with mess. We do not even see it as mess. If we grow up in riches, we will attempt to preserve these. If all we have known are lacks, we will not feel at home with abundance until we change our expectations. Like a guided missile, we will seek and manifest what our consciousness allows based on the images we house in our minds. These set our comfort levels which we struggle to maintain. We rise and fall to preserve these settings—our comfort zones. We are successful to the extent that we are content with our comfort zones.

Success rests on three groups of factors. First; our hopes, aspirations, dreams, goals, expectations, incentives and our vision for the future. Second; our abilities, skills and the actions we take based on established plans. Third; appropriate environments which include the resources we need and the relationships we establish to this environment. We are successful to the extent that we can use our hopes and aspirations to propel us into action, using our skills and abilities to mold our environment and create the realities that match our comfort zones. Successful individuals adjust their comfort zones on an ongoing basis. Thus, they are seldom content for long with what they have attained. I, on the other hand, could not adjust my comfort level even though I knew that I could accomplish far more. I had the goals, the intelligence, the skills and the appropriate external environment to be far more successful than I was demonstrating. What I lacked was the appropriate internal environment. I was driving at a low speed believing it to be the safe speed. I did not, however, feel safe. I was immobilized by fear—fear of success. For if I succeeded beyond my comfort zone, I would feel out of place and undeserving. To ensure that I did not succeed beyond my comfort level, I sabotaged myself. I applied my brakes and slowed down. I fell into a rut. Any time I attempted to go beyond my comfort zone, instantly I applied my brakes.

The human mind will not, knowingly, house incongruities. My early childhood experiences were of failure, lack, shortage, misery, abuse, struggle and indications of worthlessness. What helped me avoid total self-destruction was self-talk. I would tell myself, repeatedly, that one day these circumstances would change. I will have a better life. One day, I will be successful. However, the realities I lived took their toll. Even though I could cover the obvious aspect of low self-esteem, deeper ones remained, influencing my life. I was asleep to their hidden impacts and the havoc they were wreaking in my life. I was still afraid to succeed even though I now lived in an environment totally conducive for success. I became like a butterfly that was kept in a closed jar for so long that even though the jar was open, I still refused to fly away for I did not see the opening. Somehow, I lost my innate ability to fly free, becoming a prisoner of my own jail. Like admitting to an addiction, it is easier to get rid of a fear once we recognize its existence. Accepting the condition is the first step toward implementing a solution. So, I admitted to myself that I was indeed afraid to succeed. Realizing that I had a fear, I resolved to act.

Since my fear of success was the result of beliefs I had about myself, I had to replace these with new ones that allowed me to progress beyond my old comfort zone. Once these new beliefs took root, they helped to liberate me, release my brakes and set me free.

Here is what I did to eliminate my fear of success:

1. I brought the images of my old comfort zone with their associated sounds and feelings to the fore-front of my mind.

    I sought the origin of these images, how and why they formed, what purpose they served in the past and what role they played now. I saw these images as alive as I could imagine them: vivid, colorful, sharp, detailed, focused and stable.

2. I transformed the images.

    I dimmed the lights on these images, and sucked the life out of them by shrinking their sizes, rendering them colorless and de-stabilizing them. I made them slowly shrivel and disappear.

3. I immediately replaced the old images with new ones.

    I created new mental images embodying all the features desired in a totally successful and unlimited life style. I visualized intently with great feeling all the details I desired. I added color, vividness, clarity and stability. I imbued these images with positive emotions such as joy, love and thankfulness.

4. I repeated this process.

    Since it takes about three weeks of practice before a new habit forms, I repeated the above process for twenty-one days, each time caring for the new images as seeds planted in the soil of my consciousness. Slowly but surely, these seeds took root and began to grow. My mind was transformed. The weeds were replaced with desired plants. After I replaced the undesired images with the desired ones, I began to notice a difference. I felt lighter and much more energetic and I was not hesitating to take action to succeed.

It is important to realize that success or failure is a personal matter. It is of little consequence for others to consider us a success when we do not. Similarly, it should not matter much if others consider us a failure when we are doing what we want and are happy and content. What is important is how we view ourselves, our comfort level and the expectations we have of ourselves. For example; even after I got rid of my fear of success, I decided not to pursue higher challenges at work. This was a conscious decision due to other plans I have for my life. It is far more important for me to be successful at home spending time with my family than getting promotions at work. It is far more relevant for me to have enough free-time for important activities outside of work than to earn more money. To paraphrase Christ: of what value is it to gain all the money and prestige in the world at the expense of losing yourself by not doing what you value most.

## Pain and Suffering

*The art of life is the avoiding of pain.*

*Thomas Jefferson*

We cannot function optimally if we are constantly in pain and are suffering. Pain is a cross that we must bear for it is part of our biological makeup. However, like taxes, we do not have to suffer any more than we absolutely must. We can avoid pain, but once we have it, it cannot be ignored.

Pain demands our attention and immediate action at the expense of all else. We must learn to reckon with pain for it is not a switch that we can simply turn off.

Suffering is similar to pain in many respects. The major difference between the two is their cause. While the cause of pain is physical, that of suffering is mental. There are many causes for pain and suffering, some of which are self-inflicted. Athletes, such as marathon runners, gymnasts and boxers willingly go through pain to reach their objectives. So do women in labor. They accept pain as part of the reward. Greatness often involves some degree of pain. A life devoid of all pain is a life lacking the values and lessons of some of life's richest experiences. Just because we experience pain, it does not follow that we must suffer. We have a choice in whether or not we suffer. We can suffer whether or not there is pain involved.

Pain and suffering can be experienced by individuals, races and nations. It can be caused by nature, self, or others. It can be a reaction or an outright persecution. One of the tragedies of humanity is that often those who suffer the most are the same ones who inflict pain and suffering on others once they are in the position to do so. We will never end pain and suffering if revenge or "an eye for an eye" is our motive. If pain and suffering are to end, we must end them in ourselves. We must stop our participation and contribution.

One of the greatest stories about suffering is that of Job of the Old Testament. Job was a very wealthy and blessed man. He had all he ever needed to live a happy and content life, and he did nothing to deserve otherwise. It so happened that the Lord God and Satan made a wager, a bet, as to whether or not Satan could win over Job from God.

> *Now there was a day when the sons of God came to present themselves before the LORD, and Satan also came among them. The LORD said to Satan, "Whence have you come?" Satan*

*answered the LORD, "From going to and fro on the earth, and from walking up and down on it." And the LORD said to Satan, "Have you considered my servant Job, that there is none like him on the earth, a blameless and upright man, who fears God and turns away from evil?" Then Satan answered the LORD, "Does Job fear God for nought? Hast thou not put a hedge about him and his house and all that he has, on every side? Thou hast blessed the work of his hands, and his possessions have increased in the land. But put forth thy hand now, and touch all that he has, and he will curse thee to thy face." And the LORD said to Satan, "Behold, all that he has is in your power; only upon himself do not put forth your hand." So Satan went forth from the presence of the LORD.*

Job 1:6–12

Job experienced a tremendous amount of suffering. Everything he had was taken away from him; his children, his wealth and his health. After a prolonged period of agony, even his wife encouraged him to renounce God. However, Job did not renounce God and the Lord God won the wager with Satan.

Regardless of what Satan was doing in the presence of the Lord and the wagering that went on at an innocent man's expense, one thing is clear: suffering is the womb out of which character is born. It is we who decide how long the labor will be and what to make of the experience. Even with his great and prolonged pain, Job adhered to his mental framework. He was thankful even as he suffered.

We, too, can train ourselves to look for the good in things. For every experience has two sides to it. The same experience can be the cause of agony for some and exhilaration for others. Life can, at times, be like a roller coaster ride. We can scream our heads off with excitement and exhilaration or out of fear and trepidation. If there is a **season** for everything under the sun, there is a **reason** for everything as well. Picking the reasons that empower us instead of the ones that disable us is our ultimate choice and the noblest exercise of our freedom of will.

Pain evolved as a means of alerting us that something is wrong within our system. Pain compels us to pay attention to a particular area, or to change the way we treat the body. We could have as easily evolved a painless system, like a switch that lights up whenever we needed to be alerted. We did not. Pain evolved because of the critical roles it plays. Until we understand these and find alternative ways to achieve the same results, pain will persist. If we want to eliminate pain from our lives, we must learn its lessons some other way. We cannot depend on pain for our important lessons and not want it at the same time.

We learn through our experiences. However, for our experiences to have value, we must feel their effects. We invite pain into our lives because it helps us feel life intensely. Pain and suffering are optional. As long as there is a need for pain and suffering, they will be with us to stay. Once they serve no purpose in our lives, we will cease to experience them.

The following are some of the functions pain and suffering play in our lives. They:

1. help us wake up;
2. enable us to let go;
3. aid our learning and growth;
4. prepare us for pleasure;
5. remind us of our ignorance, or "sin";
6. polish our character and personality; and
7. link us to humanity.

### 1. Pain and Suffering Help Us Wake Up

We are feeling beings. Often, we need to feel something before we appreciate its value. Even though we can learn through reason, we are much less rational than we assume to be. We are fundamentally emotion-oriented people. That is why pain and pleasure are our greatest motivations.

We mostly live out of habit. Even though habits can make our lives easier to manage, they can also bind us to ways that do not serve our purposes. We often persist in our useless ways because it is not easy to break well-established habits. Pain and suffering can force us to rethink our habits.

Inertia is a powerful force. We get used to our routines and find comfort in our rut. We resist change and refuse to take positive action. We wait until we are forced to act. Often, this force for change is pain and suffering. Pain forces us to decide, act and implement change. I drank coffee habitually and my brother smoked heavily for many years. I persisted until I started getting bad headaches anytime I altered my habit of drinking coffee. He resisted change until he had a heart attack. It was only then that we decided to change our habits and get rid of our dependencies on caffeine and nicotine. The headaches and the heart attack helped us to re-evaluate our routines. As a result of the pain, we consciously replaced undesirable habits with more beneficial ones.

Suffering is mental anguish and can result from financial loss, broken friendships and other unpleasant experiences. At times we need to lose something before we appreciate its full value. Other times, we must "pay a price" before we learn a valuable lesson. As a simple example, I know that I should clean my furnace filter monthly. I kept ignoring it until one extremely cold day, the furnace shut down. My family and I had to endure the cold for two days before we managed to get a heating specialist to inspect the furnace. It did not take him long to diagnose the problem. The culprit was a dirty filter. After paying the emergency bill, I resolved to always keep my furnace filter clean.

We do not readily appreciate free-ware. Pain and suffering are the price we pay to discern the true value of something. Once we pay for what we get, we appreciate it more than if it were free.

## 2. Pain and Suffering Enable Us To Let Go

We can never possess the ever-changing, yet we try. We cling to material things beyond their usefulness. We become jealous and possessive. We believe that we can possess anything we desire, including people, especially our children and spouse. How can we assume that we can possess anything when these "possessions" are in a constant state of change? Nothing remains the same. Everything has the "Midas Touch" associated with it. Time is Midas. What time touches does not change to gold, but it changes never-the-less. The belief in our ability to possess and hold onto things that are transitory in nature, is the root cause of much of our pain and suffering.

One of Christ's fundamental teachings is the admonition to give up possessiveness. Christ teaches this valuable lesson by the example of his life.

> *And Jesus said to him, "Foxes have holes, and birds of the air have nests; but the Son of man has nowhere to lay his head."*
> *Matthew 8:20*

The tenets of Christianity as presented in the Sermon on the Mount, reflect a fundamental reality of life: it is impossible to possess for we cannot arrest the flow of life. Therefore, give freely and freely you shall receive.

> *To him who strikes you on the cheek, offer the other also; and from him who takes away your coat do not withhold even your shirt. Give to every one who begs from you; and of him who takes away your goods do not ask them again.*
> *Luke 6:29–30*

The intent behind these verses is not senseless giving. It is understanding the law of life which states that nothing stands still. Everything is a process. We will give up our possessions one after another, sooner or later, for one reason or another. When we are children, we accumulate lots of toys believing that we will always have them. Where are those toys now? We either outgrow the usefulness of our possessions, or they simply wear out, break down, or get lost. Ultimately, when we pass away we leave it all behind. We then give all we have whether we want to or not. Possessiveness is a futile attempt to arrest the flow of life. If life is a flow, our lives must be a flow as well, giving and receiving, freely and joyfully.

Unless we let go of the old, we cannot experience the new. Unless we allow newness into our lives and grow, we stagnate and die. We live by letting go. The more we attempt to hold on, the more we shut ourselves out from the abundance that can come our way. Life is like love. If we only keep it within us and hold onto it without letting it flow, it does not grow and flourish. The more we express love (give), the more it grows and the more we end up with. As we give and let go, we make room for better things to flow into our lives.

When we give up possessiveness, we end up with less to worry about, defend and even pay taxes on. This does not mean giving up owning things. We can own all we want with the understanding that these commodities are transitory in nature. They come our way, we use them, and we let go of them once they serve the purpose for which we acquired them. We then put them back into the flow of things. We circulate and allow others the opportunity to use what we used and thus multiply the benefits of each item by sharing it. As more people share an item, more people will experience abundance as a result of that single item.

After a long while, even our bodies cease to serve a useful purpose. When too many of the body's functions and abilities deteriorate, we lose our vigor, enthusiasm and passion for living. Yet some are afraid to let go of their bodies and die in peace. They attempt to hold onto their bodies at all cost and for as long as they possibly can. They hold onto their bodies believing that they are holding onto self and life. The stronger we hold onto something, the greater the incentive we will require to let go. This incentive is often pain. Because of severe pain, the balance eventually tilts in favor of letting go and overcoming the fear of the unknown. Thus, through pain we let go of something as dear as the body itself. Pain emancipates us from our last perceived possession.

The desire to live and the knowledge that we must die are not contradictory. We can live as well and for as long as we want. But when the time comes to die, we must do it willingly and graciously. We are a mere cell in the body that is humanity. The cell must die so the body may continue to change, adapt and evolve. Even though the cell appears to have died, it merely undergoes transformation. The cell must transform for the body to grow. We must die individually for humanity to continue unfolding.

### 3. Pain and Suffering Aid Our Learning and Growth

If life is a school, pain is often the principal teacher. Pain is the water that softens the ground and prepares the soil for introducing new seeds for growth. Pain is what helps us value and appreciate states we took for granted earlier. Pain helps us prevent disasters by forcing us to take care of inconveniences. When we experience a toothache, we learn to take better care of our teeth. If we ignore our toothache, we might end up losing the tooth.

Pain has been a great teacher for me. From my suffering and lack of family life, I resolved that I would value and esteem my family—as my best friends, partners and beloved. From seeing how my father mistreated his wife and children, I resolved to treat my wife and children lovingly. My wife and I would share responsibilities and support each other. She would be my partner, sweetheart and best friend. Together, we would have only as many children as we could provide for, nourishing and nurturing their material, mental, emotional and spiritual needs. I would show my love for and share my time with my wife and children freely. My early pain was a laboratory from which I learned, grew up and became transformed.

Our option is not whether or not we will learn for we must learn and we will learn. The choice we have is in how we learn. We can learn through awareness and intelligence, or we can do it through pain and suffering.

**4. Pain and Suffering Prepare Us For Pleasure**

Living with pain is like being held hostage. The terrorists in this case are the conditions under which we live. We do not need to be held hostage, but having lived under pain, we can learn from it and use it to appreciate our freedom even more as we get rid of the pain. A hungry person will appreciate food more than someone who has never missed a meal. A traveler will miss his family more than someone who has spent his entire time with them. Similarly, a person who has experienced pain will appreciate pleasure and freedom from pain even more having lived under its yoke.

We tend to take everyday miracles for granted until we can no longer perform them. By experiencing pain in conducting normal activities such as walking, bending, running, sleeping and eating, we appreciate these activities even more once we regain our abilities and the pain is gone. Generally, the longer it takes for the pain to go away, the hungrier we are for that experience without the pain. If we lose our jobs and suffer as a result, then that pain prepares us to enjoy our new jobs even more once we get employed. Lack not only makes the heart grow fonder, it teaches us value and appreciation as well.

Unless we are living with excitement, we are not living at all. Unless we are enjoying life, we might as well be dead. For all practical purposes, unless we live with awareness and can exhibit the qualities of life, we are already dead. Christ alluded to this when He stated:

> *Another of the disciples said to him, "Lord, let me first go and bury my father." But Jesus said to him, "Follow me, and leave the dead to bury their own dead".*
> Matthew 8:21–22

## 5. Pain and Suffering Remind Us Of Our Ignorance and "Sin"

While growing up as a young man in the Middle East, some religious fanatics frequently attempted to convert me to their point of view. The foundation of their argument was often the premise that Jesus Christ came and died for *my* sins. They insisted that He came to die for *me*. They attempted to convince me that my sins were so terrible that only the blood of the Son of God could cleanse me. They asserted that everyone was guilty of sin just for having been born. For, according to them, we were conceived in original sin and born into it. They attempted to instill in me the belief that sin was our fate and we could not escape it unless we repented and accepted the Son of God (Jesus) as our personal savior.

I never succumbed to this argument. I could not believe that I was bad enough that anyone should die for me, let alone the Son of God. By accepting the premise that Jesus came to die for our sins, we are simply absolving ourselves of our responsibilities for what we did to Him.

Ignorance and sin are analogous; one is mental while the other is spiritual. According to Christianity, there are two conditions under which everyone is born. One is sin:

> *Therefore as sin came into the world through one man and death through sin, and so death spread to all men because all men sinned—.*
> Romans 5:12

The other is pain:

> *To the woman he said, "I will greatly multiply your pain in childbearing; in pain you shall bring forth children, yet your desire shall be for your husband, and he shall rule over you."*
> *Genesis 3:16*

Our world is full of pain and suffering. Many suffer as a result of ignorance. They simply do not know any better. Others believe that they deserve to suffer because they have "sinned" and the wages of sin are pain, suffering and eventual death.

Sin means different things to different people. For me, sin is a state of ignorance of our true nature. We are "sinful" to the extent that we feel separate from our source because we are ignorant of who we really are. If "sin" is a state of separation from God, our source, ignorance is a state of separation from knowledge and truth. Traditionally, the source of knowledge and Truth is God, or if you prefer, the Cosmic Intelligence. Hence, sin and ignorance are separation from God and the flow of life. The price we pay for being in sin, or in ignorance (separation), is pain, suffering and ultimately death. Being ignorant, we make mistakes. Living unaware of our nature and source, we struggle, suffer and eventually die.

Pain and suffering are the result of ignorance, not a punishment for ignorance. Having the freedom of will entitles us to make mistakes, or even sin. We must, however, bear the consequences of our acts. We are not only free, we are held accountable as well. If we would like to reduce pain in our lives, let us work on reducing our ignorance and isolation from our source.

The price of sin is not pain and suffering after death, but prior to death. Sin, however, is not something we do against God. We do it to ourselves and against nature. I do not believe that God gets offended by our acts if they are based on ignorance. God will not punish us for acting foolishly. We punish ourselves through the consequence of our acts which follow naturally and automatically. We are not born perfect, or meant to be perfect. Only God is perfect. While perfection is our destination, we are never expected to attain it.

Our lives are not governed by chance or fate. They are the result of the decisions and the actions we take. The more we are aware and act responsibly, the less we are apt to make mistakes, suffer and experience pain. Pain is an equal opportunity affliction. Nature is fair in that the same laws apply equally to everyone. If we violate the laws of nature, we experience the consequences as pain and suffering. Through these, we learn to assume responsibility for our lives.

## 6. Pain and Suffering Polish Our Character and Personality

We are born as babies, immature, but with tremendous potential. We live to actualize as many of these potentials as we can. We are each like a tiny universe and just like the universe itself, we are constantly expanding. We can expand at will by actualizing more of our potential. We have a choice in what we pursue and which potential aspects become realized. Often, what causes us to choose one over another is the memory of pain or the expectation of pleasure.

Experiences make us who we are. Often we require pain to bring our best forth. Many of our geniuses had to experience intense pain before they could produce their greatest creations. Ludwig von Beethoven, Mozart and Van Gogh are among the many who because of their suffering produced masterpieces.

If life is a school, our ultimate choice is how we learn. We can do it through pain and suffering, or we can learn through intelligence. For many, pain and suffering are the only way some of life's more important lessons are learned. In the school of life there are many teachers. What matters is education, not where or how we learn. We continue to encounter our limitations and suffer until we learn. When we learn, all these negative conditions will vanish.

### 7. Pain and Suffering Link Us To Humanity

We might not have any idea what the rest of humanity is going through unless we go through comparable experiences ourselves. If we were never cold or hungry, how would we know what the poor and hungry feel like? If we never lost a job, how would we understand the plight of the unemployed? How can we appreciate the pain and suffering of a cancer patient, or the agony of a parent having lost a child, or the mental state of someone who has been through a natural disaster? Our painful experiences join us with the rest of humanity. They are the links that bind and hold us together. Humanity is a gigantic body. If a part of this body is in pain and suffers, the rest must feel the pain and come to the rescue. *The body can heal itself; the aching part, on its own, cannot.*

Pain and suffering link us to each other and to all of life. Through pain we are born and because of pain we wake up and live. Pain can drive us to serve a higher cause and an ideal. If we know what it is like to be discriminated against, we might never want anyone else to have such an experience. We might dedicate our lives for such a cause. Pain and suffering are not inherent in our nature or inevitable. They are states of being. They are real while we experience them, but they do not have to last or have dominion over us. Negative states lose their power once the positive appears. Darkness cannot remain once light shines. Pain cannot abide once pleasure arrives. Fear evaporates in the face of courage and ignorance dissipates in the presence of knowledge.

Painful experiences are like sand paper. They help polish us and smooth our rough edges to reveal the beautiful sculpture hidden within. We are a work of art, a miracle to behold, but only after we are polished and seasoned through the trials and tribulations of life. The more polished we get, the more the light within us, our essence, shines forth. With this light, we see clearer—not only ourselves, but the world as well.

* * * * *

Ignorance, fear, pain and suffering are some of our major brakes. Releasing these requires awareness and effort. We must persist until all of our brakes are released. When we finally release our brakes, we will attain the freedom to transform our drab earth into a vibrant heaven; a heaven created by us, for us and for all the living. With our brakes finally released, our burdens will lighten up considerably. We will be free to soar and live the possible life instead of the mediocre one. By replacing our ignorance with knowledge, we gain true and lasting power. By letting go of our fears, we attain the freedom to soar in the realization of our potential. By eliminating our pains, we can immerse ourselves fully in the joyous experience of living. When we eradicate our suffering, we are then ready to devote our lives to live our purpose and ideal.

STAGE 7

# Take it Easy, Enjoy Yourself, and Do What You Can

*To live is the rarest thing in the world. Most people exist, that is all.*

*Oscar Wilde*

To enjoy life, we must enjoy ourselves for that is all we can enjoy. We must greet each day with enthusiasm if we want to live life abundantly. If you are a woman, revel in being a woman. If you are a man, celebrate being a man. Savor every stage in your life and every role you get to play. When you are a spouse, a parent, a student, or a laborer, be the best you can be for this is your moment in history to demonstrate what you can do in each situation. We are actors and actresses in our current role. This is our opportunity to stamp the event with our uniqueness. We go through each stage of our lives once and for a short duration. If we learn to appreciate whatever comes our way and take full advantage of our opportunities to make a positive contribution, then what we can enjoy and cherish is limited only by our imagination.

Everyone and everything is a perfect expression of the

Cosmic Intelligence. No one can play our role of being who we are better than ourselves. Just as a flower is the perfect flower it can be and a cloud is the perfect cloud it can be, we are also perfect as an expression of the Cosmic Intelligence. There is nothing commonplace in life. There are only common eyes. Even a "common" activity such as talking, walking, or cooking is magical. When we see and experience magic everywhere, we carry that sense of wonder with us. We become transformed and our lives become filled with peace, joy and gratitude. Living becomes sacred.

We are unique to the extent that we distinguish ourselves. Nothing within us or without us is unique in and of itself. Our cells, tissues, organs and systems are not unique. We all share the same human features and characteristics. It is action that sets us apart. It is what we do with what we have that distinguishes us as unique individuals. Thus, even though we have eyes, ears, noses, hands, feet, minds, friends and acquaintances, what we make of these is unique. We can use our eyes, for instance, to see opportunities where others only see obstacles, employ our ears to hear and understand people's needs and concerns, while others pretend to listen. We can create a master-mind group from our relationships, while others get together to gossip, quarrel, or simply kill time. The greatest power we have to shape our lives is the power to think, feel and act with awareness and intent. Through these we can sculpt our lives and fashion our circumstances.

The key to success in life is to either recognize our uniqueness and make the most of it, or to specialize enough and stand out as unique. We do not have to be exceptional to succeed. All we need is to do a few things exceptionally well. If we select a few fundamental activities and become remarkably good at performing them, we can achieve greatness. There are only a few basic laws that govern the universe. There are a little over one hundred elements, out of which the entire universe is composed. There are only twenty-six letters in the English alphabet, out of which the entire language is formed. Of these twenty-six letters, only five or six are vowels. There are only three primary colors, out of which millions of shades of color are created. There are only a few musical notes, a few amino acids and a mere four nucleotides, out of which all the music, all the proteins and all the genetic material are formed. Thus, if we focus our efforts on a few critical skills to live by, such as the seven discussed earlier, then as surely as effects follow causes, we will live healthy, joyous and fulfilled lives.

We must not wait for grand events to make us happy. Rather, we should celebrate each moment with a spirit of gratefulness for the gifts of life. Being thankful is a vitamin that aides our health and hastens our blossoming. To assist us in this process, we can make a list of items for which we are grateful, beginning with being alive, having family and friends.

If we learn to be happy enjoying ourselves, then we will constantly be happy for we always have ourselves. To enjoy ourselves, we should not take ourselves too seriously. We need to relax, laugh and take it easy. If we practice taking it easy, we will not harbor stress and store negative emotions. If we do not accumulate stress, we live longer, healthier and happier lives. Quite often we already have everything we need to be happy.

Once we learn to enjoy ourselves, we must extend outward—determine to enjoy nature, our family, community, country and the world. Just as we can never love anyone more than we can love ourselves, how much we enjoy others is limited by how much we can enjoy ourselves. In a way, to enjoy is the same as to love, for if we love someone we automatically enjoy that person. Hence, to enjoy nature, family, community and the world is to learn to appreciate and love them.

It is easiest to appreciate someone if we can recognize an aspect of ourselves in that person. We can start loving others by noticing common features that we both share. Before we recognize aspects of ourselves in others, we must get to know ourselves—the traits we have, our weaknesses and strengths, our abilities and handicaps, our likes and dislikes. We can only reflect what is within us. If we know what we are and why we are the way we are, we can accept others for being the way they are. The more intimately we know ourselves, the better we can know, appreciate and love others.

We can learn to love others if we view them as family and friends. It is common practice to consider only blood relatives as family and non-family members that we like and do things with as friends. This is a narrow and parochial view. A more expansive outlook would be to consider as family anyone and everyone with whom we establish close, loving and abiding relationships. Thus, people belonging to the same organization who share the same ideals and work for a common purpose are also a family. Anyone we relate to, deeply and profoundly, we establish family ties with. Even though we have been blessed with one natural family, how many more we create is only limited by how involved we decide to get.

Taking a closer look at my life, I note that the closest people to me are my wife and two daughters. How did they assume such prominence? My wife was a total stranger until I met her and got to know her. My children did not even exist until they were born into my family. These two, spouse and children, came into my life and became its most important aspects. My wife became my family by invitation and through choice. My children, on the other hand, came in, though invited, but without much choice as to who they should be. Hence, there are two ways we can convert people into family: choice and invitation on the one hand and acceptance of what life brings our way on the other hand. We can learn to enlarge our circle of family and friends by exercising choice—selecting individuals to whom we want to relate—and by incorporating into our lives whomever life brings our way through circumstance.

Even though we naturally share many interests and characteristics with family members, not everyone relates to family members equally. Some focus on differences rather than the shared characteristics. Hence, instead of developing deep and loving relationships, they harbor ill-feelings and live lives of strife. Even if our parents did not do a good job raising us, or our siblings, relatives and friends fell far below our expectations, that is all in the past. We must not harbor ill feelings toward anyone. We must let go of anger. We must accept that people do the best they can under the circumstances. We cannot judge people for we do not know all their circumstances. Through loving our families, we have the greatest opportunity to develop the noblest power of all, love. If we cannot love our family members with whom we share so much, how can we ever love anyone else with whom we share far less? Once we learn to love our family, we can extend this love to our neighbors, community and eventually to the world. Our family plays a much greater role in our development than we are aware of. For by learning to relate to the diverse members of our family, we develop and master the ability to relate to the diverse world at large.

The first to love is our spouse—the one with whom we fell in love and chose to marry and share our joys and sorrows. Our spouse must occupy a special place in our heart and life that no one else does. With and through our spouse, we have an opportunity to break away from our self and share with another in a manner we can never share with any other individual. We can share our bodies, emotions and minds. Our spouse usually has many of the qualities we admire but lack ourselves. Without our spouse, we are only male or female. But relating intimately to our spouses, loving them, being one with them, we have the opportunity to be whole once more—both male and female, man and wife, a complete couple.

Next to love is our children. Children require the most attention, but the rewards of healthy relationships with them are incomparable. If we have children in our family, then we have a unique opportunity, not only to help them grow, but to understand, develop and grow ourselves.

Our children are most like ourselves. They are the only ones we can know longer than we have known ourselves. We know our children from their birth. We only know ourselves from the time we acquired self-awareness. With our children we have a chance to establish deep and lasting relationships; to discover a boundless universe and to share love, memories and experiences. We can view our children's needs as demands and be resentful, or we can realize that these days will not last and this is our opportunity to give to our children with joy. Thus, to drive a child early in the morning to swim practice can be drudgery, or a chance to bond and share love.

Our children can teach us a tremendous amount about ourselves and we, in turn, can teach them a great deal. With our children, we have an opportunity to see how we might have been as children: how we learned, how we felt, how our abilities developed or might have developed had we the proper opportunities. By learning to relate to our children deeply and profoundly, we develop our power to love and establish contact with the flow that is life. It is easy to have children; it is far more difficult to raise them competently. We must raise children who love and think highly of themselves. We must raise children who are happy and content to be themselves. Children require a great deal of time, effort, love, praise, care and encouragement. We tend to raise children for obedience and submission as if they were pets, rather than for self-esteem, creativity, individuality and accountability. We tend to raise "dependents" rather than *individuals* who are in the process of unfoldment.

Next to have loving relationships with are our neighbors, work colleagues and the rest of our community. It is easier to establish great relationships with them if we consider them to be just like us with similar needs, hopes and aspirations. We need to love and be loved. So do they. We like to be appreciated, praised and respected. So do they. Before we judge anyone, we need to develop the ability to place ourselves in their situations and understand their circumstances. In all of our relationships, we must be fair, compassionate and supportive. We cannot want things for ourselves while denying others the chance to acquire the same for themselves. To have good friends and neighbors, we must be good friends and neighbors. To be understood and appreciated by others, we must understand and appreciate others. We must always start with ourselves, creating in ourselves that which we seek in others.

Christ taught that unless we learn to love those whom we see and deal with, we cannot love God whom we do not see. We can only love and serve God vicariously—through the ones we love and serve in our everyday experiences.

> *Then the King will say to these at his right hand, "Come, O blessed of my Father, inherit the kingdom prepared for you from the foundation of the world; for I was hungry and you gave me food, I was thirsty and you gave me drink, I was a stranger and you welcomed me, I was naked and you clothed me, I was sick and you visited me, I was in prison and you came to me." Then the righteous will answer him, "Lord, when did we see thee hungry and feed thee, or thirsty and give thee drink? And when did we see thee a stranger and welcome thee or naked and clothe thee? And when did we see thee sick or in prison and visit thee?" And the King will answer them, "Truly, I say to you, as you did it to one of the least of these my brethren, you did it to me." Then the King will say to these at his left hand, "Depart from me, you cursed, into the eternal fire prepared for the devil and his angels; for I was hungry and you gave me no food, I was*

> *thirsty and you gave me no drink, I was a stranger and you did not welcome me, naked and you did not clothe me, sick and in prison and you did not visit me." Then they will answer, "Lord, when did we see thee hungry or thirsty or a stranger or naked or sick or in prison and did not minister to thee?" Then he will answer them, "Truly, I say to you, as you did it not to one of the least of these, you did it not to me."*
>
> Matthew 25:34–45

Through another parable, Christ showed us who our neighbor really is.

> *But he, desiring to justify himself, said to Jesus, "And who is my neighbor?" Jesus replied, "A man was going down from Jerusalem to Jericho, and he fell among robbers, who stripped him and beat him, and departed, leaving him half dead. Now by chance a priest was going down that road; and when he saw him he passed by on the other side. So likewise a Levite, when he came to the place and saw him, passed by on the other side. But a Samaritan, as he journeyed, came to where he was; and when he saw him, he had compassion, and went to him and bound up his wounds, pouring on oil and wine; then he set him on his own beast and brought him to an inn, and took care of him. And the next day he took out two denarii and gave them to the inn keeper, saying, 'Take care of him; and whatever more you spend, I will repay you when I come back.' Which of these three, do you think, proved neighbor to the man who fell among the robbers?" He said, "The one who showed mercy on him." And Jesus said to him, "Go and do likewise."*
>
> Luke 10:29–37

Our "neighbors" are anyone and everyone we choose to relate to. They are all opportunities to serve, appreciate and love. They are our means to give so we may receive accordingly. Our neighbors are the ones we bless so our lives may be blessed. Our neighbors are mirrors that reflect back to us what we are and how we act. Our neighbors are life and all that we encounter daily. We create our neighbors based on the way we act and treat people. Our love baptizes those we touch and converts strangers into neighbors, enemies into friends and aliens into family. As love binds two in matrimony, extended love binds humanity into a family.

If every time we meet a person we recognize it as an opportunity to relate, know and be known, then we have loved our neighbor as ourselves. However, like any skill that we want to master, we must practice it repeatedly until it becomes second nature and a habit forms.

The difference between family, neighbors and strangers is the degree to which we relate to them and the quality of our relationships. Relationships are exchanges. Exchanges take place on all levels and with varying intensities. As we exchange, we impart part of ourselves and in return we take on aspects of those we exchange with.

In the physical world, the ultimate currency of exchange is the electron. Electrons in atoms revolve around their protons and form an energy field. This constitutes their "self." If electrons revolve only around their self, the universe remains as individual atoms—a very simple existence. However, as atoms learned to trust each other and extend their electrons in a "handshake," molecules formed. Electrons graduated from revolving around their small self to revolving around their new and enlarged self, the molecule. Thus, the first family unit was born. Families soon "multiplied" and "children" were born to them. These are the compounds, the organelles, and, ultimately, the cells—the basis of all life forms. As cells learned to relate to each other intimately, they multiplied and formed tissues, organs, and systems. Then, individuals appeared.

In the social world, the currency of exchange is money, both credit and cash. Money is the means for exchanging time, skills, goods and services. This exchange enhances the quality of our lives. Society is a gigantic market place where all participate in a commerce of giving, receiving, and adding value. The more value we add to our social world, the better our returns are.

In the emotional world, the currency of exchange is feelings. As we exchange these with each other, we barter "pieces" of ourselves and become different as a result.

In the mental world, the currency of exchange is thought. As we exchange thoughts with each other, we influence and mold our world.

On the spiritual plane, the ultimate currency of exchange is love. To the degree that we freely give and receive love, to that degree our spirits blossom. By joining with others, we become larger and our capacity and power grows. By giving of ourselves, sharing our experiences and by learning from each other, we speed up our evolution.

## Doing What We Can

> *If I can stop one heart from breaking, I shall not live in vain.*
> *Emily Dickenson*

Being and doing are the two serpents of the caduceus. They are eternally entwined. We are to the extent that we do and we do to the extent that we are. As we do, we become and as we become, we acquire new abilities. Hence, we are a duality of what we now are and what we are becoming. What we can become is based on what we know and what we decide to do. As we act, we experience, learn and change. Thus, doing shapes being and being determines the nature of what we do and become.

We are not expected to have a major impact on the world as we pass through it. Even minor improvements made by the billions of individuals will have a major impact. What we are expected to do, though, is to learn and share what we learn with others and to gain mastery of our environment by attaining mastery of ourselves.

The first step in mastering our environment is to stop

## Take it Easy, Enjoy Yourself, and Do What You Can

complaining about it. Complaints are a waste of time. Only actions achieve results. Instead of complaining about what we have to work with, let us open our eyes and wake up to their possibilities. Just as Botanist George Washington Carver found several uses for peanuts, there can be a number of uses for almost anything. A cucumber, for example, might be a mere cucumber for most to be eaten by itself or as part of a salad. But a cucumber can have several other uses. It can be used as a pickle, in making creme, medicine, shampoo, pet food and compost. It can be used for seed to grow more cucumbers, and a host of other uses known and yet to be discovered. In the movie "Forrest Gump," Forrest is in Vietnam with his best friend, Bubba. Bubba wants to be a shrimper and shrimp is all that he thinks and talks about. Bubba would talk for days about all the different ways one can cook and eat shrimp. If the uses of shrimp can be so vast, how much more there is to us. We must see ourselves and each other not only as we now are, but as the possibilities that we hold and all that we can be. All we need are trained eyes that see beyond the immediate. Instead of letting things happen and then complain, we must plan, will and act with energy, enthusiasm and inspiration. We must shape and create what we want from the circumstances we find ourselves in. These are our raw materials and like an artist, we must transform them into what we seek.

Just as a plant uses the simple elements in the air and soil to create itself and the foods we enjoy, so must we. We must excel at taking full advantage of our circumstances—what life provides us—and transform these into valuable goods and services. What we have to work with is the same for everyone: ourselves and our environment. We are our abilities, skills, knowledge and relationships both apparent and latent. Our environment is the air, soil, water, sunshine, animals, plants, people, equipment, time, space, money, opportunities and challenges. These are not equally available to everyone, but if we start with what we have and can work on right now, more resources and opportunities become available to us.

We function best where we are. Where we are is the ever changing moment, the launching pad to where we want to be. It is our present—the seat of our power. Therefore, we must not concern ourselves with the past and heap blame on parents, circumstances and others. Similarly, we must not focus too much on the future and waste our precious time in day dreams. Instead, we must focus on the rich and abundant reality that is right before us, take action and change the circumstances, ours and the worlds.

Our sphere of influence extends only to the areas we are actively involved in and intimately knowledgeable about. We extend to the extent of our involvement; we shrink with our pulling away and remaining aloof and uninvolved. Too often we concern ourselves with events we can do little about, while ignoring the ones we can impact and influence. We fantasize about changing the world, getting rid of dangerous views and eliminating corrupt systems. We dream of establishing peace all over the globe, even if it requires some form of imposing it. Aim for the stars, we are told. Do not sell yourself short, and have grand visions, for everything is possible. The adage "think global but act local" is wonderful advice. Our sphere of influence extends only to the areas we are actively involved with. We can achieve a lot, it is true, but how involved in the affairs of the world are we? There is a price to pay. We must get involved and take action beginning from where we are. Our involvement must be with our entire being: body, mind, emotions and spirit. Just as a seed must be buried in the ground to establish roots in the soil in order to grow and be the plant it can be, we must "bury" ourselves in our daily "soil" as well. Our soil is our immediate environment—our daily challenges and opportunities. As we put more of our skills and abilities to productive use, we grow.

We must be selective as to where we invest our time and

energy, getting involved only with whatever is in line with our missions and ideals. Additionally, we must not be discouraged by the behavior of others. We are here for our own growth and the contributions that we can make. Others have their own reasons. Additionally, we must view everyone as valuable contributors with their unique point of view. By exercising detachment when the situation calls for it, we can learn to view the larger picture created by the involvement of all.

One of the best ways to get involved is to join organizations that are concerned with the same values that you hold. Just as the human body can achieve far more than any of its individual parts can ever achieve separately, the power of the group is much greater than the power of its disparate individuals. The activities of the group whose members are committed, focused and fully involved take on a life of their own. An organization in synergy is the surest way to excel.

An organization does not have to be large. What is more important than numbers is the dedication and enthusiasm of each member and the degree of their commitment and involvement. Involvement is contagious. The more we get involved, the more energy we can generate. The more energy we put into an organization, the more energy that organization has and the more effective it is. This attracts others to join and get involved. Thus, the more involved we are in the activities of an organization, the better our chances are to animate, direct and shape those activities and through them, be in touch with the larger events of the world.

We should not be too harsh on ourselves if we face setbacks occasionally or seem to have shortfalls. If we do what we can, we can trust that all else will fall into place. We have our limitations. We are not responsible for the world. What we are responsible for is ourselves, our actions and reactions. We need to keep things in perspective, relax, take it easy and be concerned only with what we *can* do.

Our actions are based on the way we see and perceive. We

do not see clearly if we look with colored glasses (biases, prejudices and ignorance). We cannot appreciate uniqueness if we always compare. Comparing, we judge. This leads us to see ourselves and others as inferior or superior. Comparing individuals is a waste for we can always find some who are "better" and others who are "worse off." Additionally, comparing individuals denies their individuality and uniqueness. Instead of looking at others to compare and judge, we should observe others to learn about ourselves. We can learn a lot about ourselves by observing others, especially children. We can look at a newborn and realize the miracle that it is. We all entered the world the same way. We started as a miracle just like everyone else. We are each a unique wonder to behold, accept and appreciate.

We are born to fill a void. We do not have to struggle to know what this void is. We are guided from within by our intuition and from without by the circumstances of our lives. Life is a book that we both read and write into. We write into life automatically through our thoughts, feelings and actions. It is more difficult to read the book of life. It requires us to be still, listen and observe. If we cultivate our vision, develop our logic and employ our intuition, we can read the guideposts of life and find our way around.

Observing the flow of life in ourselves and in nature leads us to an obvious conclusion: life is progressing towards *increased organization, enhanced abilities, greater awareness, and ever more freedom and power.* These appear to be the goals of evolution. Our living should reflect these same goals.

Our bodies are composed of atoms. These are in a constant state of change; most are replaced within a year. These atoms organize themselves into molecules and compounds, eventually arriving at the next level of organization—the cell, some 50 trillion of them. Cells organize themselves into tissues, organs and systems, eventually arriving at the next level of organization—the individual. Individuals incorporate themselves into higher and higher forms of organizations: the family, the community, the nation and the world. With each level of organization, the goals of evolution become more apparent.

Organization is a form of incorporation. For to incorporate is to form the "corpus" which is the body of that organization. This body can be at the level of the cell (composed of organelles), the individual (composed of systems), the community (composed of individuals), the country (composed of communities), or the world (composed of nations). Earlier in this book, I stated that there are four general and three specific fundamentals that we must master to live full, meaningful and joyous lives. These seven ensure the flow of life and express the goals of evolution. Being alive and a corporation, we must do both: exemplify the seven fundamentals of life and express the properties of the best corporations. Corporations excel when they incorporate seven basic principles of success. Not surprisingly, these seven principles are equivalent to the seven fundamentals of life. What is true of life is equally valid at the corporate and the individual levels. The seven corporate principles of success are:

1. clear and focused mission;
2. action plan;
3. focus on customer satisfaction;
4. communication and other skills;
5. integrity;
6. employee empowerment, recognition and commitment to excellence; and
7. willingness to change.

### 1. Clear and Focused Mission

> Nothing contributes so much to tranquilize the mind as a steady purpose — a point on which the soul may fix its intellectual eye.
>
> Mary Wollstonecraft Shelley

Every successful corporation has a clear and focused mission with stated strategies and initiatives for the realization of its mission. We must do likewise if we want to be successful. Our mission must be clear and succinctly stated. Every aspect of our corporation (body, emotions and mind) must know this mission and adopt it as its own. All of our activities must be in compliance with this mission and must enforce and substantiate it.

Our mission is like the constitution of a country. It must be broad and stable. This mission provides us the vision to plan our lives, prioritize our activities and utilize our resources effectively and efficiently.

Our mission is the yardstick against which we evaluate our priorities. Our daily activities must reflect our mission so that anyone by merely observing us can know what we stand for and what our values are. To keep the flame of our mission burning brightly, we must form the habit of daily examining our lives and evaluating our activities against our mission. Just as we grow by metabolizing one meal or experience at a time, we must learn to progress toward the realization of our mission one day at a time. To live ample lives, we must live **each day** as amply as we can.

### One Day At a Time

*Life is not lost by dying; life is lost minute by minute, day by dragging day, in all the thousand small uncaring ways.*
                                                    Stephen Vincent Benet

A day is one revolution of earth around its axis. As earth rotates, it changes; yet, it maintains its movement around the sun. Our mission in life is to maintain our movement around our sun—ideals and values. Even though the starting and ending points of a day are arbitrary, we will assume that the day starts when our consciousness returns in the morning and ends when we lose consciousness at night in sleep. Thus, we will conveniently divide up the day into three segments: morning, daytime and night. Here is how to best utilize each interval of a day.

**What to Do In the Morning:**

> *As soon as e'er thou wak'st in order lay*
> *The actions to be done that following day.*
> Pythagoras' advice for the morning

It is best to wake up naturally prompted by daylight. As soon as you are awake, give thanks for being alive and for having another opportunity to live and experience. Before you get up, be aware of your body, one part at a time and then the entire body as a whole. Relax and attune your mind and body. Mentally vitalize every aspect of your being. Bathe each aspect—family, friends, job, community, health, money, leisure—with appreciation and love.

Get up, shower, dress and go to an area where you can be alone. Review your purpose, objectives and goals. Mentally review what you generally want to accomplish this day and set your priorities. Mentally see yourself accomplishing each task as well as you can, taking everyone involved into consideration. Simulate and mentally rehearse. It is the easiest way to perfect your actions. Use the power of autosuggestion and self-talk. Know that what the mind dwells upon with feeling, the body acts upon.

Next, take a leisurely walk, or exercise if you feel like it. If you feel hungry, eat a rejuvenating light breakfast. When you are ready, step outside into the world where all dreams can become reality. Face the world with confidence, anticipation and enthusiasm. Here is your chance to make the potential actual and the unpredictable future take shape through your intention and actions.

**What to Do In the Daytime:**

*There is no security on this earth. There is only opportunity.*
General Douglas Mc Arthur

Live passionately. Engage in activities with zest, awareness and ease. This is the only chance you will ever have to do these at these times. Living is like being in a school. You go through each grade once unless you fail and even then it is not the same. This is your chance to exercise your skills and excel. Do the important and difficult things first. Focus on what you want to do, the critical few and ignore all the others, the trivial many. Create the opportunity you want from the possibilities surrounding you.

Live as you would drive a vehicle, or ride a bicycle. Keep your sight on the distant goal, while you are aware of your immediate surroundings. Focus on one activity at a time. Once you complete that activity, you can move to a new one. Learn what you can and teach whoever wants to learn. Share yourself. Accept yourself and others for who and what each is.

Take time to enjoy yourself, smile and laugh. Express who you are and do what you can. At the same time, let others be and lend them a helping hand to be whatever they want for themselves. Be guided by your innermost feelings and your highest ideals at all times. Be true to yourself. You live with yourself more than you live with anyone else.

Eat when hungry and never to fullness. Your stomach is like a furnace. It needs room to mix and "burn" the food. As much as possible, eat your main meal at noon within your most active periods. If you feel like taking a short nap in the afternoon, do so.

Be content, yet never fully satisfied; always hungry for new opportunities to experience and learn. Remain attentive and inquisitive, appreciative of what is at hand and thankful for what is yet to come. Enjoy your current achievements.

In the evening, lessen your activities. Relax, play and enjoy the simple things life has to offer. Spend time with your loved ones. Shower them with your joy, appreciation, affection and love. When you are ready for your evening meal, let it be light, relaxed and in the company of loved ones.

**What to Do At Night:**

> *Nor suffer sleep at night to close thine eyes,*
> *Till thrice thy acts that day thou hast o'er-run*
> *How slipt? What deeds? What duty left undone?*
> Pythagoras' advice for the evening

Review the activities of the day. Relive the well executed ones. Mentally edit the activities you would prefer to have done differently. When you are ready to sleep, prepare for bed. Give thanks for the opportunities of the day. If you like, play some soft and relaxing music. Mentally preview what you will be doing the next day. Anticipate the coming day with joy. Relax your body, every part of it. Lose yourself in peaceful sleep.

**2. Action Plan**

> *Our grand business is not to see what lies dimly at a distance, but to do what lies clearly at hand.*
> Thomas Carlyle

Having a clear and focused mission is like knowing where we want to go. It is not enough to get us there. We must have a plan, a map and a blueprint of how we intend on getting there. We must plan our actions and act out our plans. The best way to do this is to set goals for ourselves in accordance with our priorities.

Goal setting is like engaging in sports. It is an activity with an end result. The end result is achieving the goal. In a game, the end result is winning or losing. In the game of life, we win just for having played because when we participate, we learn and improve.

Just as every game has fundamentals, so does goal setting. Goals must be written, specific, measurable, attainable, and personal. Obviously, goals can be for the short, intermediate, or long term. Daily goals are the same as our daily task list. While goals provide us the plans, our daily activities enable us to carry out those plans.

We must never cease examining our lives to ensure that the life we are leading is the life we want to live. If we learn to evaluate our experiences against our goals, we will realize that we can ignore the vast majority of our sources of irritation that cause stress. Most of our experiences are transitory, with little long-term impact. It is toward the critical few that we should devote and direct our attention, time and energy. We know what is critical and what is trivial by their effects. The critical few are indeed very few. They have long term impacts. They aid the attainment of our purpose.

### 3. Customer Satisfaction

*One thing I know: the only ones among you who will be really happy are those who will have sought and found how to serve.*
                                            Dr. Albert Schweitzer

A corporation exists to provide services or sell goods. Both of these activities require satisfied customers. We, too, are a corporation with many customers to satisfy. We must begin by satisfying ourselves. Once we are content, we can proceed to satisfy our families, serve our communities and ultimately the world. The best way for us to prosper, is to serve others as well as possible. When we give the best that we can offer, we gain satisfied customers and reap an abundance of rewards.

It is not evil to seek riches and enjoy abundance. Money is not the root cause of any evil. Money is neutral. It is a currency for exchange. Its use determines its value. It is a wonderful tool if used constructively and it is a terrible resource if used destructively. We must understand the difference between greed and ambition for there is a vast difference between the two. Ambition is a constant striving to improve and live abundantly. Ambition recognizes that there is a price that we must pay. This price is service and satisfied customers. If we do great work, we can expect to be rewarded amply. If we help others achieve prosperity, we can expect abundance ourselves. Greed and avarice, on the other hand, are the desire for riches without paying something in return.

When the disciples of Christ discussed among themselves who was the greatest, they displayed ambition. Christ did not rebuke them or ask them to cease aspiring. He simply showed them the way: *service.*

> But they were silent; for on the way they had discussed with one another who was the greatest. And he sat down and called the twelve; and he said to them, "If any one would be first, he must be last of all and servant of all."
>
> Mark 9:34–35

We can have abundance, riches and greatness. We must simply do what it takes, and what it takes is service. By serving, we give. As we give, we create a vacuum. Since nature abhors vacuum, rewards rush in.

## 4. Communication and Other Skills

> Commune with thyself, O man! and consider wherefore thou wert made. Contemplate thy powers, contemplate thy wants and thy connections; so shalt thou discover the duties of life, and be directed in all thy ways.
>
> Unto Thee I Grant

A corporation cannot meet and exceed its customers' needs unless it first knows what the customers want. Developing excellent communication skills, listening and being attentive to detail are key ways that a corporation can find out what are needed and how to best provide them. We must do likewise. We must learn to listen, pay attention to detail and communicate effectively to meet and exceed needs. We can begin by listening to our inner promptings and the people we come in contact with.

We are among the highly successful creatures on earth not because we have the keenest eyes, strongest claws, sharpest teeth, or because we are the fastest, biggest and most powerful. Even our brains are not the largest in the animal kingdom. They are, however, the most developed. This is because in the small space of the cranium, billions upon billions of neurons are organized in the most efficient and effective way possible. There are more neural **connections** in the brain than there are stars in the galaxies. These neurons are interrelated and in constant communication. It is these connections and the relations between them that give us our true and amazing power. This gives us an indication of the amazing power and capabilities we can have if we learn to communicate with each other the way our neurons communicate among themselves.

Communications are relationships and the quality of our relationships is the quality of our communications. Relationships are critical to our success as well as our happiness. Plato realized ages ago that it is useless to achieve success if we did not have someone to share it with. The more people we know and relate to, the easier it is for us to succeed and the better the quality of our lives. For it is through people that most of our successes are attained, needs fulfilled and pleasures derived.

Our relationships must be loving, caring and trusting. Establishing loving relationships with others should be a primary area of focus for our daily activities. This requires awareness and commitment. Living with awareness transforms simple living into a sacred art.

## 5. Integrity

*An honest man's the noblest work of God.*

*Alexander Pope*

A corporation must have integrity to endure. So must we. Integrity is being true to ourselves and others. Integrity demands that we be sincere. Sincerity means that we are not phony or hiding anything. We display our strengths as well as our weaknesses. When we make a mistake, we do not deny or defend the mistake. We accept it, learn from it and make amends.

If integrity is being true to ourselves, then we should never compromise our ideals to suit a situation. We should be willing to compromise at all times, *except* when it comes to our ideals. We must be true to our own self before we can be true to anyone else. Our actions must be compatible with our beliefs. We should clearly know what we believe in, and only believe in what we know and are willing to live by and defend.

One of the easiest ways to live a life of integrity is to live a simple life. A simple life does not mean a life devoid of luxuries. Rather, it reflects a life style uncomplicated and unencumbered by unnecessary possessions that ensnare and enslave us. Living the simple life requires us to carry along only what we need for our journey of life. What we need is mostly weightless, formless and free. We need: love, joy, sincerity, fortitude, appreciation, contentment, trust and purity of heart. The Desiderata, a passage found in a church in Baltimore, Maryland, speaks about living the simple life.

### *Desiderata*

*Go placidly amid the noise and haste and remember what peace there may be in silence. As far as possible without surrender be on good terms with all persons. Speak your truth quietly and clearly; and listen to others, even the dull and ignorant; they too* have their story. Avoid loud and aggressive persons; they are vexations to the spirit. If you compare yourself with others, you may become vain and bitter; for always there will be greater and lesser persons than yourself. Enjoy your achievements as well as your plans. Keep interested in your own career, however humble; it is a real possession in the changing fortunes of time. Exercise caution in your business affairs; for the world is full of trickery. But let this not blind you to what virtue there is; many persons strive for high ideals; and everywhere life is full of heroism. Be yourself. Especially, do not feign affection. Neither be cynical about love; for in the face of all aridity & disenchantment it is perennial as the grass. Take kindly the counsel of the years, gracefully surrendering the things of youth. Nurture strength of spirit to shield you in sudden misfortune. But do not distress yourself with imaginings. Many fears are born of fatigue and loneliness. Beyond a wholesome discipline, be gentle with yourself. You are a child of the universe, no less than the trees and the stars; you have a right to be here. And whether or not it is clear to you, no doubt the universe is unfolding as it should. Therefore be at peace with God, whatever you conceive Him to be, and whatever your labors and aspirations, in the noisy confusion of life keep peace with your soul. With all its sham, drudgery and broken dreams it is still a beautiful world. Be cheerful. Strive to be happy.

## 6. Employee Empowerment and Recognition with a Commitment to Excellence

*One that desires to excel should endeavor in those things that are in themselves most excellent.*

*Epictetus*

Excellence is not directly due to the performance of a corporation. It is the result of the conscientious activities of the members of that corporation. As it is individuals who carry out activities, then these individuals must be em-

## Take it Easy, Enjoy Yourself, and Do What You Can    293

powered in accordance with their skill levels and responsibilities. The more empowered an individual feels, the higher the productivity. Excellent products are built by committed and motivated individuals.

Empowered employees occasionally make mistakes. This should be expected. It is far better to act and make a mistake than to be afraid of making a mistake and not act. Even though it is important to allow employees to make mistakes, it is far more important to recognize them for doing something right. Recognition can be with rewards or in praise. Praise is powerful, free and readily available. It must be sincere, timely and specific. Praise enriches employees self-esteem and reinforces the positive act.

Even though a corporation has various departments with department heads, everyone is an employee of the corporation. Everyone has a role to play and a contribution to make. Rewards should be based on contribution and merit alone. While compassion is a virtue, favoritism is not.

In our physical corporation, the body, contributions are made by atoms, molecules, organelles, cells, tissues, organs and systems. The health and vitality of the body depends on the health and vitality of its various parts and the cooperation among them. This cooperation is the key that allows specialization and advanced functions. Fundamentally, all atoms are a variation of the simplest atom, the hydrogen. All cells are a differentiation of a basic stem cell. A cell can grow into any cell type for as long as the cell is "embryonic in nature"—young and not specialized (undifferentiated). The type of specialization a cell assumes depends on its location and the needs of the body. Just as each cell has the capacity to be any cell type, so must each employee within a corporation. The corporation is at its best when each member finds his or her natural niche based on qualification, performance and proclivities.

We, too, can grow into any occupation or career we choose for ourselves. Like our cells, we are guided by two factors: our abilities and our perceptions of needs in society. Just like our cells, if we remain flexible and specialize, we can achieve what we want. To be successful, we must determine what the needs of society are and align those with our aptitudes and passions. We then, must empower ourselves to do our best—specialize and excel. We must remain responsive to the needs of our community. When the needs of the community change, so must our services and deliverables. We must also recognize and celebrate the achievements of our family, friends and acquaintances and reward ourselves through vacation, play and fun.

## 7. Willingness to Change

*Change alone is eternal, perpetual, immortal.*
Arthur Schopenhauer

Matter is condensed energy. Energy is motion. Motion is change. Thus, as long as we experience matter, we will experience change. We either direct the course of change and cause the results we want, or change will overtake us. Corporations and individuals who remain resilient and adapt to change survive and prosper. Those that do not adapt to change become obsolete.

It is not easy for large corporations to change. The movement of massive bodies generates tremendous momentum. This momentum manifests as inertia and expresses itself as the "culture" of that organization. Culture is the set ways of doing business. It is the internal environment of that organization. If the needs of society change, it will require a great deal of energy to overcome a large corporation's inertia and change the direction of its movement. That is why change for a large organization is often difficult and agonizing. Cultural changes are slow and gradual to allow for adaptation. Rapid change in a well established culture can lead to disaster or even extinction. One way to overcome this obstacle is to compartmentalize a large corporation the same way that the human body is compartmentalized into organs and systems.

Individually, we are a gargantuan organization of physical, mental, emotional and spiritual configurations of matter, energy, awareness and intelligence. Since sudden, large changes introduced to huge organizations can lead to disaster, we must change gradually. It is far easier to adapt to incremental change. When a frog is placed in water that is too hot, the frog will jump out instantly. If, however, the frog is placed in water at room temperature and the temperature of the water is then slowly raised, the frog will stay there and cook. Similarly, businesses that raise their prices gradually do not face stiff opposition. Sudden, large changes are not as readily accepted. When the oil companies raised the price of gasoline by 10 cents a gallon all at once, consumers complained bitterly and the government had to act. Over the next two years the price of gasoline rose steadily, but very gradually and the incremental changes were easily accepted and adapted to.

Similarly, humans can adapt to change if change is introduced gradually. Large changes introduced rapidly can lead to death. This is why, something as small as a bullet, kills a large and fully developed human being. If too much damage (change) is introduced too quickly, the body has no time to adapt.

Since we face change frequently, it behooves us to develop ways to cope with these changes with as little stress as possible. We have little control over external changes, but a great deal of maneuverability over our internal states. Since the manner in which we deal with change is as important as the change itself, we can handle any change if we remain mentally flexible and cultivate an attitude that anticipates and welcomes change. Change can bring us benefits and provide us advantages. Change is an opportunity if we choose to take advantage of it.

We do not have to react to every change. Most changes have no long term impact and should be ignored. We must cultivate wisdom in dealing with change, evaluating them prior to responding. At times we must seize the moment and act swiftly. At other times, we must evaluate the risks. Our inner promptings and past experiences should be our guides.

We are not in the world to change people. We are here to live, be happy, learn, grow and help improve the quality of life for everyone. To want to change others assumes that we are right and they are wrong. We are not better than anyone else. It is far easier to change ourselves than change anyone else. If we work on changing ourselves, we only have one to work on. If we strive to change everyone else, we get overwhelmed. To paraphrase Native Americans: it is far easier to place a piece of hide under our feet to protect our soles, than to carpet the world. If we change ourselves, the rest will often take care of itself. If we change ourselves a little bit at a time and improve consistently; over time, we will notice a big difference in our circumstances.

*Part Three*

# Repeat the Seven Step Process — Each Time, Waking Up on a Higher Plane

> *We live between two worlds; we soar in the atmosphere; we creep upon the soil; we have the aspirations of creators and the propensities of quadrupeds. There can be but one explanation of this fact. We are passing from the animal into a higher form, and the drama of this planet is in its second act.*
>
> W. Winwood Reade

Each morning we wake up to the dawning of a new day. This day is *not* the same as yesterday or tomorrow. As earth rotates around itself, it gives us the cycles of day and night. As earth revolves around the sun, it gives us the cycles of the seasons. The sun is not static, however. Earth, sun and all other celestial bodies are on a journey into vast space. Where everything is going, no one knows. We do know, however, that with each morning we wake up to a new day, in a new location in space and time.

Cycles are not mere repetitions to dull our senses. Instead, they give us on-going opportunities to take advantage of circumstances not recognized before. Cycles are a recurring phenomenon that give rise to the spiral of being. We are a mere "rung" on the unfolding spiral of life. Which rung we are depends on the level of our awareness and the abilities we express.

As we go from one experience to the next, we accumulate memories, gain insights and increase our awareness. We move up the "ladder". Eventually we reach the critical mass required for a chain reaction and a change in phase. Just as day follows night, wakefulness follows sleep and attainment follows struggle. Since we have been in the dark for a long time, our awakening must be gradual to allow us time to adapt to the brilliant light of the sun—the symbol of our ultimate awakening. Just as accumulated variations lead to the formation of new species, our accumulated experiences propel us into a new state of being. As we enter our new state, we shed our denser garments and scales fall off our eyes. We become lighter and begin to see clearer. As we become lighter, the hold of gravity on us weakens. Eventually, we attain escape velocity. We graduate, lift off and move up to the next higher quanta. As we do, we find ourselves on a higher dimension.

## Dimensions

*Reality is more fluid and elusive than reason, and has, as it were, more dimensions than are known even to the latest geometry.*

*George Santayana*

When is 1 greater than 97? When is 482 less than 2? When 1 and 2 are of a higher order. If 1 is a dollar while the 97 are cents, then $1 is greater than 97¢. Similarly, if the 2 are years, while the 482 are days, then 482 days are less than 2 years. To understand dimensions, we must stretch beyond our familiar confines, shift gears and function from a higher perspective, or quanta.

A snake cannot devour a prey larger than its head unless it first loosens it jaws. We cannot comprehend the higher dimensions unless we first unhook ourselves from our common and routine realities. By detaching ourselves, we become free and can stretch beyond our normal selves. We accomplish the seemingly impossible. We peak into the higher dimensions.

The Random House College Dictionary defines dimension as *a magnitude that serves to define the location of an element within a given set, as of a point on a line, an object in a space, or an event in space-time.* We are an element. If we consider our set to be our world and the universe, where do we fit? What "location" do we occupy?

Where we are is our dimension. There are many dimensions each with a specific world view, an assortment of paradigms (belief systems) and a distinct level of awareness. If being is like a city, each dimension is like a building. Each of us lives in this building occupying a floor that forms our world and sets our boundaries. Some are content to live in their rooms all their lives. Others change rooms frequently while remaining on the same floor. Some progress and occupy rooms on gradually higher floors with more panoramic views. Active evolution is discovering the existence of the upper levels and exercising the freedom to move conscientiously to a higher floor.

Each dimension has three distinctive features:

1. degrees of freedom,
2. scale of mysteries, and
3. level of awareness.

### 1. Degrees of Freedom

Mathematically, a one-dimensional being has two degrees of freedom: movement forward or backward. A three dimensional being, on the other hand, can move forward or backward, to the left or to the right and up or down. The higher the dimension we occupy, the less controlled and restricted we feel and the more options (degrees of freedom) are available for us. If we are on the 97'th floor of a building, less obstructions block our view than for someone on the 10'th floor. With fewer obstructions, we can see further.

## 2. Scale of Mysteries

In the movie *To Fly*, a balloonist had just taken off when he spotted a man in a boat going down the river. The man in the boat could not see that he was approaching a dangerous water fall. The man in the balloon could, so he warned the man in the boat about the approaching danger and perhaps saved his life.

The higher the dimension we occupy, the fewer the mysteries that face us. From that perspective, the view is more panoramic, unobstructed and more information is available to avoid accidents.

Rising to a higher dimension is like growing up. When we were young our understanding was limited and confined to our immediate environment. We evaluated everything based on our immediate needs and wants. When my daughter Emily was ten-years-old, she told me what a nice teacher she had. When I asked her what made her teacher so nice, she told me that compared to last year's teacher who gave her a lot of homework during the winter holidays, this nicer teacher gave her none. As children, it is hard to stretch into the future and see the value of something based on its future worth.

Functioning at the lower dimensions, we are born, grow up, age and die—if we are lucky and do not meet an accident along the way and die prematurely. Our lives are fraught with accidents, unknowns and mysteries. We see only our immediate vicinity. We cannot see the car approaching from around the corner or what else is taking place in the neighborhood. We cannot see the actual causes of events. On the lower dimensions, life is both roses and thorns. One day we experience the joy of smelling the fragrance of the roses and the next day we might experience the pain of being pricked by the thorns. Attempting to live the abundant life becomes a struggle, a trial and error, with many challenges, disappointments and frustrations. These are the thorns that come along with the roses that we seek. Functioning at the higher dimensions, we discern the true causes of events. We encounter fewer accidents and our lives become more abundant.

## 3. Level of Awareness

Our level of awareness determines the dimension we occupy. As long as we are parochial in our views, we function on the lower planes. To function on the higher planes, we must rise above our limited view and see the larger picture. To rise higher in our awareness, we must become lighter. To be lighter we must shed some of the heavy burdens that weigh us down and keep us earthbound. Some of these burdens are ignorance, fear, jealousy, false pride and selfishness. These and other restrictive beliefs are powerful chains that tie us down. If we are tied down, we can only function to the extent of our "leash."

### The Lower Dimensions

We are familiar with dimensions from the study of mathematics. Length, width and height can each be considered a dimension unto itself. Even though it is easy to understand these three, it gets progressively more difficult to comprehend the higher dimensions. This is because we have little in our daily experiences to relate to the higher dimensions. To understand the higher dimensions, we must first graduate from the school of the lower dimensions. The gateway to the higher is through mastering the fundamentals of the lower.

## The First Dimension

Extension along one direction forms a line and constitutes one dimension. A stationary point, by definition, has no dimension since it does not extend or has a magnitude. When a point moves by extending beyond itself, a line forms. A line is one dimensional since it is a measure of length. Extension in length allows two degrees of freedom, since a point in a line can move forward or backward (X-axis). To go from no dimension to one dimension (from a point to a line) requires an extension along an axis not found in the stationary point.

## The Second Dimension

Tracing the movement of a point along the two directions of length and width forms a plane. A plane is two dimensional. Extension in length and width allows four degrees of freedom, since a point in a plane can move forward or backward, and to the left or right (Y-axis). To go from one dimension to two requires an extension along a new axis.

## The Third Dimension

Tracing the movement of a point along the three directions of length, width and height forms the outline of an object. Objects are three dimensional. They extend along three axes. This allows six degrees of freedom, since a point in an object can move forward or backward, left or right, and up or down (Z-axis).

## The Higher Dimensions

In 1980, I was working as an electron microscopist at Walter Reed Army Medical Center in Washington, DC. After a painful and agonizing period in my career, I was forced to take a new look at my occupation. After a period of intense questioning, I decided to make a career change. I concluded that, fundamentally, I was a creative individual capable of anything I decided to undertake. I was in my current job as a biologist only by training and circumstance and not through choice or an innate nature. With this shift in my consciousness, I was reborn into a new realization of myself. A whole new world opened up for me that only a short while ago did not exist. I then applied for and took the programmers test offered by the Internal Revenue Service at their National Headquarters in Washington, DC.

The test consisted of math, comprehension and series-reasoning questions. The math and comprehension questions were easy, for I was used to such tests. I had never taken series-reasoning tests before. I was given a series of numbers, letters and shapes and was asked to extrapolate what came next. The following are examples of simple number series-reasoning questions:

1)  9   12   15   18   21
    (A) 21   (B) 27   (C) 25   (D) 24   (E) 23
2)  7 8   6 7   5 6   4 5
    (A) 2 7   (B) 3 9   (C) 3 4   (D) 5 8   (E) None
3)  2 8   3 7   5 6   8 5
    (A) 10 6   (B) 11 3   (C) 11 4   (D) 12 4   (E) 12 6

In the first example, the numbers are multiples of three. We simply add three to a number to arrive at the next one. Thus, the answer to the first question is (D) 24.

In the second example, each two numbers represent a pair. Both the first and second number of the pair are decreased by one. Thus, the next number pair is (C) 3 4.

In the third example, each two numbers are also a pair. To get the first number of each pair, we simply increment the previous number by one, then two, then three and so on. To get the second number of the pair, we decrement the previous number by one. Thus, the answer to the third example is (D) 12 4.

Even though the above are simple examples, we can learn a great deal from series-reasoning exercises. We can extrapolate the answers because our minds are capable of deducing the rules and the patterns that govern these progressions. Once the patterns are discerned and the rules are known, it is easy to arrive at the answer. What is important in this type of reasoning is that we can know not only the one answer, but the next several numbers that follow and precede. In the first example we can know not only that the succeeding numbers are (24, 27, 30, and so forth), but also what the preceding numbers are as well (6, 3, 0, −3, and so forth). This is true with all series-reasoning exercises.

One way to understand dimensions, is to treat them like numbers or figures in series. The first number is the first dimension, followed by the second, the third, the fourth, the fifth and so forth. Once we identify the rules that govern the progression from one dimension to the next, we can know the characteristics of preceding and succeeding dimensions. In the above example of series reasoning, we placed a series of numbers in sequence and then proceeded to "reason and calculate" the next sequence. If we place the three lower dimensions in series, we can proceed to "reason and calculate" until we extrapolate the rules that govern their progression. If we place a point, a line, a plane and an object sequentially and consider them dimensions in series, what patterns and rules of progression can we identify? P.D. Ouspensky describes some such rules in his book *Tertium Organum: A Key to the Enigmas of the World*.

1. **Each higher dimension consists of an infinite number of the lower dimension.** A line contains an infinite number of points. A plane contains an infinite number of lines. An object contains an infinite number of planes. Therefore, the fourth dimension must contain an infinite number of third dimensions, and the fifth dimension

must contain an infinite number of fourth dimensions, and so forth.
2. **The higher dimension is the medium for the tracing of the movement of the lower dimension.** A line is the medium for tracing the movement of a point. A plane is the medium for tracing the movement of a line. An object is the medium for tracing the movement of a plane. Therefore, the fourth dimension must be the medium for tracing the movement of a three-dimensional object, and so forth.
3. **We experience only dimensional segments, never the dimension in its entirety.** A line, a plane and an object, as concepts, begin nowhere and extend indefinitely. We never experience The Line, The Plane, or The Object each in its entirety. What we experience are line segments, plane representations and samples of objects. These are confined. They begin, extend and end. They can be measured and comprehended. Similarly, we can not experience the fourth and higher dimensions in their entirety since each is limitless. We can only experience samples of the fourth and higher dimensions.
4. **When two higher dimensions intersect, a lower dimension results.** At the intersection, the lower dimension possesses features from both parent dimensions. When two lines intersect, a point results. When two planes intersect, a line results. When two objects intersect, a plane results. Therefore, the third dimension is the result of the intersection of two fourth dimensions and the fourth dimension is the result of the intersection of two fifth dimensions and so forth.
5. **A higher dimension results from a paradigm shift and an extension into a totally new realm.** Thus, for a point to become a line, it must extend beyond itself. For a line to become a plane, it must extend into a new direction. For a plane to become an object, it must break its boundaries and extend in a new dimension as well.
6. **Each lower dimension is a segment of a higher dimen-

sion. Yet the segment never fully represents the higher dimension entirely. Thus, even though a point is a segment of a line, we cannot arrive at an understanding of a line by studying the features of a point. Similarly, even though a line is a segment of a plane, and a plane is a segment of an object, we cannot know what a plane is by studying a line, or arrive at an understanding of an object by analyzing a plane.
7. **A higher dimension binds several separate lower dimensions into a cohesive whole.** The line binds several separate points, the plane binds several separate lines, and an object combines several separate planes. Thus, the fourth dimension must bind several objects into a cohesive whole and the fifth dimension must bind several fourth dimensions into a cohesive whole, and so forth.

**The Fourth Dimension**

We know that extension along four directions gives rise to the fourth dimension. What exactly is the fourth dimension? Using the above discussed patterns and rules, we can postulate that *space-time* is the fourth dimension.

**Analysis:**
1. Space-time contains an infinite number of three-dimensional objects.
2. Space-time is the medium that houses the tracing of the movement of three-dimensional objects.
3. Space-time cannot be experienced in its entirety, but a representation which is confined and limited can be experienced as local space-time.
4. When two fourth dimensions intersect an object results (?).
5. To arrive at an understanding of space-time requires a paradigm shift, an extension in a new direction, and a breaking away from the confines of the third dimension.

## Repeat the Seven Step Process

6. We cannot arrive at an understanding of the fourth dimension by merely studying an object. The features of space-time are beyond the added features of objects.
7. Space-time binds several separate three-dimensional objects into a cohesive whole. To see the unity of apparent separate objects, we need to view these objects from a higher dimension. Objects are connected in space-time the same way that fish are connected in the medium of water.

Can space-time be the fourth dimension?

Every three dimensional object exists in the medium of space and time. For to exist is to occupy space and to move requires an extension in time. Extension in space is along the three coordinates of length, width and height, while extension in time is along a fourth coordinate. These extensions along four coordinates allow eight degrees of freedom, since a point in the fourth dimension can extend forward and backward, left and right, up and down, in space and in time.

The human body is an example of the fourth dimension. For the body to exist, it must extend in space. For the body to change, it must extend in time. As we extend in space, we cover specific areas. As we extend in time, we change (grow and age.) Our bodies are constantly changing. The medium that makes it possible for anything to change is its higher dimension. A point cannot change unless its movement is contained in the line. A line cannot change unless it is done in a plane. A plane cannot change unless it is done in the third dimension. Similarly, the physical body cannot move and change unless it is carried out in the fourth dimension—space-time.

We experience several bodies, yet only one at a time. The body appears miraculously in space-time as a fertilized egg, grows, matures and then mysteriously disappears. Between appearing and disappearing, the body continuously changes from one form into the next. This change is our indication that we are indeed fourth dimensional.

The fourth dimension, like any dimension, is similar to Plato's world of concepts. Just as a line has no beginning or end since, by definition, a line is an infinite extension, so is a plane, an object and space-time. These exist as concepts and lie beyond our three-dimensional physical realities. Even though we seem to experience lines, planes and objects, these are mere representative samples of the concepts of lines, planes and objects. Concepts do not have beginnings or ends, only representations do.

Our experiences are of the relative and not the absolute. We experience a body, but not The Body; beautiful expressions, but not beauty; just or unjust situations, but not justice; demonstrations of power, but not power itself. We do not know truth, life and consciousness. We only know demonstrations of these as sample expressions. While the concept of the absolute contains all examples of relative occurrences, a relative occurrence is merely one possibility. Knowing a relative example does not imply a knowledge of the absolute. Studying few examples on the lower dimension is not enough to have an understanding of the higher dimension. To know the higher, we must experience a paradigm shift and take a quantum leap.

## The Fifth Dimension

Extension along five directions gives rise to the fifth dimension. What exactly is the fifth dimension? Using the above discussed patterns and rules, we can postulate that *idea* is the fifth dimension.

**Analysis:**
1. The *idea* of space-time contains an infinite number of (space-time)s.
2. The *idea* of space-time is the medium that houses the tracing of the movement of all (space-time)s.
3. The world of ideas cannot be experienced in its entirety.

Each *idea* is limitless. Yet a *representation* of this idea is confined and limited. For example, even though the idea of beauty is limitless, a beautiful person is confined and limited.
4. An *idea* results when two sixth dimensions intersect (?).
5. To understand *idea* requires a paradigm shift, an extension in a new direction, and a breaking away from the confines of the lower dimension.
6. We cannot arrive at an understanding of the sixth dimension by studying an idea, even though each idea is contained in the sixth dimension. We do not know the higher dimension by merely studying the lower.
7. An *idea* binds several separate (space-time)s into a cohesive whole. The idea of *beauty,* for example, binds into a cohesive whole all representations of beauty.

Can *idea* be the fifth dimension?

An idea is a medium of extension just as length, width, height and space-time are. Each idea enables us to extend into a different realm, a dimension outside our routine confines. When we get an idea and act on it, a whole world opens up for us to extend into.

Ideas are clearly beyond the realm of space-time for ideas cannot be confined by them. The ideas of love, justice and freedom for instance, extend over time and influence all-time. Ideas reside in their own world, as potential, until they bubble forth and are experienced. They appear out of nowhere and then disappear into nowhere. Ideas are behind our creative deeds. When we engage in activities, we are expressing the ideas behind these activities. The idea itself is hidden like an unuttered word and an unexpressed ideal. The journey of the idea from mind, where it resides, to expression is the journey of creativity and creation. It is the transfiguration of the "thought" of God into the "word" of God which then takes "flesh," and dwells among us as the "work" of God.

To better understand how *idea* can be the fifth dimension, let us consider an example.

Ideas are absolute. Representations of ideas, however, are relative. The idea of *book*, for example, is not limited to any specific book or time-period. There are many books in the world today. There were many books in the past and there will be many more in the future. There are books of varying sizes, shapes, colors, weights and contents written in different languages, some that we know, others that we can decipher and many more that we cannot decipher. Yet all these are manifestations of the same one eternal idea—the idea of book.

One book can never be a complete expression of the idea of book. Even if we take all the books that were ever written, are written, or will be written, they are still only a partial expression of the idea of book. What about all the books that could have been written but were not? These, too, are part of the idea of book. They simply remained potential and never manifested. The idea of book represents not only what manifests as actual, but those that remain potential as well. The idea is both the passive and the active, the manifest and the potential.

> But there are also many other things which Jesus did; were everyone of them to be written, I suppose that the world itself could not contain the books that could be written.
>
> John 21:25

When we read a book, we relate to an expressed manifestation of this one eternal *idea* of book. Yet, the *idea* itself remains unseen. We also gain a certain understanding from reading the book. Where did the meaning that led to the understanding come from? Was it in the letters? Was it in the mind? How was the meaning conveyed? Does the same word mean the same thing to everyone? When the word is communicated, the meaning is conveyed and understanding results. The invisible *idea* becomes tangible and can touch and influence us.

The book originates as an *idea* in the mind of the author. The journey of the *idea* from concept to manifestation requires space-time and construction. It requires effort the same way that the journey of a blue-print into a physical construct entails labor. Living is the experience of translating the *idea* that we are into the manifestation that we can be. It is the process of laying the stones of our temple. For it is through our experiences that we chisel ourselves into individual characters and personalities. That is why living entails both effort and gratification. Witnessing the temple take form is a slow and deliberate process. Because of this, the value and meaning of living often eludes us. The completion of each phase and the transition into a new one appears as aging and eventual death. This is why these two are natural because they are an integral component of the transmutation of the idea into its material counterpart.

We, too, originated as an *idea* in the mind of our author. This *idea* took flesh and manifested as a living word, as a body that is a corporation with a name. Just as we think many thoughts and entertain several ideas, so does our author. We are *each* an idea in a unique portion of space-time and at a different stage of construction. For the *idea* that we are to become fully manifest will require us to live, experience and learn. As we live, we remember and find our way back home. We are now The Lost Word in the process of waking up and becoming The Found Word. As we wake up and assume our full meaning, the beauty of the *idea* behind our manifestation shines forth.

We are in the image of the *idea* we are giving form to. We are simultaneously both the idea and the expression. As the idea, we are the hidden author of all the books we write. We write not one book, but many versions in many life-cycles, in many places and times, in many ways and forms using different languages, styles and formats. What we write or do not write makes our realities what they are.

As a manifestation, we are the body with its circumstances. The atoms of our bodies, like the letters of a book, combine and recombine all the time; and with each recombination new meanings, new values, new aspects of this eternal idea form and emerge. Benjamin Franklin's epitaph reads: *"The Body of Benjamin Franklin" (like the cover of an old book, it's contents torn out and stripped of its letterings and gilding) lies here food for worms. Yet the work itself shall not be lost, for it will appear once more in a new and more beautiful edition corrected and amended by the author).*

Authoring does not take place through blind expressions such as the writing of meaningless words. It is achieved when the expression (action) is based on *knowledge and clear intention.* **Knowledge and intention are the means to any creation.** Being an author is a great opportunity and tremendous responsibility. If living is authoring our own books, let us turn whatever we create into classics and masterpieces. For as we create, we give birth to ourselves and help shape all else. Hence, we should write (express) not only for our own enjoyment, but for the benefit of others as well. For, on higher dimensions, we are all connected. We are each a word that combines to form the paragraphs and chapters of a larger book—the Book of Life.

### The Sixth Dimension

Extension along six directions gives rise to the sixth dimension. What is the sixth dimension? Using the same patterns and rules that led us to discover the fourth and fifth dimensions, we can postulate that *mind* is the sixth dimension.

**Analysis:**
1. *Mind* contains an infinite number of ideas.
2. *Mind* houses the tracing of the movement of all ideas.

3. *Mind* as an absolute is limitless. Yet any *representation* of this mind is confined and limited. For example, even though mind is limitless, the mind of an insect, a bird, or a human is limited to the level of consciousness attained.
4. *Mind* is the result of the intersection of two seventh dimensions. Mind contains features from both parents.
5. To arrive at an understanding of mind requires a paradigm shift, an extension in a new direction and a breaking away from the confines of the old.
6. Even though each idea is contained in the mind, we cannot arrive at an understanding of mind—the seventh dimension—by studying ideas. Each idea is a mere image or a projection of mind. Studying the ideas of a person puts us in touch with the mind of that person, but does not lead us to know mind itself. We can not know the seventh dimension by merely studying the sixth.
7. **Mind** contains within it several separate ideas. Mind binds seemingly disparate ideas into a cohesive whole.

Can *mind* be the sixth dimension? What is ***mind?***

There are two aspects to mind, universal and individual. Individual mind is the portion of universal mind an individual has access to. It comprises *the collective conscious and unconscious processes that manifest as thought, perception, emotion, will, memory, imagination and dreaming.*

Mind is creative and is the birthplace of all ideas; new, old, past, present and future. By mastering the art of using our minds effectively, we can give birth to creative ideas, breakthroughs, and transform our world. We can stretch out into realms we have never ventured into before. As we expand the use of our minds, we grow in power, awareness and abilities. Perhaps the reason the universe is expanding is because the use of our minds is broadening. As we use our minds more effectively, our individual worlds expand and with them, the entire universe.

Mind is the source of matter and energy. When mind is

expanded, it is energy. When it is contracted, it is substance. Living beings plug into mind like appliances plug into electrical outlets. Each draws as much electricity (mind), as they need and are capable of utilizing. Thus, even though there is one mind, its expressions are as varied as there are appliances that use electricity. Electricity has its source in electrical generators. Mind has its source in the Mind Generator—Cosmic Intelligence, or God.

We plug into mind consciously when we think, perceive, feel, will and imagine; and unconsciously when we dream. Anytime we plug into mind and use it, we create.

An example of conscious creation is the first statement from the book of Genesis: *"In the beginning God created the heavens and the earth."* Like all creations, genesis has two phases: **ideation** which takes place in mind, or *the heavens* (ethereal and non-physical) and **manifestation** which takes place on *earth* (physical world in space-time.) The words *In the beginning* are a translation of the original Hebrew or Aramaic word *Brishit*. This word has two meanings in Aramaic: 1) *In the beginning,* or 2) *in the head* (the mind). In other words, creation takes place in the head, or more accurately, in the mind. The mind is where all ideas are first born as immaterial *heaven* before they manifest in the material as *earth*. There are many accounts in ancient Egypt where the gods begin creation in the mind first. Once an idea is created in the mind, it is only a matter of time before it manifests in physical reality.

Not all minds are equally creative. Minds, like fields, produce after the image of the thoughts planted there. Passionate thoughts based on knowledge and clear intention are naturally more creative than the thoughts we entertain in passing. To realize the impact of creative thinking, let us take a look at the following statement in *Matthew 5:27–28:*

> *You have heard that it was said, "You shall not commit adultery." But I say to you that every one who looks at a woman lustfully has already committed adultery with her in his heart.*

When I first encountered the above passage, I was a teenager and my instinctive reaction was, "I am doomed." How could I live my entire life without ever looking at a beautiful woman and desire her in my heart? I could not understand why Christ would make His teaching so difficult and, in a way, impractical and unnatural. How could looking at a beautiful woman and desiring her in the heart be equal in crime to someone who actually commits physical adultery? If the wages of sin are the same whether one actually commits a crime or simply thinks of doing it, why would one opt to sin by mere desiring instead of the actual act?

As my awareness of natural law increased, the meaning of this statement became clear. The reference to lust is as much about sin as it is a restatement of *the law of creation*. Christ was teaching us how creation takes place beginning in the mind and the heart before it manifests in physical reality.

Lust is a powerful **desire** coupled with vivid **imagination**. It is based on **knowing** who and what you want. Creation starts in the mind as a vivid impulse, as an idea. If this idea is coupled by a desire for its manifestation, action will follow and the idea will materialize. *Any idea accompanied by lust without fear, worry, or doubt, **will** manifest as actual reality.* The more positive the expectations, the clearer and more detailed the visualization, the easier it is for that idea to take form and manifest as reality. Therefore, to create a desired experience, we must first fashion it as an idea in the mind and desire it passionately in our hearts. We must see the details of the visualization with great clarity, feel the effects of having achieved the desired end, and with heightened expectation, crave it. This is the law of creation. This is why if we lust for a woman, we have already committed the act. The first phase of creation—ideation—has already taken place. The second phase—manifestation—will inevitably follow.

This law of creation can be used to acquire anything we desire, or to realize lofty ideals. Looking back, I now see that this is exactly how I immigrated to the United States, found my job, asked for my wife and met her, and wrote this book. This is how I achieve worthwhile goals. I first see the desired outcome clearly in my mind and desire it in my heart. I build the picture in my mind until it is alive and vibrant, and then I release the idea from my mind, trusting that it is done. Once created in the mind, it will manifest physically unless interfered with or sabotaged by doubt, fear and worry.

If creation is as simple as this, it is within the reach of all to partake of its fruit. We are co-creators with God. We create our own destinies, whether we are aware of it or not. It is all in what we choose to "lust" for, expect confidently to attain, and act according to what we desire. Ultimately, what we lust for, becomes our reality.

An example of unconscious creation is our dreams. Dreams are the creations of our individual minds. They bring to light our unresolved concerns, hidden obsessions and can provide us creative solutions to problems that are of concern. We can learn a great deal about our minds from studying our dreams carefully with an open mind. Even the simplest dreams can reveal deep and true aspects of our minds. A simple dream I had, focused on a dental assistant:

> "I never seem to have any luck with men," she was complaining to me. "I seem to always end up with the one not right for me. I simply cannot believe that, once more, my boyfriend is leaving me."
> I tried to assure her that everything would be all right.
> "You don't understand. I have gone through this before. How many disappointments must I endure?" She said.
> I persisted, "It is all for the best. Disappointments are necessary to pave the way for the right relationships. You now know what does not work and who is not right for you. Next time you will fare well."
> She began to cry. "I am tired of going through these painful relationships. Nothing seems to work. When I meet someone I

*think to myself, this is it. But then I end up disappointed one more time."*
*I put my arms around her. "Things will work out for you, I promise. The next one has to be much better than this last one." As hard as I tried I could not console or reassure her. Finally, I found myself telling her: "I promise you that the next relationship will be the right one for you. If it is not, then **I will be your boyfriend..**"*

I woke up shocked. How could I make such a promise? How could I forget that I am already happily married and have a family? Totally absorbed into the events of the dream, I did not remember anything about my current state.

The dream, on its own merit, made sense. The pictures were as real as anything I have seen in my wakeful state. Yet, it was illogical that I did not remember my wakeful state. Most of my dreams do not involve my wife, children, or my current status in life. How come? Even when they do, they are altered drastically from what is really taking place. My mind seems to have a dual existence like Jekyll and Hyde. While awake, its intelligence enables me to live and function. As soon as I fall asleep, this same mind seems ignorant of the basic facts of my life. It seems to forget who I am, where I live, my marital status, age, nationality and other vital "facts." While I am asleep, my mind does not even remember who is alive and who has departed. For this mind allows me to dream of departed ones just as naturally as I do of living ones. How can this be?

Is it possible that my mind is not as forgetful as I assume? Perhaps what I lack is the *knowledge* of the basic nature of this mind and the higher dimensions. It is possible that the reason we dream of departed ones is because the experiences of the mind are not limited to the same dimensions to which we are restricted when we are awake? It is also possible that the mind can visit other dimensions as easily as we visit other countries. The mind does not have to travel anywhere to enter into other dimensions. It simply has to free itself of limitations. We do that when we fall asleep.

I seem at home in my dreams. While dreaming, I seem to know who I am and who everyone else is. I am never alarmed that I do not remember what my wakeful state is. I am never concerned about finding myself in unusual situations and unfamiliar surroundings, with people I have never known or seen in my wakeful state before.

In my wakeful state, I am comfortable only in circumstances I am familiar with. I am completely focused in the present. However, over the years, I lived in different places and under various circumstances. I spoke several languages, ate a multitude of ethnic foods and interacted with people of many religions, races and nationalities. I have been child and adult, single and married, employed and unemployed, poor and well-off, sick and healthy, hungry and full, happy and miserable. Even though consciously I am now focused only on my current circumstance, I am at ease with many different environments because of my past experiences. I can relate to children, soldiers, clergy, natives, foreigners, those in favor and those out of favor, for I have been in each state myself. Similarly, is it possible that the reason I am not alarmed by my strange dreams is that they are not strange after all?

While asleep and dreaming, I am not restricted by my circumstances. I can go backward and forward in space-time and experience anything I want. *My dreaming mind is not limited to its conscious memories.* It can draw upon the subconscious as well as the super-conscious. More importantly, the dreaming mind is not confined to one lifetime. It can access the memories of many lifetimes or cycles of reincarnations.

Does the mind create the dream experience, or does it visit other dimensions in which these experiences take place? Does the mind paint all the intricate details of people and places—some known, others unknown—or does it go to different dimensions and encounter these? Is it possible that the dreaming mind is in touch with other realities that we are not aware of because of the noise that fills our wakeful mind, just as the stars are always in the sky, yet we only see them in the dark?

What appears separate and apart, contradictory and absurd, past and future, on the lower dimensions, actually coexists and make total sense on the higher dimensions. We cannot use the measuring tape of one dimension as a yard stick in the next dimension.

**The Seventh Dimension**

Extension along seven directions gives rise to the seventh dimension. What is the seventh dimension? Using the same patterns and rules that led us to discover the fourth, fifth and sixth dimensions, we can postulate that **The Cosmic Intelligence,** or *God* is the seventh dimension.

**Analysis:**
1. *God* contains all minds.
2. *God* is the medium that houses the tracing of the movement of all minds.
3. *God* is absolute and limitless. Yet, representations of *God* such as a human, nature and a solar system are confined and limited.
4. The seventh dimension results when two eighth dimensions intersect. The result contains aspects of both higher dimensions. We cannot know the validity of this statement since we do not know what the eighth dimension is.
5. To get to the seventh dimension requires escaping the confines of mind. To arrive at God, we need to go beyond mind.
6. We cannot comprehend *God* by merely studying mind.
7. God binds the seemingly disparate minds into a cohesive whole.

God is to the universe what our mind is to us. Our mind is a unique aspect of God—an image that reflects the multifaceted nature of God. Our mind is the portion of God that is dedicated for our use. God is public property. By using our mind, we privatize God and make God our own. God is the beginning and the end of all individual minds. God is the unity of consciousness, the highest level of awareness, the peak from where the unity of all is self-evident. In God everything is united and through God nothing is separate. God is the unity of all opposites. God is the *One* that is the perfect union of the two. These two manifest as idea and manifestation, mind and body, positive and negative, and as masculine and feminine. These two always coexist, but in varying degrees.

We mirror the dual nature of God. However, we are not yet one which is the perfect union of the two. We are polarized. We are more positive or negative, more masculine or feminine. We mirror what we are in our beliefs and behavior. As we evolve, we will balance our nature and ultimately become like God—one that is a perfect union of the two. Humanity began the trek to civilization starting at the masculine pole. We needed brute force to hunt, build, and survive. As we evolved tools and our consciousness began to rise, we slowly moved toward the feminine pole. I believe that we are currently mid-way between the two poles. Our history is highlighted by the dominance of the masculine aspect of our nature and hence the masculine nature of God as well. This is evident in the gods we chose to worship—combative, demanding, expansionist, subjugating, domineering and power hungry. Accordingly, nations took up arms, conquered and subjugated other nations. Might became right and brute force ruled. At this stage of our evolution, the feminine aspect of humanity and God were subdued, dormant and inconspicuous.

When Akhnaton occupied the throne of ancient Egypt as Pharaoh, he attempted to restore the balance by emphasizing the feminine aspects of God and humanity. He declared *Aton* as god. Akhnaton shunned wars, domination and subjugation. He advocated the arts, simplicity and family relations. He declared that men, women and warring nations were all equal in the sight of *Aton*. Akhnaton chose the sun as a symbol of *Aton* because no one owns the sun. Everyone could claim it as their own. Even though no one could see *Aton* directly, anyone could see the representation of *Aton*—the sun. Thus, *Aton* as sun was not only distant to be experienced by all, but local and easily experienced individually as light and warmth touching us daily through the rays of the sun.

> *Thy dawning is beautiful in the horizon of heaven,*
> *O living Aton, Beginning of life!*
> *When Thou risest in the eastern horizon of heaven,*
> *Thou fillest every land with Thy beauty;*
> *For Thou are beautiful, great, glittering, high over the earth;*
> *Thy rays, they encompass the lands, even all Thou hast*
>   *made.*
> *Thou art Ra, and Thou hast carried them all away captive;*
> *Thou bindest them by Thy love.*
>
> *Akhnaton*

The sun is a befitting symbol for God for each of us is like a ray emanating from the Sun, our source. Even though each individual reflects its own color, all abide in white, the color of our source and destiny. While the physical sun is the source of **light**, the cause of earthly **life** and the provider of heat and **warmth**, God as Spiritual Sun is the source of **spiritual light** or knowledge and awareness, **spiritual life** or experience and evolution, and **spiritual warmth** or love. This reveals the deeper nature of the deity—God as the trinity of Light, Life and Love.

God, however, is only what we understand Him/Her to be. This understanding is a reflection of our level of comprehension. We can believe God to be masculine and revengeful, or feminine and love. Akhnaton's attempt to live and teach the feminine nature of God failed. The concept of a gentle God did not take hold in the hearts of the masses. Humanity was not ready for peace, sharing and love. Years later, when Christ strove to do the same by adopting and living love as a way of life, He too mostly failed. We remain infatuated with war, power and domination. We seem unable to live in peace, harmony and love.

The swing from the old concept we have of ourselves and God to a new one continues. Eventually we will arrive at the feminine pole. When we do, we will see and know that what we sought in the masculine as power, dominion and subjugation can only be had through the feminine. True power is not over others. It is power over our lower nature. What must be dominated is not the others, but our circumstances. Instead of subjugating people, we need to subjugate our uncontrolled lust for money, power, and conquest. Once we master self, we have all the power we need. While the pursuit of external power is transient, the acquisition of internal power is lasting.

The ancients, especially the Hermetic philosophers, emphasized that *all is one.* This One manifests as God and nature, spirit and body, matter and energy, cosmos and intelligence. These philosophers also stated that *God is One.* Therefore, God and all must be one and the same. Viewing earth from outer space, we can see that all earth is one. All the life forms on earth are intricately entwined. Because we are all connected, each of us can make a difference, influence outcomes and contribute to the destiny of earth. Therefore, we are significant. Additionally, since we are all linked, whatever we do to each other we do to ourselves and to God.

*And the King will answer them, 'Truly, I say to you, as you did it to one of the least of these my brethren, you did it to me.' Then he will say to those at his left hand, 'Depart from me, you cursed, into the eternal fire prepared for the devil and his angels; for I was hungry and you gave me no food, I was thirsty and you gave me no drink, I was a stranger and you did not welcome me, naked and you did not clothe me, sick and in prison and you did not visit me.' Then they also will answer, 'Lord, when did we see thee hungry or thirsty or a stranger or naked or sick or in prison, and did not minister to thee?' Then he will answer them, 'Truly, I say to you, as you did it not to one of the least of these, you did it not to me.'*

*Matthew 25:40–45*

It is difficult to comprehend the notion of being connected to each other and to God unless we rise to a higher dimension from where we can view and experience this reality. P.D. Ouspensky, in his book *Tertium Organum: A Key to the Enigmas of the World,* describes several analogies that can help us better understand this concept. Let us consider an analogy to elucidate the concept of oneness as it is experienced from the vantage point of two dimensions.

A thin sheet of living tissue, for all practical purposes, is a two-dimensional entity. Its world is that of the plane. Assuming that a three-dimensional worm can pass through the tissue, without tearing it and remain intact, how will the tissue experience the worm? Since the awareness of a two-dimensional entity is confined to its plane of existence, the tissue can only experience shapes and figures on its flat surface. It cannot experience anything outside the boundaries of the plane. Objects outside the plane simply do not exist for the tissue. Thus, when something enters the world of the plane by touching its surface, it is realized as having appeared out of nowhere. When the experience of the tissue with the worm ends, the worm simply disappears into thin air. It no longer exists because it does not touch the surface of the tissue.

The worm exists prior to entering the tissue and after it leaves it, but not for the tissue. As the worm passes through the tissue, it is experienced as a series of rings that traverse the surface of the tissue. *The worm will never be experienced as a worm by the tissue.* It will only be sensed as a series of concentric circles that appear from nowhere and then, after a certain duration, disappear into nowhere. What is above or below the plane will not exist for the tissue. What is on the surface of the tissue—its plane—is experienced as the present, what is below it has already been experienced and constitutes the past, what is above the plane has not been experienced yet and constitutes the future. Neither the past nor the future exist for the tissue. They are merely ideas in the mind.

Like capturing the picture of a three-dimensional object on a two-dimensional paper, the three-dimensional object will lose its third dimension upon entering the world of the plane. Cubes, pyramids and anything else that has a square base will be experienced as squares. Perpendicular lines collapse upon themselves when viewed from the plane level; therefore, only slanted lines are experienced as lines by plane beings. Moving lines will be experienced as possessing special attributes such as life. Curved lines will be experienced as moving lines, while straight lines will be experienced as immobile since no change is detected even though there is movement.

The world of the two-dimensional is so limited compared to the world of the three- dimensional that it is impossible for a three-dimensional being to communicate with a two-dimensional being. How can we explain to the living tissue, that the entire worm exists all at once and as a complete worm? How can we explain that there is in fact no past, present, or future and that it is the limited level of awareness of the tissue that is inducing these relative states? How can we explain the life of the worm to a two-dimensional being?

With our knowledge and understanding, we would appear as gods compared to the two-dimensional tissue. We would know the causes of events, be aware of the past, present and future, and we would have the power to change outcomes. What appears as separate to the two-dimensional tissue we will see as connected. If a parsley plant were to pass through the tissue instead of a worm, the parsley would appear as hundreds of separate and unrelated circles or shapes. A being on the second dimension would not be able to experience all of these shapes at once because they are too numerous and too scattered. Yet for a being on the third dimension, all these apparently diverse shapes and sizes appearing on the surface of the tissue belong to *one* plant—the parsley. How could we explain that even circles with identical features appearing on a plane do not have to come from identical sources? For the circles and other shapes made by the passage of a live parsley plant, that of a plastic parsley and that of a fern might appear identical to the plane being, even though the sources of the impressions themselves are very different .

Two-dimensional beings will never experience reality as we know it. They will experience only shadows and projections of three-dimensional realities on the two dimensions of the plane. Analyzing and studying cross sectional "pictures" of a three-dimensional object as it passes through the plane will never lead to an understanding of the three-dimensional object.

We can look at a picture on a two-dimensional paper and know what that picture represents if we have seen the three-dimensional object before. For example, having seen a car, we can know by merely looking at the picture of a car what it represents. If we had never seen a car before, we would never be able to know what that picture represents. Two-dimensional beings, having never experienced a complete three-dimensional reality, cannot comprehend the meaning of pictures as they are formed on their surface by passing three- dimensional objects.

Just as a two-dimensional tissue can only experience a three-dimensional reality—a worm—one section at a time, so it is with us when we experience a higher reality. While on the third dimension, we can only experience the fourth-dimension one segment at a time as a series of three-dimensional "figures" moving and changing in space and time. A fourth-dimensional "plant," for example, will appear as a seed, get planted, go through its unfoldment, grow into a tree and produce fruit, and then eventually die and wither away. All of these events will appear as separate and individual states associated with the seed and the plant. Each state will be experienced as a separate segment appearing in space and time, undergoing change and then disappearing. We will never experience the complete life-cycle of the plant as one higher reality. We will not be able to see all phases of the plant's life-cycle at once. We will experience the plant with a past, present and future. What is gone is gone forever, what is to come is not here yet. Only the present exists. Unfortunately, even the present is extremely illusive. It is always changing into the past as it extends into the future.

This is how we experience our bodies. Each of our bodies is like a cross-section, a shadow and a picture of the higher-dimensional body, which is one, connected and existing as a whole on the higher dimensions. Just as the portion of the worm that resides above or below the plane surface does not exist on the second dimension, our past and future bodies do not exist for us. Just as the entire worm exists on the third dimension, our entire "body" exists on the higher dimensions. We, however, being focused on the third dimension, can only experience our present bodies. If we are middle-aged now, the middle-aged body is all that we have for a real body. The infant body we had is gone forever. The body of old age is nowhere to be seen.

We are different from a tissue. We are on a higher dimension. Even though our current awareness is in the present, it is connected to the past and the future. The present is always the point of our power. From it we can alter the past and shape the future. Reality, like a worm, intersects the surface of our awareness at a certain angle based on our interpretation of the event. If our interpretation of an event changes, it is as if the angle of intersection changed. This affects the position of what we experience. Hence, by changing our interpretation of an event, we change not only our present reality, but the past and the future as well. Our mind is the fulcrum on which hinges the outcomes of not only the present, but the past and future as well. By mastering our mind, we master life.

The higher our level of awareness is, the more unity and connection we see and experience. If our level of awareness is only three-dimensional, then we only know what we can see, touch, taste, smell and hear. Our physical senses would be the limits of our awareness. If our level of awareness is four-dimensional, we employ our psychic senses as well. We experience a higher unity. Perhaps we get to know our bodies as a complete life-cycle and a continuum with all the bodies coexisting at once. This is a higher reality, for the body of the infant contains the body of the adult and visa versa, just as the seed contains the plant and the plant lies as potential in the seed. Christ alluded to this when He talked about His relationship to His Father:

> *Jesus said to him, "Have I been with you so long, and yet you do not know me, Philip? He who has seen me has seen the Father; how can you say, 'Show us the Father'? Do you not believe that I am in the Father and the Father in me? The words that I say to you I do not speak on my own authority; but the Father who dwells in me does his works."*
>
> John 14:9–10

Fourth-dimensional awareness allows us to see **The One** with all of its possible transformations coexisting. Fifth-dimensional awareness enables us to see not only the simultaneous existence of the entire life-cycle of a three-dimensional body, but the connections of all three-dimensional bodies. On this plane, we will experience the "leaves," "branches," "stems," "trunks," and "roots" as connected and belonging to the one tree—*the tree of life*. What appears as air, water, wind, soil and sunshine are connected and belong to the same plant, animal, or human being, and each, in turn, belongs to life. We will also know that none of these apparently separate parts have a life of their own—their life is due to the life of the whole.

We are alive because we are connected to a higher reality. Ultimately, at the seventh dimension, everything is connected to the one reality we call God. Perhaps the closer we come to understanding **The One**, the closer we will come to knowing our true self. The more we know ourselves, the more of the ultimate *truth* we will know and be part of. The closer we get to the truth, the freer we will be. When our consciousness rises to the seventh dimension, we come face to face with God—our ultimate self. At that instant, we will shed all the veils that have been obstructing our view. We will know the Truth and the Truth will set us completely free. From that lofty position we can declare that finally, we, too, have risen!

### Rising to Higher Dimensions

Formidable barriers separate one dimension from the next. To move to a higher dimension demands a change in phase and transformation. To transform, we must break away from gravity, attain escape velocity and undergo a change in phase. This requires the expenditure of energy. For ice at 0°C (centigrade) to become water at 0°C (a change in phase), 80 calories per gram of water—heat of fusion—must be expended. For water at 100°C to become water vapor at 100°C (another change in phase), 539 calories per gram must be expended. So it is for us to go from one dimension to the next. We must expend enough energy to transmute to the higher dimension. However, the energy we require is not in the form of heat, rather in the form of gained knowledge, accumulated experiences and a higher level of consciousness.

Just as changes in the environment force us to evolve, difficulties in life provide us the incentive to break loose from our current dimensional limitations, make a paradigm shift and extend into new territory. Difficulties are the heat that ripen the fruit. If necessity is the mother of invention, difficulty is the father of growth and unfoldment.

We can wait for difficulties to force us to change, or we can make a conscious effort and employ tools to speed up the transition from one phase to the next higher one. Once more we have a choice. Some of the tools we can use are:

1. acquiring knowledge;
2. thinking;
3. adopting an ideal;
4. practicing detachment;
5. conscious dreaming;
6. living the inspired, passionate and creative life;
7. acts of heroism and noble deeds;
8. meditation and prayer;
9. communion; and
10. loving and relating deeply and profoundly.

**1. Acquiring Knowledge**

Knowledge is a "ladder" we can use to climb to higher dimensions. Since a dimension is characterized by its degrees of freedom, number of mysteries, and level of awareness, acquiring knowledge gives us more freedom, reduces the number of mysteries, and raises our level of awareness. Knowledge is a key that unlocks dimensional barriers. It changes the level of our understanding, what we see and experience and the results that follow.

There is a hierarchy of knowing. As we acquire more knowledge, we move up the ladder, we evolve and eventually occupy a higher dimension. Our evolution has been a steady progress in the acquisition of knowledge and increased awareness. Through knowledge, awareness and action we participate in our evolution and the shaping of our destiny.

## 2. Thinking

Thinking is employing perception, emotion, will, memory and imagination. Thinking takes place in the brain. The brain has a right and a left hemisphere. The left hemisphere is sequential, causative, quantitative and logical. It deals with our expressions and controls speech, decision making, body movement, the five senses, learning languages and math. The right hemisphere, on the other hand, is holistic, qualitative and intuitive. It mostly deals with our perceptions and controls imagination, sleep and wakefulness, knowing, learning the arts and religion. We need to use both hemispheres of the brain if we want to use our minds more effectively.

Thinking is not something that happens to us. It is something we do intentionally. Thinking is establishing contact with a higher dimension, gleaming the required information and bringing this knowledge down to our dimension. It is stealing fire from the gods and bringing it to humanity. Thinking requires clarity of purpose, dedication, focus and persistence. We can think for synthesis, or for inspiration. To think for synthesis is to dwell on an issue, to concentrate, reason and analyze. It is to persist until a satisfactory answer appears. Thinking for inspiration is knocking at the gate of the higher dimensions until a doorway opens. It is praying until the prayer is answered. It is meditating until an experience is had.

We are surrounded by opportunities to think. We know little and there are so many mysteries to be solved, challenges to be tackled, inventions to be made, gadgets to be created, poems to be composed, books to be written and works of art to be rendered. There is so much to do and so little thinking going on. We can remedy the situation by thinking on a regular basis.

### 3. Adopting an Ideal

Ideals reside on the fifth dimension, in the world of ideas. If we adopt an ideal, then by association, we will rise to the level of that ideal. Living for, and through an ideal, is a worthwhile way to live.

We can adopt any ideal, but it makes sense to choose one which we have a natural affinity for. Because of our unique situation, each can select from a variety of ideals such as: Service, Peace, Love, Justice, Kindliness, Beauty, Harmony, Knowledge, Compassion, Sympathy, Tolerance, Unity, Communion, Quality, Virtue, Temperance, Fortitude, Excellence, Perfection, Nobility and Altruism. A benefit of adopting and living an ideal is that we will not blindly side with one individual or group against another. We side only with our ideals. We detach ourselves from individuals, parties, religions and politics. By attaching to our ideal, we rise above the parochial. By rising, we are not affected by what takes place below. Like a plane in air, we will be above the street traffic jam and the fight for access. We will have the entire sky open for us to fly through.

### 4. Practicing Detachment

We become what we identify with. If we identify with our appetites, greed, pride and the ego, we remain three dimensional, trapped in our current circumstances. If, on the other hand, we identify with our ideals, we break our limitations and set ourselves free. By detaching from the lowly, we are free to rise and attach to the lofty.

What we identify with is what we plug into. We either plug into what gives us energy, joy and satisfaction, or what drains us of our energy, causes us stress and leads us to disease. If we are afraid, we are plugged into what causes us fear. If, on the other hand, we plug into our source for guidance and power then we can live the life we want with courage, gratitude and contentment.

Practicing detaching, we rise above our objects of attachment. We see solutions and exercise options not available before. Through detachment, we can be in a situation but not part of it, be in the world but not of it. We get to know that "our kingdom" is not of this world. By detaching ourselves, we create a gap that gives us "time" to act instead of react, to live intelligently instead of out of habit.

## 5. Conscious Dreaming

We detach ourselves daily from our physical world when we enter the world of sleep and dreams. Through sleep we silence the physical and allow the deeper aspects of self to surface and take center stage. When we sleep, we leave the realm of the dense behind. We enter the higher worlds where transformation takes place. We enter the world of thought, ideas and creativity. Here we take part in creation. What we create in the mind, we experience instantaneously as reality. What we create in dreams reside in the mind, yet we experience them as if they are taking place in space and time. When we wake up we realize that the movements in space-time that we experienced while dreaming were figments of our mind. Is it possible that what we experience while awake as space, time and movement are figments of a higher mind? Is it possible that just as we create our dreams, we create our other experiences and, in turn, this is how God creates the worlds? We create while mostly asleep. God, on the other hand, who is always awake creates through conscious dreaming.

Dreams are thought-paintings, "living pictures," and the **creations of our mind experienced as reality.** Dreams are aspects of our creativity. Perhaps the reason we sleep is to perfect the art of dreaming and creating. Even though dreaming is relegated to the subconscious, we can claim dreaming back and make it a conscious activity. We can dream without having to sleep by day dreaming consciously. This is akin to visualization. The more vivid, detailed and clear the images we paint, and the more feelings we attach to them, the more power they have to move us into action. Realities created in the higher dimensions must descend to the lower realms to become physical. The less obstacles we place in their path and the more positively we anticipate their arrival, the better chance they have to "take flesh and abide with us."

We sleep and we dream because we are multi-dimensional. We exist not only on the dimension we are aware of, but others as well. While we are physically focused in the third dimension, our minds are part of the sixth dimension—Mind. As we fall asleep, we shed many of our limitations. We travel to the fourth, fifth and the sixth dimensions. In these higher dimensions, we witness and participate in creations, dramas and rituals. When we wake up, some of the activities of sleep bleed through and affect our thoughts, feelings and actions. They also manifest as inspiration and intuition.

## 6. Living the Inspired, Passionate and Creative Life

To live the inspired life, we must remain connected to a source that inspires and moves us. We must remain in touch with our deeper aspects. We must learn to read nature, ourselves and each other. It helps if we live a simple and an unencumbered life.

To live passionately is to live with excitement, energy and anticipation. It is to grow roots and establish strong connections with life. To live passionately most of the time, we must maintain our interest, curiosity and purity of heart. It is much easier to maintain these if we first identify what we can be passionate about and pursue these. When we act upon our passions, we allow a higher reality to guide us and take charge of our affairs. When we live our passions, we do what we love and love what we do. Since passion is contagious, living passionately empowers others to do the same. Living passionately is the best example we can set for our lives. It is the healthiest, happiest and most productive way to live.

To live creatively, we must give birth to new ideas. Creativity requires an incubation period and a birthing process. The birth will take place at its own opportune time and place. This could be while we are awake or in a dream. Creativity requires that we remain open, flexible and trust that the answer will appear. Creativity is achieved when we use both hemispheres of our brain. It is enhanced through detachment from the accepted and the expected.

What and how we create is limited only by our imagination. The Egyptian god Ptah created the world through uttering the word of his mind. We, too, can create through the spoken and the written word. Kneph, the ancient Egyptian serpent god, breathed on the waters and its breath impregnated the water, producing matter and life. We can do likewise by breathing life into the dull, and by infusing energy and vitality into the otherwise lifeless and drab. We create anytime we think, feel and act.

## 7. Acts of Heroism and Noble Deeds

When we act heroically, altruistically and perform noble deeds, we transcend our limited selves and are in touch with the higher self of humanity. Any time we transcend our limited selves, we rise above our current dimension. We touch a higher truth. By touching the higher, we transform ourselves and all the ones we come in contact with.

It is interesting that most heroic acts are performed without much thought of the self. We delve into acts that endanger our individual selves in an attempt to save others. We do this, not because our subconscious fails to protect us, rather because deep down we know that we are all connected. What we do for others, ultimately we do it for our Self. We do not live just for ourselves, we live for humanity as well. We also know that our contributions are important, especially if they are acts of heroism and noble deeds.

### 8. Meditation and Prayer

Meditation is entering the realm of silence, quieting the body and the mind, and then becoming totally passive and receptive. It is shifting the focus of our awareness from our immediate environment to the one beneath it. It is shutting out the distractions to become aware of the subtle and profound. Meditation is dimming the light so the stars may appear. Through meditation we can delve deeply into our nature and experience our buried aspects that are as real as the obvious and physical ones. When we shift our focus from the body and its senses, our deeper aspects make their presence and reality self-evident. When we connect to our deeper selves, we can be passive to receive impressions, or become active and visualize our desires and form seeds that we drop in the cosmic mind as causes for effects we want to attract into our lives.

Prayer is focus on God to petition for services or express gratitude. The more unselfish we are in prayer, the easier it is to establish contact with the higher dimensions. This is because selfishness focuses on self, while unselfishness detaches from self and focuses on the higher Self. Additionally, the more passionately we pray and the more confidently we expect a response, the more effective our prayer is. The answers to our prayers can come from anywhere. Since all are connected, God and the Cosmic can talk to us through anything and everything. If we open our senses and are receptive, we can detect our answer in any guise.

## 9. Communion

Communion is immersion into and union with another. When we commune, the two become one and what takes place in one takes place in the other. Communion is the highest form of marriage. It is the abandoning of the partial for the sake of the whole. We can commune with another, God, or nature. We can commune through love, profound appreciation and through the living of an ideal. Through communion, what was once apart and separate, coalesces and unites. If gaining knowledge is a stairway to the higher dimensions, communion is a fast elevator that can take us there the accelerated way.

## 10. Loving and Relating Deeply and Profoundly

Love is essential in our lives because it leads us to the ultimate reality: the oneness of all. Through love, we learn to relate deeply and profoundly and hence, know oneness— our innermost reality. That is why when two people love each other they desire to commune and become one with each other. Socially, this is often carried out through the sacrament of "marriage." Marriage is the ritual where two, through love, renounce their individuality by claiming their unity.

> "For this reason a man shall leave his father and mother and be joined to his wife, and the two shall become one flesh."
> Eph 5:31 RSV

Perhaps that is why God is not just **One**, but **Love** as well. For to love is to bind with and become one with another. And to love all, is to bind with all and make them one.

> He who does not love does not know God; for God is love.
> 1 John 4:8

Just as we are in the *image* of God, we are a mere *image* of love. We have the potential to become real by adopting love, living it and becoming one with it. When we finally become love, we shed the image and assume the reality of our nature—Godhood. God is not only our source, but our destination as well. Hence, love is equally our source and destination. Through love we express not only our true nature, we live our ultimate reality as well.

> *O love that knoweth of no fear.*
> *A love that sheds a joyous tear;*
> *O love that makes me whole and free,*
> *Such love shall keep and hallow me.*
>
> *Rosicrucian Chant*

# About the Author

Shahan was born in Aleppo, Syria where he lived for the first fifteen years of his life. At the age of 15, he left for Lebanon where he joined a monastery to study and prepare to be a monk for the Syrian Orthodox Church of Antioch. After two years in the monastery, he left to continue his education.

Shahan graduated from the American University of Beirut with a Bachelor's degree in Biology. At the age of 24, Shahan left for the United States, became a United States citizen while serving three years in the Army at the medical laboratory of Fort Meade, Md. After working as a Histologist and an Electron Microscopist at the Walter Reed Army Medical Center for 7 years, Shahan started a new career in computers. He is currently employed with the Department of Treasury, the Internal Revenue Service, as a Computer Systems Analyst.

Shahan lives with his wife Barbara and two daughters, Olivia and Emily, in Adelphi, Md., a suburb of Washington, DC. Shahan has been a public speaker conducting workshops and seminars for over fifteen years. Shahan is a Regional Instructor for the worldwide Rosicrucian Order, AMORC (The Ancient and Mystical Order Rosae Crucis). He serves his community as a soccer coach, speaker at community functions and as the president of the Adelphi Recreation Inc., a community recreational facility.

For more information about Shahan's workshops, seminars, and availability for speaking engagements, please write to:

Worthwhile Publications
P.O. Box 8748
Langley Park, MD 20787

# Order Form

Direct your order to:
**Worthwhile Publications**
P. O. Box 8748
Langley Park, MD 20787

Make checks payable to:
**Worthwhile Publications**
(All prices and charges are in U.S. Dollars.)

| Quantity | Price each | Total |
|----------|------------|-------|
| _____ | _____   | _____ |

Maryland residents add sales tax _____

Shipping Charges _____
First copy $3.95
Add $1 for each additional copy

**Ship orders to: (please print)**

Name _____

Total _____

Address _____

City, State, Zip _____

Daytime phone number ( ) _____
(in case there is a question abour your order)

**Attention organizations, spiritual centers, and schools of self-actualization:** Quantity discounts are available on bulk purchase of this book for educational purposes or fund raising. For information, please contact Worthwhile Publications, P. O. Box 8748, Langley Park, Maryland 20787.